Moral
RELATIVISM

A SHORT INTRODUCTION

Moral
RELATIVISM

A SHORT INTRODUCTION

Neil Levy

ONEWORLD
OXFORD

MORAL RELATIVISM: A SHORT INTRODUCTION

Oneworld Publications
(Sales and Editorial)
185 Banbury Road
Oxford OX2 7AR
England
www.oneworld-publications.com

ISBN 1–85168–305–4

Cover illustration by Andrzej Klimowski; cover
design by Perks-Willis Graphic Design.
Typeset by Saxon Graphics Ltd, Derby, UK
Printed and bound by Bell & Bain Ltd, Glasgow

CONTENTS

INTRODUCTION

On 11 September 2001 an American Airlines jet crashed into the north tower of the World Trade Center in New York. Eighteen minutes later, a United Airlines flight crashed into the south tower. All passengers on both planes were killed, as were the passengers and crew aboard two other flights: an American Airlines flight that crashed into the Pentagon in Washington, and a United Airlines flight that crashed near Pittsburgh. Worse still were the casualties on the ground. As I write, estimates of the number killed in New York still vary, from around three to five thousand. Office workers, waiters in the restaurants, fire-fighters and passengers; all perished in the fire, or in the collapse of the twin towers.

The reaction of most people around the world to these events was shocked horror. Even some of the United States' harshest critics were quick to condemn the terrorist actions as barbarous atrocities. This was murder, pure and simple, most people said, and nothing could justify it. Yet, if moral relativism is true, perhaps these events might turn out to be justifiable.

What might a moral relativist say concerning 11 September? She might point out, first of all, that the perpetrators of these acts did not believe themselves to be doing anything wrong. Far from being ashamed of their acts, terrorists are usually proud of what they have done (or plan to do, in the case of those who expect to die as a consequence of their actions). Murderers normally regret their actions, at least somewhat; terrorists exult in them. Now, we can react to this fact in one of two ways. We can say that the terrorists' failure to regret their actions makes them morally worse than the average murderer, who, we hope, feels some pangs of conscience. Or we can wonder whether the fact that the terrorist is proud of his or her act shows that it is not wrong at all, at least not wrong for him or her. It is this second course of action that relativism tempts us to take.

Strengthening the claim that the terrorists' acts are not wrong for them is the fact that they can and do cite justifications for their actions. Osama bin Laden, who most people believe was behind the attacks on America, claims that the Pentagon and the twin towers were 'legitimate targets' in a war against America. The Pentagon is, of course, a symbol of the American military, while the World Trade Center was a symbol of America's economic might. The occupants of these buildings therefore could not be considered ordinary civilians, but were engaged in the war the United States is conducting against Islam.[1] After all, the United States is by far the biggest donor to the state of Israel, which continues to oppress the largely Muslim Palestinians, and is responsible for the maintenance of crippling sanctions upon Iraq, sanctions which, according to UNICEF, have been estimated to be responsible for no fewer than half a million deaths. The attacks of 11 September were therefore justified, both by the fact that they limited America's ability to wage its war against Islam, and by the fact that they undermined US morale, thus weakening its resolve to continue to wage war.

Moreover, bin Laden claims, his war against the United States is justified upon religious grounds. 'We are carrying on the mission of our Prophet, Muhammad [...]. This is defensive Jihad [Holy War].'[2] He cites passages of the Qur'an and Muhammad's example in support of the actions of the terrorists, and as part of calling for further such acts. Spreading the word of the prophet, and protecting Islamic nations, not just against aggression, but also against the cultural influence of the West, is sufficient justification for terrorist acts.

Now, the moral relativist will not endorse bin Laden's reasoning. That is, she will not conclude, with bin Laden, that the terrorist actions were morally *right*, in the sense in which we normally use that word. But she might nevertheless think that they were *justified*. A radical relativist holds that an action is right *for someone* if and only if it is justified by the reasons available to that person (or, even more radically, if and only if that person thinks it is right). Thus, she will say that the terrorist acts were right for Osama bin Laden, for the terrorists themselves and for anyone else who shares the same set of justificatory reasons. Thus the relativist comes to a surprising conclusion: those same acts that most of us condemned as murder were (also) morally right. She applies the words of morality, right and wrong, good and bad, and so on, relativistically, asking, with regard to each of them, right or wrong *for whom*?

Thus, too, the counterintuitive implications of moral relativism do not stop there. For at the very same time as the relativist endorses the reasoning of bin Laden, she *also* endorses the views of the rest of us, of those who condemn the attacks. We point out that most of the victims of the attacks were innocent civilians, people who had nothing to do with any supposed war upon Islam. Even if there were such a war, which is very doubtful, it would not justify the mass slaughter of such civilians. Some of us dispute bin Laden's interpretation of the Qur'an; others hold that whatever the Qur'an says is irrelevant to the question of whether the slaughter of the innocent is justified. Such an act is against all civilized laws, all canons of decency, we maintain. And the relativist endorses what we have to say. The terrorists' actions were, she agrees, wrong. But, she adds, they are only wrong *for us*. Thus their wrongness is relative to us, to our reasons and our judgements, and does nothing to alter the fact that the very same acts remain right for bin Laden and those who see matters from his standpoint

We can already begin to see why moral relativism arouses such strong emotions. It is capable, we see, of generating views that are shocking – for instance, of endorsing the view that an act of mass-murder is morally right. And as if shocking our moral sensibilities were not enough, it also seems to give rise to paradoxes that are as much an affront to our intellect as its moral views are to our ethics.

For instance, it appears to say that one and the same act is both ethically right and ethically wrong, at the very same time. Moreover, the strange and apparently contradictory results of applying relativist views to this case is not an isolated anomaly. Relativism, at least in the hands of its more radical proponents, regularly comes to conclusions just as disorienting. It declares, for instance, that human sacrifice as practised by the Aztecs was right, at least *for them*, though at the very same time it might have been wrong for the Spanish conquistadors; that female circumcision as practised in North Africa, or the myriad restrictions placed upon women in Saudi Arabia and Afghanistan, are right, for the members of these cultures. And so on, for example after example. Again and again relativism tells us that some of the most objectionable practices are in fact right, at least for some people; that if we criticize those who engage in these practices, we illegitimately impose our standards upon them. No wonder so many people find relativism so strange, so shocking, so downright immoral.

And the oddities do not end here. While the opponents of relativism dismiss it as inherently immoral, some of its defenders claim that we ought to embrace it precisely upon moral grounds. They see moral relativism as the only guarantee of tolerance and respect for the diversity of cultures with which we share the world. Whereas its opponents see it as a prelude to the horrors of Auschwitz and Stalinism, its defenders argue that it is our best hope for avoiding such tragedies. How can one and the same philosophical position be believed to have such radically divergent implications?

This books aims to explore the questions to which moral relativism gives rise, a few of which we have already glimpsed:

- Is moral relativism a coherent position for us to adopt? How can a position that endorses opposing views of the same action be coherent?
- If it is coherent, is it true?
- Does moral relativism promote tolerance, or undermine it?
- What is the relationship between moral relativism and multiculturalism? Do they imply one another?
- Finally, what *is* moral relativism? Can it even be given a clear and coherent statement?

As we shall see, different philosophers have advanced divergent answers to these questions. Unfortunately, the general standard of debate has not been high. Because moral relativism arouses such passions on both sides, few people take care calmly to consider its plausibility and its implications for morality. Too many people are too busy hurling insults at one another to take the time to analyse their opponent's arguments. Most philosophers, at least in the Anglo-American tradition, believe that relativism is not just false, but hopelessly confused. Because they *know* this to be the case, they rarely are careful to construct good arguments against it. Instead, they are satisfied with mere imprecations. The proponents of relativism fare no better. They *know* that their opponents are prejudiced against it. Hence, they seem to think, they needn't bother to put forward strong evidence for it. This book will, I hope, avoid these recurrent problems. We shall analyse the strongest arguments put forward by both sides, and examine them for their plausibility. We shall consider the possible responses each side could make to these arguments, and we shall try to discover which arguments are most plausible. We shall, in short, do all those things that philosophers – indeed, anyone conducting an intellectual enquiry – are supposed to do, but in which, with regard to relativism, they have singularly failed.

This failure is important, because moral relativism *matters*. It matters philosophically, of course, but it also matters politically and ethically. Moral relativism is a doctrine with adherents far beyond the bounds of philosophy. It is found in sociology, history, anthropology – which might in fact be regarded as its spiritual home – psychology and many other disciplines besides. Whether or not it is a plausible and coherent view will, therefore, have profound implications for these disciplines, for their theory and for their practice. For instance, it has direct implications for the manner in which anthropology is conducted. Ought its practitioners attempt just to understand other people – our ancestors, our neighbours, the members of other cultures – or should they also judge them? This is just the first of the questions upon which moral relativism bears within the university. More important will be the implications it has outside the academy, for the conduct of our everyday lives and for our politics, for the way in which we all should behave, individually and collectively. Right now, in very many different parts of the world, people are being treated in ways we find unacceptable, indeed, sometimes horrifying. In many countries, women are denied the right to participate in society on an equal basis to men, homosexuals are discriminated against and sometimes punished, and people who dissent face persecution. Ought we to object to these facts? Should we put pressure on the nations concerned to behave in ways that conform to our ethical standards? Impose economic sanctions upon them? Invade them? Or should we conclude that our ethical standards have no cross-cultural validity and, therefore, that we ought not to interfere?

The puzzles posed by relativism have always been with us, and its truth a live intellectual issue. Today, however, as our world becomes increasingly globalized, these questions are more pressing than ever and are encountered more and more frequently. No longer is the truth of relativism an exotic question, of little concern to most of us outside departments of philosophy, anthropology and history; relativism is now an issue for all of us, at home and abroad. Here are two examples of the ways in which it increasingly arises, selected almost at random from amongst many. The first concerns the kind of questions that can arise in relations between countries; the second illustrates how the same kind of question can confront us within the bounds of a single country.

> In this world of trade without borders, many countries are finding it more profitable to transfer some part of their operations away from wealthy countries, to the countries of the developing world. There are frequently tax advantages to doing so, but we are here concerned with another economic incentive: the lower price of labour in these countries. Many US clothing manufacturers have relocated their production facilities to Mexico, where wages are much lower than in the USA. Now call-centre jobs are following in their wake. When the holders of some British and Australian credit cards telephone their customer-service line, they speak to someone sitting, not in London or Sydney, but in New Delhi. The reason is simple: an Australian call-centre worker earns an average of A$30,000 annually, whereas in India, call-centre workers earn the equivalent of between $A4500 and $A7700.[3]

Now, this practice raises a host of ethical questions, to which moral relativism is centrally relevant. To begin with, should workers performing the same tasks for the same company receive different amounts of pay? If Indians find lower wages acceptable but Australians do not, does it follow that such wage differentials are morally unproblematic? If moral relativism is true, does it follow that the ethically appropriate wage is set by the standards of a culture? And if that is true, which culture is here the relevant one, that of the company or that of the employee? All the data held in New Delhi by these companies are covered by Australian privacy laws; ought their employees therefore to be paid the Australian minimum wage?

Our second example is also from Australia, though cases that raise analogous issues can be found in almost every country of the world:

> Some Australian Aboriginal groups practise what is known as 'payback spearing'. Payback spearing is a form of punishment meted out to someone who has committed a serious wrong. For example, someone who is found guilty of murder might be speared in the leg as part of his or her punishment. Now, how ought we to react to the carrying out of such punishments? If I were to inflict an injury upon someone I knew to be guilty of a serious crime, I would most likely be charged with assault myself. Is that how we ought to treat Aboriginals who practise this traditional punishment? After all, most of us believe that corporal punishment is barbaric. In fact, Australian courts have taken quite the opposite view, granting some legitimacy to the practice. In several cases, magistrates have sentenced offenders to shorter sentences because they have taken into consideration the likelihood that they would be speared upon returning to their communities. People who have been charged with assault after having been involved in payback spearing have been given suspended sentences or acquitted. But surely there ought to be one law for everyone?

What (if anything) justifies this difference in the way Australian Aboriginals, as opposed to other members of the Australian community, are treated? One obvious answer (though not the only possible one) is moral relativism. If moral relativism is true, then people ought to be treated according to the standards of their culture, or so we might think. Yet this answer seems to raise almost as many problems as it solves. How ought we to identify the culture to which someone belongs? By asking them? Won't some people lie in order to escape a physical punishment they fear while others lie for precisely the opposite reasons, because they prefer such a punishment to a long prison sentence? Moreover, it is quite likely that some people genuinely won't know to which culture they most authentically belong. What should we do when Aboriginal justice and the courts disagree as to the guilt of the offender? There seems no simple way to negotiate the perilous paths moral relativism opens before us in cases like this.

At the same time, it is far from obvious that the non-relativist route is any more attractive, or less risky. If there is only one standard of justice, then are we required to treat an Aboriginal who has inflicted a traditional punishment on an offender in the same way as we would treat anyone else guilty of an assault? Ought we to stamp out such traditional practices? Can we blame people who continue to practise them, or should we excuse them on the grounds that their upbringing has led them astray?

Thus the questions with which we shall be concerned here are of immediate and pressing interest. They concern how we should, all of us, live, the policies our governments should enact, the extent to which we ought to tolerate the differences we encounter, both at home and abroad. For these reasons, they deserve, indeed require, the widest possible discussion. The truth of moral relativism matters to us all, as citizens and voters, and as thinking persons. I hope this book will contribute to promoting that discussion.

So as to be able to reach the widest possible audience, it is written as clearly and accessibly as I am able. This book ought to be comprehensible to anyone interested in the subject, provided they are prepared to spend time thinking the arguments through, regardless of whether they have any background in philosophy. However, I have not sought to 'dumb down' its contents in any way. Though it is designed to be accessible, it also aims to sort out the confusions that are endemic in the relativism debate. It is at once an introduction to the question of moral relativism and a contribution to resolving it. It will, I hope, be read with profit by professional philosophers and their students, as well as the wider public.

An overview of the book

The arguments for and against relativism are at once intellectual and moral. We are concerned both with the truth or falsity of relativism, and with its implications for morality. Of course, these two questions are inextricably intertwined, but it is helpful, at least at first, to approach them separately. A great deal of the confusion in the relativism debate stems from the failure to keep them separate, at least provisionally. Much of this book is therefore concerned with attempting to distinguish the two sets of questions and with setting out the arguments for and against each before bringing them together.

In the first chapter, however, we are concerned with laying out the terrain of the relativism debate, and that requires dealing with both the moral and the intellectual questions. Of course, our first task will be to clarify what exactly we mean by moral relativism. As we shall see, this is not the easy task that one might think. There are several different doctrines that might be meant by this term, with intricate linkages between them. As we set them out, we shall begin to consider the intellectual and moral case for relativism. That is, we will be concerned with two basic questions: How plausible is moral relativism? What are its implications for ethics?

The first question itself divides into several others: Is it a coherent doctrine? Are there good reasons to think it true? Here we shall sketch some of the reasons for the intellectual attraction, for many people, of moral relativism, though we shall refrain from subjecting them to very much in the way of analysis as yet. With regard to the second question, we shall consider whether it is the tolerant view its supporters claim, or if it is not in fact pernicious, as its detractors believe. Here we shall be concerned only with setting out the views of each side; once again, we shall refrain from assessing them for the moment.

This introduction is intended to serve as a necessary background for the deeper examination that is to follow. Once we know what moral relativism is, what different kinds of views can fall under this broad heading, we can begin to make progress in assessing the arguments for and against it. That will be the task of the bulk of the book.

Chapter 2 deepens the discussion of the intellectual case for moral relativism. It is concerned with the question of whether moral relativism is a *coherent* doctrine. It aims to discover whether moral relativism *could* be true. Is moral relativism internally consistent, or is it self-contradictory? Many of the arguments levelled against the doctrine are *conceptual*; they aim to show that moral relativism couldn't possibly be true. Thus, in this section, we will be concerned largely, though not exclusively, with a priori arguments. An a priori argument is concerned entirely with conceptual analysis; it attempts to discover what we can know before we actually look at the evidence. Here, therefore, we shall be concerned with the conceptual arguments that have been put forward for and against relativism, and with acquiring the tools we shall need for its exploration. This chapter will also set out the intellectual background against which moral relativism becomes more plausible, and which largely accounts for its spread over the last century or so. That background concerns the passing away of a metaphysical view of the world, according to which moral values are guaranteed by God, or by a cosmological order. Now that this view is no longer plausible, we need a new justification of universal morality – failing which relativism seems inescapable.

In chapter 3, we shall subject the moral case to the same analysis. As we shall see, both the proponents of relativism and its opponents are motivated largely by moral concerns. Though each side thinks that there are good intellectual reasons for their views, it is the moral implications they believe the doctrine has that motivate them. The sides claim that relativism has radically different, indeed, opposed, implications for morality. We shall therefore be concerned in this section with assessing their claims, as well as with exploring the relationship between moral relativism and some of our most pressing political and ethical concerns. In particular, we shall explore the relationship between moral relativism and toleration.

Chapter 4 turns to the empirical evidence for relativism. Moral relativism is most plausible when it is put forward as an explanation of actual moral diversity, across and within different cultures. Some philosophers, however, deny that there is any interesting moral diversity in the world. This section will be concerned, therefore, with examining actual cases that have been put forward as evidence of moral relativism. It will attempt to see whether they are best understood with reference to relativism, or whether alternative explanations are possible.

Of course, it is one thing to discover that there is a great deal of moral diversity in the world, and quite another to say that moral relativism is true. If different cultures have different moralities, perhaps some of them are simply mistaken in their moral views. Chapters 5 and 6 are concerned with different ways in which we might hope to show that they are mistaken. Chapter 5 will examine the attempt to find a foundation for morality in human nature. Perhaps moral values are not inscribed in the god-given order of the cosmos, but underwritten by the kind of animals we are, or by the evolution that has shaped us. Chapter 6 turns to the problem often called false consciousness. The question under consideration here is whether it is possible to show that people can be mistaken in the values they uphold, as a result of their socialization.

The bulk of this book delivers bad news to the opponents of relativism. It shows that their best arguments do not, as they hope, undermine the case for it entirely. Chapters 7 and 8 offer them some good news. Despite the failure of their arguments fatally to wound the relativist case, they do place substantive constraints on the contents of an adequate morality. Chapter 7 demonstrates that given these arguments, and given the argument examined in this chapter concerning the incommensurability of moral systems, no moral system can diverge radically from ours. Finally, chapter 8 sketches a middle way between relativism, as it is usually understood, and absolutism. Though we cannot, finally, vindicate a unique morality, we can demonstrate that there are moral goods that all moralities must recognize. Moral systems may diverge from each other in various ways, so that, with the relativist, we are sometimes forced to say that something that is wrong for us is not wrong for the members of another culture. But it is not true, with regards to morality, that anything goes, and very often we can justifiably condemn the culturally sanctioned practices of other peoples.

Some kind of relativism is, after all, true. But it is not a threatening relativism. It is a relativism that retains all those elements that make it attractive to many intelligent people. It helps free us from ethnocentrism, the unjustified belief that we are superior to everyone else, and teaches us respect for other ways of living. But it is also a relativism that avoids the intellectual and moral pitfalls that so worry the absolutist. It will not offer ideological cover to the fascist or to the racist; it does not undermine morality, but leaves room for its robust core. We can, in the end, say that relativism is true – but without needing to think that this commits us to saying that morality is false, or that the actions of an Osama bin Laden, or an American slave-owner, are justified.

1

WHAT IS MORAL RELATIVISM AND WHY DOES IT MATTER?

Few of the stock controversies of philosophy arouse much passion outside the academy – or, for the most part, even within its walls. Few people, apart from philosophers, are excited by the question of whether mathematical objects exist independently of us or not, for example, or even by questions that have a bearing on our lives, such as whether or not we have free will. Not even the major questions of moral philosophy – whether utilitarianism or Kantianism is true, for instance – excite much interest outside philosophy. But with regard to relativism, passions run high. Much of the left and the right is united in its denunciation, if in little else. For conservative theologian Michael Novak, for instance, '[t]he most perilous threat to the free society today [...] is the poisonous, corrupting culture of relativism',[4] while for Marxist historian Eric Hobsbawm, relativism opens the way for any crime, even genocide.[5]

The advocates of relativism are hardly less passionate. For them, too, adherence to relativism is a matter of morality as much as intellectual conviction: one should be a relativist not only because relativism is true, but because it is *right*. Thus, for instance, for the American anthropologist Melville Herskovits, adopting a relativistic position is the only way to express the respect justifiably demanded by other cultures and their members:

> The very core of cultural relativism is the social discipline that comes of respect for differences – of mutual respect. Emphasis on the worth of many ways of life, not one, is an affirmation of the values in each culture.[6]

Discovering the truth about relativism is therefore not just of intellectual interest. Relativism *matters*, or so many people believe.

Relativism differs from other issues in philosophy in another way, which also contributes to the importance of discovering the truth about it. It is one of the few philosophical questions upon which most thoughtful people seem to have a position. Students beginning philosophy are often already convinced relativists of some kind or another. They believe nothing more strongly than they believe that there are no right answers in ethics, and that, in any case, we must respect differences of opinion.

We need to know what relativism is, why it matters, why it arouses such passions – and whether it is true. The purpose of this book is to answer these questions. How did relativism come to be such a pervasive feature of the contemporary world? What are its moral and political implications, if any? Can it be stated consistently, or is it, as some philosophers believe, completely incoherent? What is the truth about relativism?

What is relativism?

Before we can make a first approach to these many and difficult questions, we need to know what relativism is. We must be sure that the term is being used consistently and in the same sense by all the parties in the debate, or our arguments will be futile. What, then, do people mean when they claim to be – or accuse one another of being – relativists?

To say that something is relative is to say that what it is is, in some way, dependent upon – relative to – something else. If I say that something has a property in a relative fashion, I might mean my attribution of that property to be understood in a comparative manner. Imagine, for instance, someone stepping outside their house on a spring morning and remarking that the air is relatively warm. By this they might mean that though the air is quite cool compared to a midsummer's day, it is warm compared to – relative to – recent days. Thus a relative judgement makes essential reference to something else, to which it is compared. The truth of such a judgement depends upon the context in which it is made. The truth of the statement 'It is relatively warm today' therefore depends not only upon the current air temperature, but also on the temperature of preceding days.

Relative judgements are to be contrasted with *absolute* judgements. A judgement is absolute if its truth (or falsity) is dependent only on facts about the object the judgement concerns, and not facts about the context beyond it. We can illustrate this, once more, with the example of a statement about temperature. If I were to say, not that 'it is relatively warm today', but that 'the ambient temperature is currently 18° Celsius', I would be making an absolute claim. The truth of the claim depends only on the current air temperature, and not on facts about preceding days, or anything else for that matter.

Now, no one disputes that the kind of relative judgement under discussion so far is often appropriate. As our example shows, some kinds of relativisms are clearly innocuous. No harm is done by claiming that the weather is relatively warm, or that the programmes on TV are relatively bad. Such relative claims are more or less explicitly comparative: they do not assert that X is (absolutely) Y, (that the air is warm, or the programmes bad) but that X is (relatively) Y; that is, it is more Y than something else, to which it is compared. Relative claims such as these do not arouse anyone's passions. But some relative claims are importantly different. When someone asserts that morality or truth is relative, this person does not just mean that some such statements are true (or false) relative to some framework to which they are compared, but that such statements can *only* be understood relativistically. Whereas with regard to temperature we have available to us an absolute measure, with reference to which we can compare all relative claims, with regard to morality no independent standards are available. Or so the moral relativist claims.

If morality really is relative, then, moral statements are only true or false relative to some standard. There is no absolute standard available, against which all the relative claims might be measured.

When someone asserts that morality is relative, what kind of relative standard does this person have in mind? What is morality relative *to*? There are two major candidates for this position. We might think that moral statements are true relative to the feelings or opinions of individuals. Or we might think that they are true relative to cultures. The first position is often called *subjectivism*, since it holds that subjective opinions set the standards of truth and falsity. It is this kind of position that people seem to have in mind when they say that morality is just a matter of opinion. The second kind of position is often known as *cultural relativism*, since it claims that cultures set the standards of moral truth.

We need to add one further point before we have full-blown moral relativism, the relativism that so many people find infuriating and dangerous. For relativism to be threatening, it must be true, not only that all the judgements made concerning a particular subject matter are true only relative to some standard, but also that the standard cannot itself be shown to be uniquely correct. If this were not the case, then relativism would, once again, be innocuous. No one would worry if all moral claims were relative to some standard, but that standard was itself known to be true, or the best available. Subjectivism and cultural relativism are threatening precisely because they suggest that the standards with reference to which we judge are not themselves justified. Subjectivism judges the truth of moral statements by reference to individual opinion; cultural relativism by reference to the standards of a culture. In both cases, there are multiple such standards. In the absence of any way of deciding between such standards, we have full-blown relativism.

We shall therefore define moral relativism as the conjunction of the following two theses:

a.   Moral claims are true only relative to some standard or framework; and
b.   This standard or framework is not itself uniquely justified.

The framework in question is almost always the culture of some group of people; this is how we shall understand it in most of what follows.

Kinds of relativism

Relativism comes in many varieties. That is, there are different kinds of things about which we can be relativists. We can be relativists about morality, about knowledge, about art, and so on. The two most important kinds of relativism, however, are relativism about knowledge and relativism about morality. We already have some notion of what is meant by moral relativism. We will now look very briefly at relativism about knowledge.

Relativism about knowledge is called *epistemic relativism*, from the Greek word for knowledge. The claims made by an epistemic relativist are very similar, structurally, to those made by a moral relativist. Thus, an epistemic relativist claims that:

1.   All knowledge claims are true (or false) only relative to some standard; and
2.   This standard cannot itself be known to be true.

Thus, epistemic relativists believe not only that our morality is no better than that of the Aztecs, but also that our science is merely one local system of knowledge among others. Epistemic relativists are usually cultural relativists; hence, they hold that every belief system reflects the way of life or the culture of a particular people, and none can be said to be better than any of the others. Generally speaking, epistemic relativists are also moral relativists. If we cannot have absolute knowledge about any subject matter, then we cannot have absolute knowledge about morality. Thus epistemic relativism is usually held to *entail* moral relativism.

Though there are a few philosophers who advocate epistemic relativism, it is not a widely held view. The overwhelming success of our science in making accurate predictions, in controlling our environment and in making our lives easier is hard to reconcile with the belief that, nevertheless, that science is no more true than premodern or Navaho physics. Worse still for epistemic relativism, it seems to be an incoherent position. People who claim that they believe in epistemic relativism seem to be contradicting themselves.

To see how epistemic relativism seems to be self-contradictory, we need to ask ourselves what the status of the relativist's own knowledge claim is supposed to be. The epistemic relativist asserts that all factual claims are true only relative to a standard or a framework. But this is itself a factual claim, and therefore must *itself* be subject to the strictures it imposes on knowledge claims. If all factual claims are only true relative to a framework, then the claim 'all factual claims are only true relative to a framework' is itself true only relative to a framework! But if it is only true relative to a framework, then we have no reason to have any confidence in it. After all, the point of the epistemic relativist doctrine is to convince us to stop believing that any knowledge claims are true at all times and everywhere. But if the claims of epistemic relativism are not themselves true at all times and everywhere, then it may be that other knowledge claims are absolutely true. At least, the epistemic relativist gives us no reason to believe that this is not the case.

The only way the epistemic relativist can avoid these mind-boggling paradoxes is by somehow excepting her own principle from the rule it states. That is, a full and non-paradoxical statement of epistemic relativism would have to claim something like the following:

> All factual claims are only true or false relative to some framework, with the exception of *this very* claim.

Though this version of epistemic relativism avoids the problems of self-contradiction, it does so only at the cost of creating new dilemmas. What reason do we have for thinking that this knowledge claim, alone of all such claims, is exempt from the effects of epistemic relativism? What features of the claim make it the case that it is so exempt? If there is one such claim that avoids relativism, might there not be more? Until the relativist provides convincing answers to these questions, her doctrine seems to be rather implausible.

There is a reply to this line of argument available to the epistemic relativist. She might hold that her view is correct, that all factual statements are only true relative to some framework. But, she might add, this claim itself is true relative to *all* frameworks. It is, at the moment, hard for us to evaluate this claim, since the notions of 'framework' and 'standards' we have been utilizing so far are vague.

Nevertheless, at this stage we can at least say this much: if it is true that some factual statements are true relative to all possible (or plausible) frameworks, then this in itself seems a sufficient basis for suspecting that any interesting relativism is false. If some statements are true relative to all frameworks, then we can concentrate our attention on these. It might, for instance, turn out that some moral statements are true relative to all plausible moral frameworks. Perhaps 'murder is wrong' is one such claim. In that case, though, we seem to have a sufficient basis to begin elaborating a morality that is, if not absolutely true, at least true for all people and at all times. What absolutist could want more? Such a morality would disarm those relativists who argue that we should never interfere with the practices of other cultures. Formulating a cross-culturally valid morality would provide us with the criteria for deciding when such intervention was justified.

Since epistemic relativity (in any strong form) is regarded by most philosophers as implausible, and since it is vulnerable to the contradiction argument, I will from now on ignore it. I will focus all my attention on moral relativism. This form of relativism is not vulnerable to the contradiction argument in the form we have so far presented it. The moral relativist claims that:

a. Moral claims are true only relative to some standard or framework.

Since this is not itself a moral claim, it is not contradictory to assert it. We can, without contradiction, say that no moral claim is (absolutely) true, while holding that nevertheless a. is (absolutely) true. Thus the moral relativist avoids the contradiction argument, at least in the form in which we have examined it.

Varieties of moral relativism

The rest of this book will focus on moral relativism almost exclusively. But moral relativism is itself a broad category. We can distinguish three basic kinds of relativism that fall under the general category of moral relativism.[7]

Descriptive relativism

By descriptive relativism, we simply mean that, as a matter of fact, different cultures or (rational) individuals hold different fundamental moral principles, which sometimes conflict. So described, descriptive relativism seems to be obviously true: we only have to look at the diversity of practices and beliefs across the world (or even within our own society) to be convinced of it. As we shall see, however, things are not so simple. Descriptive relativism is true only if moral disagreement is really fundamental; very often, however, apparent moral disagreement can be fully explained by pointing to a factual (and therefore non-moral) disagreement upon which it rests. Thus, for example, apparent moral disagreement concerning the permissibility of pornography might be fully explained in terms of a disagreement about a matter of fact: does pornography lead men to objectify women?

Moral-requirement relativism

Moral-requirement relativism is the view that what is morally required of individuals varies from group to group, culture to culture, and so forth. Thus, if moral requirement relativism is true, I may be morally required to do some things (treat everyone equally, for example, regardless of their gender or race) that some other individuals are not required to do. There may even be some things that some people are required to do that are impermissible for others. Thus, for example, it might be that an Aztec priest is morally required to sacrifice human beings to the gods, whereas similar acts are absolutely impermissible for me. As we shall see, moral-requirement relativism is true only if the kinds of moral principles that are binding upon some people, but not others, are truly fundamental. It is true and uncontroversial that different people are required to act in different ways (only those who have made promises are required to keep them, for instance), but unless these requirements concern fundamental principles, they give no support to relativism in any interesting form.

Meta-ethical relativism

Meta-ethics is that branch of moral philosophy that is concerned with the meaning of moral statements and with the foundations of ethics. Thus meta-ethical relativism is a relativistic *theory* of morality. Meta-ethical relativists assert, roughly, that moral judgements are neither (absolutely) true nor false, or perhaps that a moral statement such as 'murder is wrong' *means* something like 'my culture disapproves of murder'. These views are independent of each other, so that a meta-ethical relativist can hold one without holding the other.

These three kinds of moral relativism are importantly related to each other. In fact, each builds upon the preceding one. Thus, the truth of moral-requirement relativism seems to depend on the truth of descriptive relativism. If descriptive relativism is false – if there just is no disagreement about fundamental moral principles in the world today – then it seems likely that no one is required to act upon a fundamental moral principle upon which others are not required to act. Thus moral-requirement relativism requires descriptive relativism. But 1. does not entail 2. That is to say, though if 1. is false then 2. is false as well, it does not follow that if 1. is true then so is 2. In fact, most people who deny that normative-requirement relativism (and, for that matter, meta-ethical relativism) is true nevertheless believe that descriptive relativism is true.

Similarly, the truth of meta-ethical relativism presupposes the truth of moral-requirement relativism. Here, though, the relation is stronger. If 2. is true, then there are some fundamental moral principles that are binding on some people and not upon others. But if this is the case, then there may be some statements concerning morality that some people hold to be true and others hold to be false *without either of them being wrong*. Thus, for example, I might hold that the following statement is true:

| Killing an innocent person who is no threat to anyone is always wrong.

But an Aztec priest might disagree with me. He might hold that it is not wrong when the act is performed as a sacrifice to the gods. Now, if neither of us is mistaken in our beliefs, then meta-ethical relativism must be true, since the label 'meta-ethical relativism' attaches to any view that holds that moral judgements are never (absolutely) true or false. Thus it seems that moral-requirement relativism entails meta-ethical relativism. We shall return to these questions in subsequent chapters.

Why does moral relativism matter?

We are now in a position to understand why relativism is often held to be such a threatening, and such an exhilarating, doctrine. To see this, we have only to notice that not only are the standards by reference to which moral statements might be held to be true multiple, they are frequently also thought to be incompatible. The opinions of different people, and the standards of different cultures, often conflict. Thus it may often happen that one and the same moral statement is true relative to one such standard and false relative to another. If the relativist's thesis is true, at this point we have gone as far as we can go. We cannot, by hypothesis, judge which of the competing standards is truer or better (any such judgement will itself only be true relative to some standard!). Thus we have no rational means of rejecting either claim. We are confronted with an apparent paradox: the same statement is true and false at the same time.

The mere fact that relativism gives rise to such an apparently paradoxical conclusion is not sufficient to explain the passions that surround this debate. After all, constructing paradoxes is a philosopher's parlour game and has been since the time of the ancient Greeks. No one is roused to anger or joy by the liar's paradox, or by the paradoxes formulated by Bertrand Russell. What explains the passion upon both sides of this debate is the fact that relativism seems to threaten moral truth. Consider an example, one to which we shall return several times during the course of the book.

In Aztec society, human sacrifice was an important part of life. On major feast days, slaves, captives taken in battle and even children were slaughtered by Aztec priests, their bodies then butchered for ritual cannibalism. As many as twenty thousand people were killed as part of the dedication ceremony for one major temple. This massive slaughter was not condemned; far from it. It was at the centre of Aztec religious life, and almost everyone participated in it, from the priests who wielded the knives and the warriors who took the prisoners to the common people who helped care for the prisoners before their death and ritually consumed them afterwards. For the Aztecs, then, human sacrifice was a sacred duty to the gods. By making the blood of fellow human beings flow, the Aztecs repaid a debt to the gods and helped ensure the fertility of the earth.[8]

When the Spanish conquistadors arrived in 1519, they were appalled by these Aztec practices. I suspect that most of us share their response. We too recoil from the mass slaughter of innocent human beings, condemning it as savagery. But the relativist asks us to refrain from such condemnation. Instead, she asks us to understand the place of human sacrifice within Aztec society, its centrality to their belief system and to their entire way of life. When we condemn them, she points out, we invoke our moral standards, standards which the Aztecs did not share. If we cannot demonstrate that our standards are objectively better than others, then we have no right to impose them on people who happen not to share them. If morality is always relative to a standard, then human sacrifice is not necessarily always and everywhere wrong. It might be wrong for us, but it was permissible for the Aztecs.

We now begin to glimpse why moral relativism is, if true, such an unsettling doctrine. Aztec human sacrifice is, of course, now consigned to the distant past. The inhabitants of present-day Mexico are no more likely to engage in it than are those of London or Paris. But there are many other activities taking place right now across the world that seem, at first glance, equally objectionable or almost so. Some of these activities are largely confined to exotic places; others occur in the large cities of the First World. Consider a few examples:

☛ An estimated 135 million women and girls alive today are the victims of female genital mutilation, also known as female circumcision, a ceremony practised in many northern African and some Middle Eastern countries. In some cases, this is an almost entirely symbolic ritual, which causes no lasting damage or pain. But in many cases the victim will suffer long-term physiological and psychological harm, ranging from repeated infections to death. The professed aim of the practice is, in part, to control female sexuality.

☞   In Afghanistan under the Taliban, women were banned from
       seeking an education, being employed outside the home, or
       even travelling without male relatives. Similar, though less
       extreme, restrictions are common throughout the Middle East.
☞   The past ten years have been witness to attempts to destroy or
       displace entire populations, identified by their religious or
       ethnic identity. In the mid 1990s Bosnian Serb forces massa-
       cred tens of thousands of Croat and Muslim men, putting into
       practice a policy known as 'ethnic cleansing'. In April 1994,
       Hutu extremists in the East African country of Rwanda perpe-
       trated their own brand of ethnic cleansing, killing at least half a
       million ethnic Tutsi people, as well as thousands of Hutus who
       opposed the massacre.

These are all cases of what we are reflexively disposed to call human
rights abuses. They seem to call for our condemnation at the very
least, and perhaps for much more. Organizations such as Amnesty
International and Human Rights Watch have been set up to report
on these activities and to attempt to bring pressure to bear on the
countries concerned. An international War Crimes Tribunal has
convened in the Hague to prosecute people who took part in the
ethnic cleansing in the Balkans. These movements are all, in part, a
response to the passionate anger felt by many thousands of ordinary
men and women around the world who believe that this kind of
behaviour cannot be tolerated, that the perpetrators must be
pursued and brought to justice. Now consider one possible relativist
response to all these cases:

> When we condemn these activities, we do so by reference to our
> moral standards. But we have no reason to believe that our moral
> standards are any better than the moral standards of other people. If,
> therefore, these acts are permissible on the moral standards of the
> people who perform them, then we have no right to interfere.

The relativist might bolster this claim by pointing out that many of
the kinds of activities with which we are here concerned are permitted or even required by the cultures in which they take place. Thus

female genital mutilation is frequently held to be a religious requirement by those people who perform it, while the exclusion of women
from public life was justified by the Taliban with reference to the
Qur'an. Even the ethnic cleansing in the former Yugoslavia and in
Rwanda might be justified by the cultural views of the people who
carried it out. After all, these are animosities with deep historical and
cultural roots. Now, the relativist might argue, when you condemn
these practices, you do so in the name of your morality, which is
merely the codification of the practices and beliefs of your culture.
Why do you believe that the requirements of your culture should
take precedence over those of another culture?

If relativism is true, therefore, we seem to be left without any
principled means of condemning some of the most horrific events of
the past century, and the ongoing human rights abuses of our time.
If moral relativism is true, then there are no absolute moral standards in the name of which we can denounce the Nazi holocaust, the
slave-trade or the Spanish Inquisition; if it is true, our attempts to
pressure the governments of the world to implement moral standards that are similar to our own is unjustified. If relativism is true,
then anything goes (or so its opponents fear). Thus the urgent need
felt by many people to justify a single set of moral standards, valid
for all times and places. Thus the need to refute relativism.

It is this fear, I believe, that explains much of the passion in the
relativism debate, that motivates the opponents of relativism to
denounce it as a handmaiden of genocide and murder. But it is not
the only unsettling consequence of moral relativism, if it is true.
Let us now consider a different set of examples, this time drawn,
not from faraway places, but from the everyday lives of Western
countries:

☛ In the contemporary United States, the permissibility of abortion is perhaps the single most divisive moral issue. It is legal
   for medical professionals to provide abortions for patients, but
   so strongly do many people feel about this issue that they are
   prepared to take direct action to halt the practice. Anti-
   abortion activists often picket clinics or hold demonstrations
   outside them to make their feelings known. A few have gone

much further: since 1993, at least seven abortion-clinic doctors have been killed by activists, and several abortion clinics bombed.

☞ Every year, many millions of animals are used as subjects in scientific experiments. In the United States alone, estimates for the number of animals involved range from seventeen to seventy million.[9] Most of these animals are killed at the end of the experiment, if they do not die during the course of it. Some of the experiments involve subjecting the animal to pain. These experiments are carried out for a variety of reasons: in the course of medical research; as a part of the training of scientists; and in developing new cosmetics, for example. Many people feel that these experiments are justifiable because they have direct and indirect benefits for human beings. But others are fervently opposed to some or all of them. So passionate is this opposition that, once again, some so-called animal liberationists have been prepared to take direct action illegally. Scientists involved in animal experimentation in the United Kingdom, for example, have been the target of fire bombs.

☞ In 2001, Tom Green, a devout Mormon, was convicted of four counts of bigamy in a Utah court. Green is 'married' to five women and has twenty-nine children. Polygamy was widely practised in the Mormon church until 1890, when it was abandoned in the face of United States government pressure. However, thousands of Mormons continue to believe that polygamy is permissible or even required by God. Green does not, therefore, regard himself as a criminal, but is prepared to justify his actions (as are his wives). Indeed, his case was brought to the attention of the authorities by Green's media appearances, in which he defended his marital arrangements.

All these cases, and many others besides, bear witness to moral conflict within our societies. Moral disagreement of the most serious sort is not confined to the clash *between* cultures; it is also a pervasive fact of life *within* cultures. These cases too sometimes give rise to the sort of dilemmas we pointed to above, with regard to apparent human rights abuses. That is, here too many of us want to condemn the practices in question in the strongest possible terms. To the extent that this is so, we have a motive for rejecting moral relativism, since it would prevent us from judging the practices in question. Animal suffering, or plural marriage, just is wrong, many of us want to say, and that is all there is to it.

But these cases also give rise to another kind of difficulty. With regard to the former set of cases, the relativist could – or could at least attempt to – take a neutral stance on the matter at issue. That is, she could say that though her moral standards do not condone female genital mutilation or ethnic cleansing, she recognizes that other people have different standards and that there is no principled way of deciding which set of standards is right. Therefore, she could argue, the best course of action for us is simple non-interference. Different cultures, different morals might be her motto. But this course of action is not open to her in these cases because they do not concern exotic goings-on in far-away places. Instead, the contentious activities are taking place here and now, among us. Given that this is the case, it seems that taking a moral position upon them is impossible to avoid. Even if we believe that there is no principled way to choose between the religious views of Tom Green and the views of feminists who oppose polygamy, we cannot be neutral on the issue. Either our laws will prohibit polygamy or they will permit it. Similarly, either we implicitly endorse the exploitation of animals – by buying goods produced as a result of it, for instance, or simply by our choice of diet – or reject it, we permit abortion or we prohibit it. There is here no middle way.

If you need convincing of this fact, consider how we might try to implement a policy of neutrality. We might, for example, refuse state funding for controversial activities such as abortion clinics or laboratories in which animal experimentation is conducted. In this way, we could avoid situations in which people who are opposed to these activities are obligated to pay taxes that support them. However, this is a far cry from real neutrality on the issues. People who oppose animal experimentation or abortion do not only oppose paying for it, or having it done for their benefit. Instead they hold that it is absolutely wrong, always and everywhere. Though these measures have the effect of refusing state endorsement to these activities, they nevertheless allow them to continue unimpeded. By so doing, a supposedly neutral state is committing itself to a position on these issues. It is implicitly committed to the view that these activities are not criminal. They are not the kinds of thing that, like murder and robbery, ought to be outlawed. Thus the state seems committed to the view that these activities are not wrong, or at least that they are not seriously wrong. If this is the case, however, then the attempt at neutrality fails.

For this reason, the relativist cannot easily adopt a neutral position upon these issues. Moreover, as the world becomes increasingly globalized, more and more moral issues come to resemble these cases more than they do the case of Aztec sacrifice. Female genital mutilation and the position of fundamentalist Islam on the status of women are no longer matters that arise only at our borders. Instead, with the immigration of African and Islamic communities to Western countries, they now arise at the very heart of all countries. Once again we are forced to take a stand; to decide whether we are going to permit these practices or to ban them. But if relativism is true, then there is no principled way to decide which we ought to do.

Relativism is unsettling, therefore, not just because it denies us the means to condemn strange rituals in exotic locales, but because it undermines our ability to take moral stands, here, at home. But, as we have seen, we have to take such stands: we cannot avoid or duck these issues. Relativism thus threatens to pull the moral rug out from under our feet, leaving us with no way of making decisions that have nevertheless to be made. No wonder it is so unsettling. No wonder its opponents denounce it with much the same ferocity they reserve for crimes against humanity.

We can now begin to appreciate the passion exhibited by the opponents of relativism; why they believe that refuting it is so important. We are not simply committing an intellectual error in subscribing to relativism, these critics contend, we are, willingly or not, complicit in crimes, in abuses of human rights. We give intellectual aid and comfort to dictators and rapists, torturers and murderers, at home and abroad. But why the passion from the other side, from the advocates of relativism? In part, of course, this passion could be explained by the very fervour of its opponents: when someone is accused of tacit complicity in the worst of crimes, this person's response is likely to be a little heated. However, this is very far from being a full explanation of the zeal with which advocates of moral relativism promote their cause. In fact, the passion felt by advocates of relativism is not just a reaction to that expressed by its opponents. They, too, believe that relativism is fundamentally important. Relativism matters, for its supporters as well as its opponents, and it matters morally.

Why, then, might we think that moral relativism is not only true, but also right; that is, *morally* right? Perhaps the strongest reason lies in one common response to the history of European colonization and imperialism. Earlier I mentioned the Spanish conquest of South America. This conquest was itself justified, in part, by reference to morality. The Spanish saw themselves not just as military adventurers seeking plunder, but also as missionaries, spreading the word of God. Cortes, the leader of the conquistador expedition against the Aztecs, reports that he personally cast the Aztec idols out of their temples and in their place put images of Catholic saints. Thus the slaughter of the Aztecs, the destruction of their temples and the torture of their king all were justified on moral grounds, as necessary for the salvation of the immortal souls of the Aztecs themselves.

The pattern was repeated across North and South America, Africa, Australasia, the Pacific and much of Asia. Colonies had to be established and the people subdued so that the message of Christian morality could be heard. Across the world people were dying unbaptized, living in sin, without the guidance of true morality to set them aright. Missionaries had to be sent to teach a docile population to cover their nakedness, to respect private property (especially that of their betters!) and to work regular hours for the greater glory of God. No doubt many of these missionaries were sincere in their beliefs. But when we look at the actual results of colonialism, it is hard to avoid concluding that this moralistic talk was no more than an ideological cover for brutal exploitation. From colony to colony, the story was depressingly familiar. The indigenous population was slaughtered or enslaved, cowed not by the evident truth of Western morality, but by the rifles the invaders carried. Whole civilizations collapsed, as in the case of the Aztecs. Religious structures crumbled, kinship systems fell apart, peoples were left dispirited, sick, herded into reservations. Meanwhile the natural resources of their lands were ruthlessly plundered. Aztec gold poured into Spain, at the same time as black slaves were transported to the cotton plantations of Virginia to work for the profit of their – Christian – owners. Though the entire enterprise was justified by frequent invocations of our morality and our duty toward our inferiors, we cannot help but suspect rather baser motives.

When relativists review this sad history, with its ongoing legacy of disease and poverty where once functioning societies lived and prospered, they see a lesson in it. They see that exploitation is often justified by invoking morality. When Western nations decide to intervene in the affairs of another country because they disapprove of some of its practices, the results are too frequently much worse than were the abuses they aimed to stop. It might have been far better, in the long run – there might have been much less suffering and death – to leave the Aztecs to their human sacrifices. In any case, the relativists add, who are we to judge? What gives us the right to say that our morality is better than theirs? We have, most of us, by now lost the confidence to say that our *religion* is better. Even the believers among us usually call for tolerance of different belief systems, not for casting the idols out of the temples. Isn't it about time we extended the same tolerance to different moralities, the relativists ask? Let us leave the Muslims to their ways, and the Mormons to theirs. We have no way of proving, even to ourselves, that our moral system is better than theirs, but we do know that intervening to change their beliefs will likely end horribly.

Thus relativism is often justified today in the name of tolerance. We ought, relativists argue, to treat all the peoples of the world with equal respect. But we can only show this respect by allowing every-one freedom of conscience, which includes the freedom to formulate and follow one's own moral beliefs. Imposing one's system of moral beliefs upon other people is not only rationally unjustified, it is also morally objectionable.

Thus the absolutist and the relativist each has a *moral* case to put for and against moral relativism. Each believes that the truth or falsity of this doctrine is not of mere intellectual interest, but also of moral importance. The absolutist accuses the relativist of giving aid and comfort to Third-World dictators, by refusing us the right to judge the actions of an Idi Amin or a Saddam Hussein. The relativist accuses the absolutist of adherence to a fundamentally intolerant doctrine, a doctrine that is closed to the diversity of people and their beliefs, that wants to homogenize the world, to destroy other cultures and propagate the standards of the United States, until the world is one flat featureless sameness. Thus the passion in the debate, the heat with which it is conducted.

Surveying the moral arguments for and against relativism, however, leaves us with more questions than answers. Each side justifies its position by pointing to the disastrous moral consequences of adopting the other. But surely they cannot both be right. Relativism cannot simultaneously entail respect for diversity and tolerance of different ways of life, and complicity in the abuse of human rights – can it? Where does the truth lie? What are the moral implications of relativism? Equally, whatever its moral implications, have we any reason to believe relativism true?

We need to explore the ethical implications of moral relativism in much more depth. But before we do so, we must discover whether moral relativism is a minimally coherent position. The task of the next chapter, then, is to make a preliminary examination of the arguments for moral relativism. We have seen some of the moral reasons that lead many people to embrace moral relativism; it is time now to set out the intellectual arguments for the view.

2

MORAL RELATIVISM: THE INTELLECTUAL CASE

People come to embrace moral relativism in many different ways, and for many different reasons. Very often, they are not at all clear about why they come to think that it is true. Nevertheless, their views are usually formed by arguments, more or less lucidly grasped. It will be the task of this chapter to set out these arguments.

In general, I believe, the usual route to relativism is through reflection on the source of our values. Thus our first task will be to explore our moral values. What are values? What role do they play in our thought? How do we acquire them? And how do the answers to these questions bear upon moral relativism?

Value and relativism

Belief in moral relativism is usually motivated by a view I shall call the *enculturation thesis*.[10] This thesis states that each of us has the values we do as the result of a process of enculturation; that is, as a result of having been brought up in a particular society, in a particular manner. Thus the enculturation thesis holds that we each have the values we do as a result of the same kind of process as that which led us to speak our first language. We were exposed to this language, and those values, and we simply absorbed them.

What is the evidence for the enculturation thesis? As we have previously had occasion to notice, moral relativism owes much of its current prestige to the work of anthropologists, and the evidence for the enculturation thesis is largely anthropological.[11] As they studied exotic cultures, anthropologists were struck by the sheer diversity of the moral views they encountered. More importantly, they noticed that these views varied systematically. Though there is individual variation and disagreement in every human group, the broad outlines of a moral conception are shared by almost the entire group. Thus we can speak of the morality of the Inuit, or the Aztecs, and so forth. Each group holds its own conception of what is worthwhile, what is important, what is required, and so on, a conception that conflicts, sometimes radically, with the views of other people. Thus values vary systematically from culture to culture.

The enculturation thesis is advanced to explain this variety and the systematic form it takes. Moral conceptions and values vary in exactly the same way as do human languages and customs. But languages and customs are obviously acquired as a result of enculturation. In fact, the comparison with custom or etiquette is here revealing. Each culture has its own set of customs, to which its members are strongly attached. Custom plays a similar role in human life to morality. It allows a large number of people to exist alongside each other with a minimum of friction, and even to co-operate with each other, by producing behaviour that is relatively predictable. Moreover, our emotional responses to custom following, and to violations of customs, are very similar to those we are prone to feel with regard to morality. This is particularly clear in the case of that sub-group of customs we call etiquette. Many people are moved to outrage by violations of etiquette; they might, for instance, hold that it is intolerable for someone to chew food with an open mouth, or to belch at the dinner table. Thus they feel that everyone *ought* to follow the rules of polite behaviour. Yet, as we all know, what these rules require differs from culture to culture; in some cultures it would be considered rude *not* to belch at the dinner table.

Given the similarities between customs, which we know to be produced by a process of enculturation, and values; given the fact that the values to which people subscribe vary from place to place and time to time, the conclusion seems inescapable: the enculturation thesis is correct. Each one of us has the values we do largely as a result of enculturation. It is characteristic of our culture to place a high value on certain things that are, at best, peripheral in other cultures: individual autonomy, for instance. The best explanation for this variety and the systematic form it takes is that the values we hold are the result of a process of enculturation.

Now, in what way does the enculturation thesis lend support to moral relativism? Proponents of relativism point out that recognition of the centrality of enculturation has several implications. First and foremost, it has the effect of shaking our confidence in our own values. Imagine the experience of the anthropologist, as he encounters an alien set of values. At first, he confidently concludes that where he and his subjects differ, he is right and they are wrong. After all, he might say to himself, they are wrong about so many other things – about science and medicine, for example. But as he reflects further, his confidence is shaken. He realizes that his subjects have acquired their moral views as a result of a process of enculturation. They were not given the opportunity to reflect upon their values. Indeed, they could not have been given such an opportunity; we can only deliberate ethically against the background of values. If we do not already think some things are worthwhile and others trivial, that we have obligations and duties, and so on, we would not be able to engage in ethical reflection at all, since we would have no reason to prefer anything to anything else. Thus, the anthropologist realizes, values have to be acquired through enculturation. But if this is the case for his subjects, then it must also be true for him. He, too, acquired his values simply as a result of a process of enculturation. Hence, as he realizes, he has exactly the same reasons for embracing his values as his subjects have for embracing theirs: he has been taught them. His confidence that his values are better justified than theirs is shaken.

The further our anthropologist reflects on his values and the manner in which he acquired them, the less confident in their timeless validity he becomes. He realizes that he has his values largely as a result of an accident of birth. If he had been born elsewhere, into a different society, at a different period in history, he would have had different values. In fact, he realizes with a start, had he been born into the culture he is now engaged in studying, he would have shared its values. And if he had, he would have been just as confident that they were uniquely justified as, just a few minutes earlier, he had been that his current values were uniquely justified. Now, this thought is enough to make us wonder whether our confidence in our values really is justified. We had thought that our values reflected the moral structure of the universe itself; now we realize that we have them only as a result of an accident of birth.

Though these reflections might shake our confidence in our values, they probably will not cause us to lose it altogether. Nor should they. After all, it is not just our values that we come to embrace as a result of enculturation. In fact, a great many of our beliefs we hold only because we have been brought up to do so. Most of us take most of our scientific views on trust, for instance. We are in no position to verify them for ourselves. Even scientists cannot check the validity of many of their most basic beliefs, at least not directly. Just as we all can only engage in moral reflection from the perspective of some set of values, so the scientist can assess theories and beliefs only against the background of yet more basic theories and beliefs. She cannot stand entirely outside her theories to compare them with physical reality. As many philosophers have pointed out, our very perception is 'theory-laden', which is to say that our theories influence what we see and how much importance we ascribe to it.

Yet the fact that we come to have our scientific beliefs in the same way as our moral values, through a process of enculturation, does not cause most of us to lose confidence in these beliefs. There is, or at least there seems to be, a fundamental difference between scientific beliefs and moral values, which leads us to lose faith in our moral views much more easily than our scientific beliefs. In fact, there are several differences, all of which centre around one single claim: our scientific beliefs are held to reflect objective reality, whereas few of us have much confidence that the same can be said for our moral values.

Nietzsche's challenge

What explains the apparent difference in the ease with which our confidence in our scientific beliefs and that in our moral beliefs is shaken? At first sight, the parallels between the two sets of beliefs are extensive. Both are acquired largely as a result of enculturation. Both give rise to seemingly intractable disagreement, at least on occasion. Scientific beliefs that have, in the past, been held with absolute certainty we now reject with equal certainty. Yet none of these facts leads us to doubt that our science is, largely, true. Why this difference between the two sets of beliefs?

I suggest that the explanation of this difference lies in the fact that it is very plausible to think that there is something independent of our scientific beliefs, something that makes them true or false. Though we might have some trouble perceiving it accurately, due to the fact that our perception is theory-laden, there is an objective reality, and scientific theories will be true to the extent to which they reflect or conform to that reality. Of course, much the same can be said for our other beliefs about matters of fact. My belief that there is a table in this room is true just in case there is a table in this room: my belief must somehow match a reality independent of it to be true. Thus, there is a characteristic method of settling disputes in science, as in other areas of life. Such disputes ought to be settled by presenting evidence of a particular kind, and that evidence is *empirical*. That is, the evidence relevant to this kind of question is the kind of evidence that is collected by observation: we look through a telescope, or take geological samples, or subject specimens to certain well-defined procedures. In practice, of course, things frequently are very much more complicated. We discover, for example, that scientific questions cannot be settled *merely* by collecting the relevant sorts of evidence, but that that evidence needs to be explained and interpreted. To do this work of explanation, we formulate theories, which are hypotheses that attempt to account for the evidence we have gathered. It sometimes happens that two or more theories account as well, or nearly so, for all the available evidence, and then we might have a protracted dispute. In any case, it is clear what general kinds of evidence are relevant for settling scientific disagreements. That evidence is physical fact; the very stuff of the universe. It is simply 'out there'; independent of us and waiting to be discovered, quantified and explained.

Since scientific theories aim to explain evidence that exists independently of these theories, we are, most of us, sure that there is a fact of the matter in science. If the dispute resists all efforts to bring it to a close, we simply conclude that we have not yet gathered sufficient evidence, or that we have not formulated a fully adequate theory, or perhaps that one of the sides to the controversy simply and irrationally refuses to accept the facts. With regard to many such disputes, it is plausible to believe that we never will satisfy all the contending parties; nevertheless, we are all sure that even with regard to these hard cases, there is just one right answer. Since there is an independent physical realm to which our theories aim to conform, we have no doubt that at bottom science deals with facts. Of course, exactly the same thing is true for other areas of human enquiry. There is a matter of fact concerning, say, how many soldiers were involved in the Battle of Waterloo (though the evidence remaining to us may well be insufficient for us ever to know the answer); it is certainly the case with regard to our everyday observations. With regard to none of these questions are we tempted to argue from the fact that people disagree to the conclusion that here there simply is no right answer.

What is the evidence that our scientific beliefs are made true (or false) by somehow matching a reality independent of them? Most importantly, there is the continuity between scientific and everyday beliefs. My belief that there is a table in this room is confirmed or disconfirmed by observation. A glance will quickly show that I am right (the theory-ladenness of perception is a real phenomenon, but its effects are subtle; it cannot cause us to see a table where there is none). Thus, my belief is true to the extent that it matches a reality outside itself. Similarly for scientific theories. Here observation is much more difficult, and often involves special equipment. Moreover, our observations often need to be interpreted before it becomes clear whether or not they support a particular theory (this is often true of everyday observations as well). Nevertheless, though scientific theory testing brings with it its own complications, it is clearly continuous with everyday observation in many ways.

Two other, closely related, facts about science lend plausibility to the belief that it reflects a realm of independent facts. The first is its great *success*. Modern science allows us to predict and control the world around us to an unprecedented degree. We use it to shape our immediate environment, to travel distances and at speeds never before imagined, to extend our lives, and in many other ways besides. Its products entertain us, feed us, heal us and enhance our lives. Even when it goes wrong, when its products turn out to be dangerous or unhealthy, it is science itself to which we turn, if not to fix the damage then at least to understand it.

Now, it is very plausible to maintain that the best explanation for this spectacular success is that scientific theories are largely *true*. To say that they are true, however, is to say that in some manner they match the world. We can use science to predict and control the world only because its theories reflect that world. Science is true to the extent that it conforms to a reality independent of it.

The second remarkable fact about science is its great success at attracting converts. We have remarked upon the moral diversity of the world, the extent to which values vary from culture to culture. This kind of diversity is much less to be seen with regard to scientific beliefs. In fact, precisely the opposite phenomenon is to be observed. All over the world, the same fundamental physics is taught, doctors are trained to understand physiology in the same way, to treat disease with the same drugs and the same surgery. Scientists in Burkina Faso use the same technical vocabulary as those in São Paulo, Singapore and San Francisco; they meet at the same conferences to work on common problems. Scientific views and theories around the world *converge*: everyone who reflects seriously on these problems comes to share more or less the same theories, with disputes largely confined to the margins.

This convergence is no doubt explained by the remarkable success of science. People seek the most efficient way of controlling their environment, of growing crops and saving lives. Science offers all this to them. Though the scientists might come from cultures that, in the recent past, attributed illness to sorcery or the gods, or believed that thunder was caused by clouds crashing together, they seem to feel no nostalgia for the traditional beliefs of their culture. Certainly, they give no sign that they think that these beliefs are as valid as those of Western science. Instead, they simply abandon these traditional beliefs, trading them in for views that better reflect the way the world really is.

Now, if all this is true of scientific beliefs, why not of moral theories as well? Why not think that they, too, reflect an independent realm of facts, moral facts? If we could so conclude, then it would follow that a moral belief was true to the extent to which it matched moral reality, that values were more or less correct, according to their conformity to this realm. Some people do believe just this. They speak of the 'moral law', as though it were a reflection of some timeless realm of moral facts. But most of us are more impressed by the differences between scientific enquiry, and indeed everyday observation, and moral values then by the similarities. And we explain these differences by holding that unlike scientific theories, moral values do not reflect an independent reality.

What are these differences? They are the mirror image of the features of science that we have been enumerating. Moral values and theories do not seem to offer us the ability to control or predict the world. At least, no moral theory seems to do a better job at this than any other. We cannot, therefore, speak of the success of moral theories. Perhaps for this very reason, people do not tend to converge on the same moral theories. When they gather at an international conference, scientists from all over the world are able to discuss their work with one another with no difficulties, but if the conversation turns to morality, not only might the scientists disagree violently, they sometimes even have difficulty understanding one another's point of view. Moreover, they would most likely find themselves unable to agree even upon a method for resolving their dispute. Scientific disputes are settled by observations, at least in principle, but what would they observe to settle a moral dispute?

What explains the manner in which moral beliefs differ from scientific beliefs? Why do we have so much more confidence in the latter than in the former? I suggest that the best explanation will hold that scientific beliefs reflect or match a reality independent of them, whereas moral beliefs do not. Thus we cannot settle moral disputes in the same way as, in principle at least, we can resolve scientific controversies: by simply adducing observational evidence. The evidence for and against moral claims is not independent of those claims, but in some way bound up with them. There are no moral facts outside of us and our moral beliefs, in the way in which there are scientific facts that are independent of what we believe and do.

To be sure, some philosophers have believed that there are such facts. Plato, for instance, perhaps the greatest philosopher of antiquity, thought that there was, besides this physical world, an independent sphere; the so-called 'realm of forms'. This realm contained the forms, instantiations of universal concepts such as goodness and justice. Thus, Plato held, something was good to the extent to which it partook of this form; that is, to the extent to which it shared in the essence of goodness. Other philosophers have produced a more conventionally religious view, analogous to Plato's, in which something is good in so far as it partakes of the idea of goodness as it exists in the mind of God. Thus these philosophers have postulated an independent world of moral facts, along the lines of the world of physical facts, so as to make moral enquiry more closely analogous to scientific research. If there were such a realm, then we would be able to settle moral disputes in just the same kind of way as scientific disagreements, and moral disagreement would be rendered innocuous.

Today, however, the idea of such an independent moral realm has lost its plausibility. We live in a highly sceptical world, and we do not easily lend credence to claims concerning the existence of the supernatural; and an independent moral realm would seem to be, quite literally, supernatural. We live, as Nietzsche dramatically put it, after the death of God. Nietzsche's madman speaks for our age:

> 'Whither is God?' he cried; 'I will tell you. *We have killed him –* you and I. All of us are his murderers. But how did we do this? How could we drink up the sea? Who gave us the sponge to wipe away the entire horizon? What were we doing when we unchained this earth from its sun? Whither is it moving now? Whither are we going? Away from all suns? Are we not plunging continually? Backward, sideward, forward, in all directions? Is there still any up or down? Are we not straying as through an infinite nothing? Do we not feel the breath of empty space? Has it not become colder?[12]

We have not all become atheists, as Nietzsche's madman might lead us to think. Nevertheless, the Europe of Nietzsche's time had undergone a change almost as significant. Perhaps most people continued to believe in God, but, for intellectuals at least, the burden of proof had shifted. It was no longer possible simply to assume God's existence. Instead, one needed evidence, or, like Kierkegaard, one needed to make a leap of faith despite the lack of evidence. This was, as Nietzsche so clearly saw, an event of the greatest significance. Previously, God had been the guarantor of moral order, had been surety that there was a sense to existence. Now, the belief in his existence was shaken, and the prospect of a universe without meaning opened before our eyes. The very horizon toward which we moved has been wiped away, our sun has set permanently and we find ourselves lost in the dark without landmarks to guide us.

Nietzsche saw that nowhere would the consequences of the death of God be more momentous than with regard to morality. Up until the great cultural shift that Nietzsche records, the belief that there is an independent moral realm, conformity to which made our moral beliefs true, when they were true, was plausible. God was the guarantor of that realm, indeed, very often the realm was identified in some manner with God. God's law, embodied in the Bible, was timeless, and punishments awaited those who transgressed it. So long as God was in his heaven, all was right with the world, and the notions of good and of right were clear and distinct. But with the death of God, the transcendent moral law itself passes from the world. Like God, people could and did continue to cling to faith in it, but it was no longer compelling.

If transcendental morality has fled the world, Nietzsche thought, then it is up to us to make our own morality. Thus he called for a 'revaluation of all values'. We ought, he held, to impose our own wills upon morality, shape it in the manner we like, and do so in good conscience. He proposed what he took to be a naturalistic morality, a morality that glorified strength of the will, one that was justified by the struggle for existence he thought he saw in the natural world. We must become hard, he argued, hard enough to defeat the treacherous blandishments of traditional morality, now exposed as a fraud. He replaced virtue with the will to power.

Nietzsche's proposals, in a bastardized and ill-comprehended form, were among the influences upon Nazism. Nazi functionaries saw themselves as Nietzschean supermen, who had hardened themselves against the tugs of compassion.[13] Of course, we cannot object to the uses the Nazis made of Nietzsche on moral grounds if Nietzsche was right; if it is indeed up to each of us to create our own values. Why think that our values are better than theirs? We shall have to confront this question head on in the course of this book. For our present purposes, however, the importance of Nietzsche lies elsewhere. It is not Nietzsche's solutions to the problems he diagnosed that interest us, but the clear-sighted way in which he registered the cultural upheaval that his times were enduring, and the implications that, as he foresaw, this seismic shift would have for ethics. Nietzsche did not cause the death of God. He did not wipe away the horizon of significance that had once been in place, nor did he explode the realm of transcendental moral values. He merely registered a transformation that was already well under way. But he was the first to see that we cannot simply ignore the death of God and go on as before. We cannot now act as if our moral values are as well grounded as, formerly, we had believed them to be. Instead, we must find an alternative justification for them, or acquiesce in the face of revaluations of values, be they as extreme as those of the Nazis. In a famous phrase often attributed to Dostoyevsky, the Nietzschean contention is encapsulated: 'if God is dead, everything is permitted'.

How is the so-called 'death of God' related to our topic? I have suggested that fundamental disagreement, the diversity of views and the enculturation thesis are all much more threatening with regard to morality than they are in science. I pointed to the systematic differences between science and morality, especially with regard to the manner in which disputes are characteristically settled. We can now add to and amplify these points. Scientific theories are true or false according to the extent to which they conform to a reality independent of themselves. With regard to morality, however, it simply is no longer plausible to maintain that there is such an independent reality. If people differ, if there are systematic differences between the moral values of different cultures, we begin to wonder if there is any way of choosing between their beliefs. Given the truth of the encul-turation thesis, given the absence of a transcendental moral realm to which we could point in attempting to settle moral disputes, the pressure to assimilate moral beliefs to custom and etiquette becomes almost overwhelming.

Morality as a system of conventions

What would be the consequences of this assimilation? Can we live with the idea that morality is merely conventional? Let us examine the notion of a convention, in order to explore whether assimilating morality to convention would constitute a threat to the kinds of things we want and need from morality. A convention is a way of getting along that a certain society devises for itself. Philosophers often think of conventions as solutions to co-ordination problems. Such problems arise when people engage in activities that might be inefficient, costly or even dangerous if they are not governed by rules. Think of the activity of driving a car. Obviously, it would be dangerous if everyone drove in any way they liked. So we formulate a set of conventions: for example, we all drive on the left-hand side of the road. So long as everyone obeys the new rule, the co-ordination problem is solved. Several things are immediately obvious about this solution, all of which might also be true of morality:

- ☞ the solution to our co-ordination problem works; it makes driving much safer than it would otherwise be. But
- ☞ at least one other solution that would have worked equally well was open to us. We might have decided to adopt another convention, such as all driving on the right-hand side of the road.
- ☞ There is now a fact of the matter as to what side of the road one should drive on. Everyone ought to drive on the left-hand side of the road, at least in countries that have adopted this rule. But
- ☞ nothing makes this true beyond the fact that the convention has been adopted: it is not conforming to an independent realm of driving facts that confers truth here. From all of this it follows, finally, that

☛ if a different culture adopts a different rule – as, of course, many have in this case – there is no fact of the matter which is right. There is more than one adequate solution to this co-ordination problem. Hence we cannot rationally criticize other cultures for failing to conform to our rule (nor, of course, can they criticize us).

If morality is merely conventional, then, it seems, moral relativism is true. There cannot be any fact of the matter which culture has got morality right, on this view. Indeed, this claim is implicit in the very notion that something is conventional. We only develop conventions when there is more than one equally well justified way of doing things. Hence if morality is conventional then no one morality is uniquely justified.

Before we conclude too quickly that moral relativism is true, however, we should notice that there seem to be significant differences between morality and typical conventions, such as road rules. Road rules are explicitly formulated, laid down in law. Thus we know them to be merely human inventions. But moral rules are not simply laid down in law; though of course laws often attempt to reflect them. Indeed, we sometimes criticize our laws in the name of morality, holding that they ought to be altered so that injustice is prevented. Doesn't this suggest that moral laws pre-exist written legislation, and that therefore the analogy with road rules fails? After all, it would be nonsensical to criticize the road laws in the name of the ideal of correct driving, at least when the road laws are mere conventions.

Unfortunately, the relativist has a ready reply to this objection. She might point out that though it is true that moral rules are different from road rules in important ways, there is at least one set of conventions that are importantly similar to moral rules. These are the conventions of language. This is a set of *implicit* rules. They too pre-exist explicit legislation: it makes sense to criticize a grammar book in the name of correct language use (grammar books are, for most languages, a relatively recent innovation). Here too there is such a thing as going wrong; failing to make the verb 'agree' with the noun, for instance. But obviously here too the only thing that makes a linguistic error a mistake is failure to conform to the usage of fluent speakers. And of course here too cultures differ as to what is correct – so much so that we speak languages that are mutually unintelligible. Morality, the relativist might conclude, is a set of conventions closely analogous to linguistic conventions: a collective invention that differs from culture to culture, without there being a fact of the matter which is best or even better.

Let us summarize the argument so far. We began by noting the moral diversity of the world, and the systematic form that diversity takes. Moral beliefs are not scattered at random, but instead follow the contours of cultures. This, we suggested, was very good evidence that the enculturation thesis is true. People are born into their moral views in much the same way as they are born into their languages, their system of etiquette, and other such conventions. We suggested that this fact by itself was not enough to shake our confidence in our moral views. Other kinds of knowledge are also acquired largely through enculturation, but we are confident that some of this knowledge, at least, is independently justified. But, as we have now seen, this confidence is founded on our ability to test this knowledge in various ways against an independent reality. With morality, there is no such independent reality. Our confidence in our moral views is now at a low ebb. When we reflect on the fact that we have the views we do merely as a consequence of having been born in a particular place and time, and on the fact that we cannot test these views against an independent reality, we begin to wonder whether we have any reason to think that our moral views are any better than those of other cultures.

Begging the question

We are not yet in a position to say that moral relativism is true. Far from it. Though we can now say, with some confidence, that we cannot rationally choose between rival moral systems in *just the same way* as we can choose between rival scientific theories, we are very far from being able to say that there is no way to choose between them at all. In fact, most philosophers today are not relativists, but few suppose the existence of a transcendent moral realm. We shall devote a great deal of this book to exploring the ways in which they have attempted to meet Nietzsche's challenge: to justifying a morality without God, and without supposing an independent moral reality.

For the moment, I will limit myself to pointing out one of the obstacles these philosophers need to confront in meeting Nietzsche's challenge. They must somehow justify their own moral views against rival views, without *begging the question* against those views.

We say that an argument begs the question against another view when one or more of the premises it uses to show that that view is false is itself rejected by adherents of the disputed view. In these cases, the premise or premises upon which the argument relies is itself in dispute. For instance, someone might argue that abortion was impermissible on the grounds that abortion is the killing of an innocent person. But this argument begs the question against people who think that abortion is permissible, precisely because they deny that abortion is the killing of a person at all. Unless the opponent of abortion offers an additional argument, which demonstrates that the foetus is a person, we have no reason to be moved by her contention. In general, then, an argument begs the question against an opposing view when it is based upon a contention that ought to be the conclusion of the argument, not a premise of it.

Arguments that beg the question are frequently encountered, in all areas of intellectual life. Why think that they have any special relevance to the question of moral relativism? I suggest that one reason many people are convinced by the intellectual case for relativism is that they believe that arguments that purport to show that relativism is false beg the question against the relativist. That is, these arguments have as one of their premises a contention that is true only if relativism is false. Consider this (frequently encountered) argument:

> Moral relativism must be false, because if moral relativism were true, then we couldn't condemn the Holocaust.

Implicit in this argument is the belief that the Holocaust was bad, indeed, a great evil. Relativism must be false because it prevents us from condemning great evil. Obviously, this argument begs the question against the relativist. It has as one of its premises the contention that the Holocaust was (absolutely and objectively) a great evil, whereas the thoroughgoing moral relativist denies that there is any such thing as absolute and objective standards in ethics. The argument therefore implicitly relies upon exactly the conclusion it claims to draw.

Now, there are good reasons to suspect that it is impossible to argue against moral relativism without begging the question against it, in one way or another. Let us return to our anthropologist, to see why this might be so. After reflecting upon the moral diversity he sees, he has concluded that the enculturation thesis is true; that people's values are to be explained as a function of the culture into which they were socialized. This was enough to shake his confidence in his moral beliefs; he realizes that it is purely a matter of chance that he has his particular set of values, and not another one. But this is not sufficient yet to tip him over into relativism. It might be the case that even though he has his values as a matter of chance, they can nevertheless be shown to be true. After all, it is only as a matter of chance that he was born into a culture that possesses a well-developed science, yet he is confident that science is largely true. We saw, however, that there are good reasons to suspect that ethics is very different from science in many ways, that the kinds of strategies open to us to settle scientific disputes will not be available to settle disputes between rival moral systems. How, then, is our anthropologist to stave off the threat of relativism? What he needs to achieve this is to demonstrate that one moral system is better than any other rival moral systems. Thus relativism will be defeated only if one moral system emerges from a process of comparison as the best justified.

But as he reflects further on what it would take for one moral system to emerge victorious from such a comparison, the anthropologist is struck by an unsettling thought. It seems to him that no moral system can manage this feat. In fact, he concludes, any argument made by the proponent of a moral system against a rival system will be invalid, because it will be guilty of begging the question.

Why should he think that all such arguments are destined to beg the question against opponents? His thought might be something like this: when we attempt to discover which of two competing moral systems is better, we can appeal to two different kinds of evidence: empirical or moral, facts or values. But, he might continue, appealing to facts cannot settle the question. In fact, the view that it is impossible to deduce moral conclusions from empirical facts alone is very widely held among moral philosophers, and has been ever since it was forcefully articulated by the great eighteenth-century Scottish philosopher David Hume. Hume argued that 'ought' statements – the prescriptions and prohibitions characteristic of morality – could not be deduced from 'is' statements alone. Thus, for example, when we conclude from

▌ Sophie promised to help Toby with his maths homework

to

▌ Sophie *ought* to help Toby with his maths homework

the argument is valid only so long as we implicitly assume a suppressed premise, which is itself moral – perhaps something like

▌ People ought to keep their promises.

From mere facts, no matter how many of them we are able to gather, we cannot draw moral conclusions. Such conclusions only follow from facts if we assume, in addition to them, the truth of at least one moral statement. It goes without saying that these fundamental moral statements cannot themselves be deduced from facts alone; such a derivation would violate Hume's law.

But if this is the case, if moral conclusions only follow from facts when moral premises are assumed, then no agreement about matters of fact will ever suffice to settle disagreements about morality. So long as the disputants hold differing fundamental moral principles, agreeing upon the facts of the case will not end the dispute. Thus, to continue our example, if Sophie believes that people are not obliged to keep their promises (or, more strongly, are obligated to break their promises) then she can agree with Toby, that she did promise to help him, and yet dispute his conclusion: that she ought to help him. It is hard to see how bringing forward further empirical facts could settle this conflict.

Thus we cannot settle disputes between rival moral systems by appealing to matters of fact. So instead we will need to appeal to values. Thus, if someone disputes the contention that Sophie ought to help Toby with his homework, while agreeing upon the facts of the case, then we will attempt to convince her by appealing to the principle that people ought to keep their promises. But it is precisely this principle that is at issue in the dispute! Thus the argument is fallacious; it assumes precisely the conclusion it claims to demonstrate. It begs the question against the proponent of a rival moral system.

The thought that is motivating relativism here is that if indeed we cannot settle moral disputes by appealing to matters of fact, then we must instead appeal to values. But since it is precisely these values that are at stake in the conflict, any such appeal will be guilty of begging the question. The principle, the relativist believes, is perfectly general. There is no way of demonstrating the superiority of one moral system over another because all attempts at demonstration will either run afoul, of Hume's law ('no "ought" from "is"') or commit the fallacy of begging the question.

Our anthropologist has drawn our attention to formidable obstacles in the way of anyone attempting to vindicate a particular moral system. Hume's law and the fallacy of begging the question close off many avenues that otherwise might have looked promising. It is far too early to conclude that relativism is true, however. Perhaps there are ways of demonstrating the superiority of one moral system over another that are not guilty of either fallacy. I do not mean this exposition of the obstacles in the way of the anti-relativist to be conclusive. It is designed, rather, to set the stage for the more detailed examination of the case for and against moral relativism to come, and to set out the reasons why rational people might come to embrace relativism. The view that relativism is true is not necessarily the product of confusion or irrationality, as too many philosophers claim, but is a response to powerful arguments, however indistinctly grasped they sometimes might be.

Universality and objectivity

I will end this chapter with a very brief discussion of two anti-relativist positions, two manners in which someone who opposes relativism might think of the status of moral judgements. It is important to enter into this question, because many people might think that the remarks above, on transcendental morality, have already settled the question. They might, that is, think that if there is no such thing as a transcendental morality, if God, or natural law, or some other supernatural force, does not guarantee morality, then relativism must be true. Indeed, some opponents of relativism seem to reason in just this way. They think, with Dostoyevsky, that if God is dead, and nothing remains to take his place, then anything goes. But they are wrong to think that the anti-relativist case requires transcendental support. Indeed, they do their cause a disservice by linking its defence to an implausible and discredited view, one that appears archaic in the modern world.

If moral values are not written in the sky, if they are not transcendentally guaranteed, then what supports them? What reality do they have? The relativist will argue that they are in some way conventional. This is far from an adequate reply by itself. It fails to account for the apparent differences between morality and mere conventions: the seeming force and motivational power of the former, and the manner in which its conclusions seem to concern matters of fact. Of course, the non-relativist who is not tempted by the view that morality is transcendental is also going to have to formulate a theory of value that accounts for its source and status. I suggest that relativist and non-relativist alike will make essential reference, in their value theory, to the needs, desires, interests and preferences of people. In some manner, yet to be spelled out, moral judgements will concern what we want, what we need, what is good for us, and so forth, and will need no more backing than that supplied by this theory.

We are now in a position to sketch one manner in which someone might oppose relativism without buying into implausible metaphysical views. We might hold that our values are in some way constituted by human needs, desires, preferences and interests, but also contend that these needs, desires, and so on, do not differ significantly from culture to culture. People everywhere, and at all times, might have the same basic needs. Given that is the case, then what is in their fundamental interests might not vary, since it is in everyone's interests that their needs be satisfied. People can be expected to prefer and desire what is in their interests (failing which they might count as insane). Thus, if values are based in some way upon needs and interests, then everyone can be expected to share much the same set of values.

If this is the case, then when two cultures dispute which has a better moral system, there will be some kind of answer to be had. Either it will be the case that they both in fact have the *same* moral system, or one will be better, on non-question-begging grounds. We shall be able to show the disputants that one is better than the other without begging the question because, though we must invoke values in our argument, we will not have to appeal to any values that both parties do not in fact share.

Let me demonstrate what I have in mind by reverting to my earlier example, concerning Sophie's promise to Toby. Imagine that we are disputing whether or not Sophie ought to keep her promise. Bloggs argues that Sophie is not obliged to do so, whereas we hold that she is. Now, we saw that we could not appeal to the principle that people ought to keep their promises in attempting to settle this dispute. That would be begging the question, since it is precisely the point at issue. However, perhaps we can convince Bloggs in some other way. We might, for instance, appeal to the *worth* of promise-keeping. It establishes trust between people, and thereby enables society to run more smoothly. If we could not rely upon people to keep their promises, we might point out, many of our everyday activities would be impossible. We could not use credit when making purchases, for example, or rely upon the mechanic to fix our car, and so on. The ramifications would be far-reaching. Now, it might be the case that this argument moves Bloggs, since he already believes that these consequences would be undesirable. We have not, therefore, begged the question against him. Rather than appeal to a principle he rejects, such as the principle that people ought to keep their promises, we have instead appealed to considerations he already accepts, and shown how his view is inconsistent with them.

It might be that all moral disputes can be settled in this manner. If this is the case, it will be because, as a matter of fact, everyone accepts the same *fundamental* moral principles (or can, in some way, be brought to accept these moral principles; perhaps because it is in their self-interest to do so). If this is the case, then relativism is false, even though there may be no such thing as a transcendental moral realm. Moral values are properly identified with our needs, interests and preferences, on this view, but as a matter of fact there is a single, uniquely justified, set of such values. This morality is *universal*, by which I mean no more than that everyone happens to share it (or, by their own lights, ought to).

On this view, the universal morality is also *objective*, which is to say that it is uniquely correct, according to criteria that are the best possible. It is, however, quite possible for someone to be a universalist without being an objectivist. We have sketched one route by which a universal morality might come into existence, by way of rational argument, but since 'universal' means no more than accepted by everyone, such a morality need not be true or even justified; it might just be the winner, as it were. Thus the possibility of a universal morality is compatible with the belief that many different cultures have, at different points in time, accepted quite different fundamental moral beliefs. It is even compatible with the view that moral relativism is now, or has at some time in the past been, true. Perhaps there used to be an irreducible diversity of moral systems but for some reason there no longer is such a diversity. Perhaps this diversity still exists but is in the process of disappearing. We need not hold that these rival moral systems are yielding to persuasion. Perhaps they are simply becoming extinct as a result of economic pressures, in the same way as many of the world's languages are becoming extinct. A universal morality might come about in any of a number of ways, rationally or not. The morality that is victorious at the end of the process need not be the best; there need not be any such thing as the best morality. It is simply the last survivor.

Someone who believes that there is a universal moral system is a non-relativist of a sort. He maintains that when two moral systems appear to give conflicting advice, one is better justified than the other, but only in an attenuated sense. One of them offers a better interpretation of the moral principles they both in fact share. A universalist who is not an objectivist does not think that these are the best possible or uniquely correct principles; merely that they happen to be universal. An objectivist, however, opposes relativism on different grounds. He believes that some moral views are objectively better justified than others, quite independently of whether the better views are widely held. There is an objective fact of the matter concerning morality, whether anyone recognizes this or not. Someone who holds this position would probably also believe that this uniquely justified morality will have the best chance of being a universally embraced morality, but might think that its truth is quite independent of its being universally accepted. Imagine that Germany had won the Second World War and had somehow succeeded in imposing fascism upon the entire world. Then there would be a universal morality, but it would not be an objectively justified morality. The whole world would have embraced a false moral system. Or so the objectivist maintains.

Philosophers who hold that morality is transcendentally guaranteed are objectivists in the sense just sketched. We might compare their views on morality with the views of a scientific realist. A scientific realist is an objectivist about scientific facts. She believes, plausibly, that the facts of science are timeless and unchanging. Thus, they are not altered in any way by what people think they are. Thus, for most of human history people have been objectively mistaken, at least with regard to a great deal of science. Their claims about scientific matters failed to conform to scientific reality. Similarly, someone who believes that morality is transcendental thinks that moral claims are made true or false by conforming or failing to conform to a moral reality that is independent of us. If fascism had become a universal morality, then people would have been universally mistaken.

Thus, everyone who believes in a transcendental morality is an objectivist. But the converse is not true. It is possible to be an objectivist without believing in an independent moral realm. So long as someone believes that there is a fact about morality, whether anyone recognizes it or not, he is an objectivist. He might think, for example, that morality is based on enlightened self-interest, that it is a kind of systematized reciprocity. He might further hold that there is an objective fact about what is in everyone's interests. Thus, people can be mistaken about what is in their interests. When they are, they might develop a morality based on this mistake. This morality could even have become universal; it would be no less mistaken for that.

In this chapter, we have examined some of the main motivations someone might have for adopting moral relativism. We have seen that it is a tempting view because it makes sense of a number of facts about our world, such as its apparent moral diversity, and because it highlights real obstacles in the way of reducing this diversity rationally. It is now time to deepen our understanding of relativism. In the first chapter, we briefly discussed the passions aroused by moral relativism, passions which stem, we said, from the implications it is believed to have for morality. In the next chapter, I want to examine these implications in greater depth. What is the truth here? Is moral relativism an apology for oppression, as its opponents hold? Or is it, on the contrary, a doctrine that teaches tolerance?

3

THE MORAL IMPLICATIONS OF RELATIVISM

When we first began to explore the topic of moral relativism, we saw that its adherents were drawn to it for ethical, as much as intellectual, reasons. They saw in it a powerful weapon against prejudice, a means whereby mutual respect and forbearance could be promoted. It is only because relativism is seen as having these implications for our treatment of other people, especially the members of cultures different from our own, that it possesses such a powerful attraction for many thoughtful people. Relativism is widely perceived by them as the only sure way to avoid repeating the crimes of the past, in which powerful colonizing powers destroyed the ways of life of millions of people, killing many thousands in the process and reducing many more to abject misery.

If it is the moral implications that relativism is often perceived to have that explains its attraction for adherents, it is equally true that opposition to it is usually motivated on moral grounds. Far from accepting the proposition that moral relativism is a bulwark against prejudices, its opponents see in it an ally of tyranny and of oppression. Proponents of relativism argue that it promotes tolerance because when we accept its truth we see that we are unable to judge, let alone condemn, the practices of other cultures. It would be question-begging to measure their behaviour by our standards;

55

therefore, we ought to refrain from so doing. Opponents of relativism agree with its proponents that if it were true we would be unable to judge other cultures, but they see in this very fact the seeds of moral catastrophe. Moral relativism leaves us unable to make necessary criticisms of human rights abuses, of the systematic oppression of women, indeed, of the very destruction wreaked by the colonial powers on their colonies. Judging other cultures is not the first step down a road that leads to genocide; it is the necessary preliminary to coming to the aid of the victims of injustice.

Can relativism be both these things at once, both ally of the despot and weapon against tyranny? Given the fact that both the powerful attraction it exerts over many thoughtful people and the equally powerful revulsion it inspires in others stem from these perceived implications for ethics, perhaps we would do better to concentrate on these implications than on the intellectual case for and against relativism. If it is shown that relativism does not promote tolerance, then its most vocal proponents will lose much of their fervour. If, on the other hand, it can be shown to be compatible with the moral judgement of other cultures, then its opponents will be better prepared to examine the evidence for it in an atmosphere of calm. If we can take the heat out of the dispute over relativism, we will be better placed to come to a considered judgement as to its truth. This, then, is the aim of this chapter: to consider the real moral implications of relativism, and to assess the extent to which these implications strengthen or undermine its plausibility.

Relativism and tolerance

The perception that relativism promotes, or is the expression of, tolerance of difference is almost certainly the single most important factor in explaining its attraction. Very probably, more people adhere to belief in it for this reason than all other reasons combined. We ought not to judge other cultures, many of us believe. To do so is the first step toward imposing our way of life upon them. It is to open the door to cultural imperialism, which leads to the homogenization of the world and the suppression of difference at best, to death, destruction and genocide at worst. We have learnt from our disastrous history: do not judge.

But is it true that relativism promotes or expresses tolerance of other groups, of other ways of life? The view that relativism is a tolerant doctrine appears to confront an insurmountable logical problem, analogous to that which makes a cognitive relativism implausible. As we saw, cognitive relativism seems to be a self-refuting doctrine. The statement 'nothing is absolutely true or false, but only true relative to a framework' is itself, if true at all, either true only relative to a framework or absolutely true. On either alternative, we run into problems. On the view that the statement is absolutely true, we face a paradox, similar to the famous liar paradox. Consider the following statement:

> This very sentence is false.

Is this sentence true? It seems that it cannot be. Since it claims that it is false, if it is true then it is false, and it can't be both true and false at the same time. So is it false? No, because if it is false then – since it claims it is false – it is true. Whichever way we go, we move in a circle. On the view that the statement 'nothing is absolutely true' is absolutely true, we face similar problems, which arise in a similar manner. The liar paradox comes about because the sentence refers to itself, claiming that it is false. Similarly the statement in question refers to itself, claiming to possess only relative truth. On the assumption that, in fact, it is absolutely true, it contradicts itself, claiming both absolute and merely relative truth at the same time. But on the assumption that it has only relative truth, it would seem to give rise to equally paradoxical conclusions. Relative to what might it be true? Is relativism true only here, whereas absolute truth remains possible *there*, in some other place or at some other time? We can barely state the forest of difficulties that confront the epistemic relativist here, much less solve them.

We saw, however, that moral relativism did not give rise to these paradoxes. Since it need not refer to itself, there is no logical reason why it ought not to be absolutely true. So long as the statement 'all propositions that assert what is morally required have only relative truth' does not itself assert what is morally required, it is not self-refuting. However, when the relativist attempts to use her doctrine to show that tolerance is required, she seems to fall back into the trap she had so far avoided. The moral argument for tolerance might run as follows:

> Since moral relativism is true, we have no reason to believe that our moral beliefs are better justified than those of any other culture. Since that is the case, it would be wrong for us to attempt to impose these beliefs upon others who do not share them. Thus moral relativism is not only true, it is also the only tolerant and therefore morally right position to take.

The problem with this argument, as philosophers never tire of pointing out, is that it wants to have its cake and eat it too. It claims that there is no such thing as (absolute) moral truth, and uses this claim as a premise in an argument for the conclusion that we are all morally obliged to tolerate the full range of moral beliefs. But what is the status of this conclusion? Is it, itself, absolutely true? Is it always and everywhere true that people ought to tolerate differing moral beliefs, so that anyone who fails to do so is guilty of immorality? If that is the case, then the first premise of the argument ('there is no such thing as absolute moral truth') is false. And, of course, if this premise is false, then the entire argument is invalid: we have been given no reason at all to believe that we ought to tolerate moral beliefs that conflict with ours.

Thus if the relativist means the conclusion of this argument to state an absolute moral truth, then the entire argument collapses. She has contradicted herself. Perhaps, then, she means the conclusion to express a *relative* moral belief. Perhaps the argument should be restated. Instead of arguing that the truth of relativism commits everyone, everywhere, to tolerance, the relativist might instead hold that it commits *us* to tolerance, given our moral beliefs. David Wong has developed this line of argument. He notes that *we* are advocates of what he calls 'the justification principle'; the principle that it is wrong to impose requirements on people that we cannot justify to them. This principle, Wong argues, together with the belief that moral relativism is true, entails tolerance. The argument runs as follows:

1. People who are members of other cultures have different values to us.
2. Therefore we cannot justify our moral practices and beliefs to them when they conflict with theirs.
3. By the justification principle, we know that it is wrong to impose requirements on people that we cannot justify to them.
4. Hence it would be wrong for us to impose our morality on the members of other cultures.

But this conclusion, that we cannot impose our morality on the members of other cultures, just is equivalent to the principle that we ought to respect other cultures.[14]

This argument seems to be valid. The conclusion it states, the principle of tolerance, is now formulated so as to be relativized to our moral standards. Since it is no longer expressed as an absolutely true moral principle, the relativist can state it without involving herself in a contradiction. Thus, the relativist may argue, though it is not true that relativism commits everyone everywhere to tolerance, for people like us, with our moral beliefs, it does imply tolerance of other moralities.

However, it is far from clear that this new and consistent manner of expressing the support relativism offers for tolerance really achieves the aims of the tolerance-motivated relativist. Our imagined relativist advocated relativism on moral grounds: she held that it was to be preferred to absolutism because it was more tolerant of rival codes. But now we see that to make her case, she has to appeal to the beliefs that, she claims, we – Western liberals – all share. Relativism only supports tolerance under certain conditions; when it is allied to tolerant moral frameworks. When it is not so allied, relativism might be as intolerant as any absolutism. Let us imagine that our relativist managed to convince a member of the Taliban, or a Nazi functionary, of the truth of relativism. What, by the relativist's own lights, ought that person to do? Ought he to tolerate rival beliefs? He has been given no reason to do so, since the relativist is barred from saying that tolerance is (absolutely) right. Tolerance is the right stance for a Western liberal who is convinced of the truth of relativism, since Western liberals believe that they ought not to impose their views on others unless they are certain that those views really are better. But, by the same token, confining women to the home is right for the Taliban, since so doing is consistent with their beliefs. And killing people they regard as their inferiors is right for Nazis, since it is entailed by their beliefs. The relativist cannot reply that the Taliban and the Nazi are making a mistake in regarding women and Jews as inferior, not if the inferiority in question is a moral category, and not one amenable to scientific investigation. For though relativism does not give any support to the claim that women and Jews are (morally speaking) inferior, nor does it give any support to the claim that women and Jews are not (morally) inferior.

In any case, the relativist vision of tolerance appears impossible to apply consistently. Who are we to tolerate? It is one thing to call upon us to tolerate the activities of people when they take place in their own home and cause no one any harm. It is quite another thing to tolerate the activities of people who are themselves intolerant. Should the world have tolerated German expansionism in the late 1930s? Perhaps Hitler would have experienced this as tolerance, but it would have been regarded as something quite different by the people of Poland, not to mention the Jews, gypsies and homosexuals of Germany itself. If we adopt the policy of always tolerating the activities of others, in the sense of never interfering with what they do, then tolerance will be extended only to the powerful, to those who are able, through force of arms or other means, to get their way. Is this really the virtue we wish to exhibit?

In general, the advocate of a tolerance justified in this manner needs to be able to give us some means of deciding whom we are to tolerate and when. We cannot tolerate any and all the actions of everyone to whom we cannot justify our intervention, not when some of those people are themselves intolerant. Ought the world to have tolerated the invasion of Kuwait by Saddam Hussein? Of course, it is very likely that opposing the invasion could have been justified to Iraq, that there was no moral principle accepted by Hussein that made the invasion permissible. But what if there had been? What, indeed, if the invasion had been mandated by a moral system? Then interference would be condemned by the justification principle, which seems to imply that we ought to be tolerant. But at the same time, the act of invasion is itself a violation of the justification principle. It imposes a brutal regime on a people against their wishes. Thus tolerating one set of acts comes at the expense of another failure of toleration. Does this apparent contradiction show that tolerance justified in the manner Wong suggests is incoherent?

In fact, Wong argues, tolerance justified in this manner can suggest a course of action to us in these circumstances.[15] If tolerance is really an important value of ours, then we ought to act to minimize the extent to which it is violated. If Iraq's invasion of Kuwait is a greater violation of the principle than our opposing it would represent, then that is what we ought to do. This remains the case even if what is wrong with the invasion is that it cannot be justified to the Kuwaitis, and we cannot justify our opposition to the Iraqis. Assuming we can find a way to measure the degree to which various actions violate the principle, we can simply do the sums and support the action that violates it to the minimum extent possible.

Wong's strategy is attractive, in that it neatly explains the commonly held intuition that relativism supports tolerance. If it is true that we accept the justification principle, then believing that relativism is true will commit us to non-interference with regard to the behaviour of those who uphold values very different from ours. Yet, if Wong is right, why stop here? If it is perfectly consistent for the relativist to act on the justification principle, and therefore to be committed to the value of toleration, then isn't it equally consistent for her to act on her other values? Perhaps accepting meta-ethical relativism, the view that there is no cross-cultural fact of the matter as regards morality, ought to lead us to accept moral-requirement relativism, via the thought that each of us ought to do what our own morality requires. After all, if what we have said about values in general is correct, then we shall all feel motivated to act upon our values, no matter what our meta-ethical views are concerning cross-cultural validity. But if this is the case, then why not go beyond tolerance and judge other cultures by our own, admittedly parochial, standards? There does not seem to be any logical inconsistency in this: we might be lucidly ethnocentric. We might accept that our values are, *merely*, ours, and yet believe that everyone ought to be judged by them. So doing would, it seems, violate the justification principle, but other values of ours might be more important to us than this principle. Think, once more, of female circumcision, as it is practised in North Africa. The practice there might indeed be accepted by the members of that society, victims and perpetrators alike. In that case, interfering with it would violate the justification principle, yet, given our stronger belief that people should not have suffering inflicted upon them for no good reason, we might think that all things considered we ought to interfere. Wong's argument seems to open the way for a wholesale imposition of our values on other people when it happens to be the case that we feel strongly motivated to do so. We shall only tolerate difference when it falls within a range of behaviours acceptable to us, not when it directly conflicts with deeply held values of ours.

Of course, it is precisely this kind of toleration for which the anti-relativist calls. He, too, holds that we ought to tolerate the practices of other cultures only when they fall within a certain range of activities that are acceptable to us. Wong's view, developed in the manner I have suggested, might have just the same implications.[16]

Relativism and respect

In any case, the opponent of relativism has a devastating reply to make to the charge that relativism alone is capable of respecting different cultures. Some non-relativists have argued that the very idea that avoiding the crimes we perpetrated against other cultures in the recent past requires the suspension of judgement rests on a fundamental confusion. What the members of other cultures require of us, with regard to their beliefs and practices, is not mere toleration, but *respect*. We ought not simply to allow other cultures to live undisturbed, but we ought also to recognize the value of their ways of life. Indeed, there is a profound sense in which failing to pay such respect to other cultures, or to minorities within our own, damages them, and therefore is incompatible with tolerance. *Mere* toleration, simply ignoring the difference between us and them, does not even meet its own minimal standards; it does not leave the other culture undisturbed, but instead is apt to damage it. This is the case because, as Charles Taylor has persuasively argued, our very identities – individually and collectively – are bound up with other people's perceptions of us. *Recognition*, the affirmation that we are worthy of respect, is constitutive of identity. Taylor claims that recognition given confirms and affirms social and individual identity, recognition withheld undermines it:

> our identity is partly shaped by recognition or its absence, often by the *mis*recognition of others, and so a person or group of people can suffer real damage, real distortion, if the people or society around them mirror back a confining or demeaning or contemptible picture of themselves. Nonrecognition or misrecognition can inflict harm, can be a form of oppression, imprisoning someone in a false, distorted, and reduced mode of being.[17]

Misrecognitions may be internalized, so that members of groups who suffer from it become incapable of taking advantage of opportunities offered to them, when and if the concrete obstacles that often confront such groups are removed or reduced. They recognize themselves in the image reflected back at them by society at large; they see themselves as less worthy, and less capable. They are, therefore, less capable.

Now, the importance of this notion of recognition, for our purposes, stems from the fact that the act of recognizing needs to have real content if it is to be successful. Recognition needs to be *substantive*, not merely procedural or formal. It is no good just saying, as liberalism would have it, that everyone has an equal right to pursue their own conception of the good life, so long as they do not interfere with anyone else, and leaving it at that. The demand for recognition must be met concretely, by affirming the value of a *particular* way of life, in its detail. In other words, recognition must be more than tolerance; it requires respect.

But we cannot simply bestow respect on other people. We cannot simply affirm the value of their way of life without first discovering what that way of life is like. What would be the value of an honour that was given to everyone, regardless of what they had done; of a gold medal awarded to anyone who turns up? This would be an empty gesture, not a real recognition of achievement. This kind of recognition fails to affirm the value of any culture, and therefore it cannot play the required role in identity-formation.

It is for this reason that Taylor insists that recognition requires a real process of judgement before it can be bestowed. If representatives of the majority culture express their respect for some minority culture while actually having no more than the slightest acquaintance with that culture, the putative recognition will be experienced as 'insufferable patronizing' by members of that culture.[18] Those who claim to have recognized that culture will not in fact have done so, for they will be in no position to appreciate its distinctive contributions. They will simply have declared themselves on its side. If we are really to recognize the value of a culture, we must first judge it, and the more detailed our judgements, the more searching the questions we put to it, the more effective any ensuing affirmation of its value will be. If we are to exhibit real respect for a culture, we must be prepared to judge it.

Thus, affirming the value of a culture *requires* judgement. If relativism were true – if we could only judge cultures by their own standards, and not by standards that are cross-culturally valid – then we would be unable to make these judgements and unable, therefore, to affirm the worth of another culture. The members of other cultures do not want to be told that their culture is worthwhile when judged by its own standards. They want to know that it is a way of life that deserves the respect of the world, one from which we all can learn. They want to know that it makes a contribution to a universal search for the good life, that it has produced art or literature or rituals that are valuable and are worth preserving. If relativism is true, they can have none of this; their culture has no such universal value. If this is the case, then we cannot show our respect for other cultures. The tolerance urged by relativism is motivated by the urge to respect difference, but it fails to live up to its own high ideals. Only if we judge, utilizing cross-culturally valid standards, can we recognize, and if we are to judge we must be able to condemn. The test of the worth of another culture must be a test that it might fail, or it fails to be a test at all.

If this argument is correct – and it seems persuasive – then not only are relativists wrong in believing that their position entails respect for difference, they are wrong even in thinking that relativism is *compatible* with such respect. Not only is the respect and tolerance for which relativists call itself a non-relative value, and therefore one that ought to have no more cross-cultural validity than any other, it cannot even be exhibited by those who believe relativism to be true. If we refrain from judging other cultures, we cannot express our respect for them, or indeed any other attitude at all. We do not accord them the recognition they desire and need.

However, the relativist seems to have a ready reply to this line of criticism. She can argue that the non-relativist is no better placed to show respect for other cultures because the consequence of assessing them would, in practice, be a kind of cultural assimilation. When the non-relativist judges other cultures, he may find them inferior, superior, or (most likely) inferior in some ways and superior in others. Whichever of these is the case, his judgement is likely to have further consequences. If he judges the other culture inferior, of course, then he refuses it recognition. He thereby exerts pressure upon its members to abandon it; indeed, if his judgement is very negative, he may feel obliged to increase the likelihood of its collapse. On the other hand, if he judges the culture to be superior to his own, then he has a powerful reason for adopting it. There would be a kind of pragmatic contradiction in asserting that another culture is, objectively, better than one's own, and yet continuing to remain loyal to one's own. In either case, the judgement delivered by the non-relativist seems a prelude to cultural assimilation.

What about the third case, in which the judge comes to a more nuanced conclusion, assessing the other cultures as a mixture of elements, some inferior to elements of his own culture, some superior? As we noted previously, this would likely be the most common conclusion; there are few societies that lack admirable elements entirely. When we come to such a judgement regarding an alien culture, we are less likely to urge its destruction or the assimilation of its members, or, on the other hand, to simply abandon our own culture for it. Yet this judgement, too, might be a prelude to assimilation. If we, members of one culture, judge that another is superior to our own so far as X, Y and Z are concerned, whereas we are superior to it with regard to A, B and C, then why not amalgamate the two? Why not adopt their practices when they are superior to ours? In this manner, the more nuanced judgement might be the prelude to a fusion of cultures.

Now, if this line of thought is correct, then the relativist has available a powerful response to the non-relativist, so far as the topic of recognition is concerned. The non-relativist had claimed that it was he, and not the relativist, who was best able to exhibit an attitude of proper respect toward other cultures, precisely because respect requires judgement. But now, it seems, the relativist can argue that judgement is merely a prelude to assimilation or fusion. The non-relativist cannot respect a diversity of cultures, because the logic of his judgement requires him to eliminate this diversity.

In a later chapter, we will examine an alternative to both relativism and absolutism, as we have formulated them so far, an alternative that might be able to ground the value of tolerance and respect for cultural difference better than either. For the moment, however, let us continue with the consideration of the moral implications of relativism.

Ought moral relativism to shake our confidence in our values?

There cannot be much doubt that some of the opposition to moral relativism stems from the feeling that accepting it will, or ought to, undermine our adherence to our own values. Morality, we feel, has a special kind of importance attaching to it, an importance incompatible with its being merely local. When we condemn the Holocaust, or human rights abuses, we do not merely mean that acting in that matter is contrary to our local principles. We mean that it is wrong, absolutely and objectively. Yet if the moral relativist is right, then in some important sense our moral principles are, merely, ours. If we are convinced of the truth of relativism, ought this fact to influence our behaviour?

We can best explore this question by examining our changing attitudes to conventions and customs. The boundary between what we now recognize to be merely conventional, and what we take to be universally binding, is a shifting one. In the past, many people were strongly attached to what we now take to be merely customs and conventions; indeed, they were downright horrified at the fact that other people ignored them. Think of the reaction of European explorers when they encountered foreign peoples. Very often, the explorers took these peoples' manner of dress as proof that they were 'savages' or 'primitives'; the very expression 'half-naked savages' became something of a cliché. Yet there can be little doubt that clothing style is essentially a matter of convention. Indeed, as recognition of this fact grows, our own standards of what counts as 'decent' clothing have relaxed. Much of the clothing worn by fashionable men and women today would have provoked an outcry in their grandparents' day.

Language, too, is a system of conventions. Linguistics tells us that there is no such thing as an inferior language; that all languages serve equally effectively as means of communication. Yet here, too, people are strangely attached to the language they know best. There is a temptation to believe that our native language is not merely as good as any other, but somehow better. Thus, for example, in his famous *Philosophical Investigations*, Wittgenstein mentions a French politician who was struck by a peculiar fact about the French language: 'that in it words occur in the order in which one thinks them'.[19] Of course, there is nothing remarkable about the fact that French word order matches the order of thoughts of someone whose native language is French, since we all think (at least in important part) in language. Thus our thought processes will largely follow the contours of our native language.

We see, therefore, how easily people slip into imputing special value to their conventions, merely because they are theirs. We are easily tempted into thinking that *these* customs, with which we have grown up, with which we are so familiar and so comfortable, must be better than *those*, which make us uncomfortable, to which we have trouble adapting. People overseas drive on the wrong side of the road, we easily think. However, when this tendency of ours to impute some kind of naturalness and superiority to our conventions is pointed out to us, the hold of these conventions on us begins to weaken. We begin to recognize that they are merely customs, that things can be done in a different way without anything being any the worse for it. Thus, it seems that recognizing the extent to which a behaviour is conventional does lead us to be less attached to it.

However, the manner and extent to which this is so is complicated by considerations we have not yet raised. Consider the example of driving once more. The side of the road upon which people drive is clearly conventional. In Great Britain and Australia, people drive on the left-hand side, whereas in France and the United States people drive on the right. Neither seems more efficient, or safer, than the other. Moreover, the fact that the side upon which we drive is conventional is very widely known. We can therefore expect that the degree to which people are attached to this convention – that is, the extent to which they feel it is uniquely right – will be relatively low.

And indeed, this seems to be the case, if we measure it in one way. If we measure it by recording the degree to which people in countries that drive on one side of the road work to have other countries fall into line, then we will conclude that the degree to which they are attached to their convention is low. There are, so far as I know, no societies for the prevention of left- (or right-) hand driving, no evangelists who go out to attempt to convert the ignorant natives. So far as the side of the road upon which people drive is concerned, it seems that we are all prepared to accept that whatever people do is perfectly all right.

In another way, however, the recognition of the fact that the side of the road upon which we drive is merely conventional does absolutely nothing to lessen the grip of this convention upon us. Measured in a different way, we are passionately attached to it. Think of how we react when we see someone driving on the 'wrong' side of the road – that is, the wrong side for us, in our country (or, as we might say, the wrong side *relative to* our conventions). Do we simply note this interesting fact, saying to ourselves that here is someone who refuses to be bound by our conventions? Of course not. In fact, we condemn this person in no uncertain terms, indeed, in the kind of terms we use for condemning moral infractions. The reason for this is obvious: by driving on the wrong side of the road, this person puts lives (including his own) at risk. The side of the road upon which we drive is merely conventional, but this is a convention it is important to observe. Driving on the left is every bit as good as driving on the right, and in that sense it doesn't matter which side we drive on, but it matters a great deal that we all drive on the *same* side of the road.

Can we draw general conclusions from this example? Does it help tell us whether or not accepting moral relativism would lead to us relaxing our grip on our moral standards, perhaps no longer thinking that they are so important? Before we attempt to draw such conclusions, we need to note that the example we have been considering has a feature that we have not yet considered. This convention is, in the jargon of game theory, a solution to a co-ordination problem.[20] A co-ordination problem arises when two or more agents interact regularly, in such a way that what is best for each person depends, at least in part, on what the other person does. Thus it is best for me to drive on whichever side of the road everyone else drives on. When we begin to analyse conventions in this way, we see that co-ordination problems are in fact pervasive. Many, perhaps all, of our conventions arise as solutions to these problems. Customs are easily analysed in this way. When I meet someone for the first time, I want to be able to signal to him or her that I am not aggressive. I wish to communicate an attitude of friendliness, so as to put the person at ease, while respecting his or her autonomy. In turn, I hope to see the same attitudes exhibited toward me. But these are attitudes for which there is no obvious natural expression (in the sense in which a cry is a natural expression of pain). So we evolve a customary method of greeting that signals these attitudes: we shake hands, or we say hello.

Could morality be a solution to a co-ordination problem? At first glance at least, it seems that large parts of it can. Indeed, one common way of justifying the demands of morality is by reference to enlightened self-interest and reciprocity. On this view, moral requirements are conventions that we obey on condition that everyone else obey them, and we do so because it is in everyone's interests that they are generally obeyed. Thus I agree not to steal your property, even when doing so is in my interests, because I do not want to undermine the convention of respect for property. Were the convention to be undermined, I would not be secure to enjoy my possessions. Thus I respect your moral rights on condition that, indeed, in order that, mine are respected in turn.

Some philosophers have gone so far as to suggest that the disposition to be moral is the product of an evolution in which seeking solutions to co-ordination problems has played a major role. We shall examine the attempt to base morality on evolution in a later chapter. For the moment, we are concerned only with the effect that understanding morality as conventional would have on our confidence in it. How does understanding the side upon which we drive as a solution to a co-ordination problem affect our confidence in this convention? Does it undermine it in any way?

In one way, and as we have already seen, it does undermine our belief in the convention. Given that we know that the rule is merely conventional, we accept that other people will do things differently. We do not proselytize for our convention; indeed, we are even prepared to give up our convention to bring ourselves into line with others (Sweden changed from driving on the left to the right in 1967 for just this reason). In another way, however, the recognition that this rule is merely conventional does not lead us to regard it as *merely* optional. This is obvious in the driving case: given the risks of driving on the 'wrong' side of the road, we object to it in the strongest possible terms. In other cases, our objection to people who violate the terms of the implicit agreement is far less strong. Nevertheless, we do object, and we back up our objections with mechanisms of enforcement. For instance, we express our disapproval of someone who wears the 'wrong' clothes in a variety of ways, from barring them from restaurants to ostracizing them completely. Why do we behave in this manner? Because the convention is a solution to a co-ordination problem (to the problem of knowing what to wear in which context, in this case). Though other solutions were possible, this one is as good as any, and better than no solution at all. Since the only alternative to this solution that is open to us right now is the absence of any solution, at least temporarily (until a new solution stabilizes) it is rational for us to maintain it, through sanctions if necessary.

Thus, the demonstration that a custom, law or ritual is merely conventional, in the sense that a different such custom would suit our needs just as well, doesn't lead us to abandon the convention; nor should it. We continue to embrace it, as a solution to a co-ordination problem, we continue to enforce it, and we are rational in doing so. Nevertheless, the demonstration that it is merely conventional changes the nature of that enforcement. We no longer regard someone who violates a mere convention as evil or sick. It is embraced by us merely as what Kant called a *hypothetical imperative*, that is, as something that is instrumental to achieving some desired end. Thus, it is no longer valued for its own sake. As a consequence, we are more open to proposals to change it. Most conventions are not like the rule concerning which side of the road we drive on. The penalty for violating this rule is death, which explains why we enforce it so vigorously. But when our conventions are not concerned with the operation of dangerous machinery, we are willing to relax them, to leave their enforcement to the vagaries of social sanction, and, sometimes at least, to let them pass unpunished.

In sum, the demonstration that some practice is merely conventional does not cause us to abandon it completely. It remains rational to enforce the convention. Nevertheless, the strength of our attachment to it decreases, and we become willing to entertain alternatives. If morality is merely conventional, and shown to be such, we can expect similar results. We shall not abandon it entirely, but, in some areas at least, we shall relax our vigilance. We might allow alternative solutions to the co-ordination problems with which it is concerned to develop. Think of the way in which we regard language. Language is merely a system of conventions, in every one of its aspects: vocabulary, accent, grammar, and so on. The recognition of this fact does not cause us to think that, with regard to language, anything goes. We continue to insist on standards of correctness in language, since we realize that if the standards were to disappear entirely, communication would be impossible. But we do not impose very rigid standards. We allow people to innovate, to bend the rules, to experiment with new words, phrases, even grammars. Our language gradually evolves as a result of this experimentation. Now, if we thought that our words reflected a transcendental reality, then we would not adopt this *laissez-faire* attitude. If we regarded our words as intrinsically important, rather than as merely instrumental to the achievement of the goal of communication, we would enforce the standards much more rigidly. Like Hindus, who take just this view of the words of the *Vedas*, we would insist on conformity in pronunciation and pitch.

Thus, the belief that morality is *merely* conventional would result in our embracing it somewhat less fervently. Moreover, a glance at our examples will impress upon us another consequence that the belief that morality is merely conventional would be likely to have. There is a big difference in our attitude with regard to conventions and their enforcement at home, compared with our reaction to foreign practices. As we saw with regard to the side of the road upon which we drive, we have no particular wish to impose our conventions upon other people, living in different countries. Though we insist upon compliance with it here, to such an extent that we demand the punishment of those who violate it, we do not attempt to generalize the convention beyond our borders. Other cultures are free to adopt their own solution to the co-ordination problem; indeed, we even accept that we ought to obey their convention when we visit them. We insist on the convention at home, and discard it abroad. Would – or should – not the recognition that morality is merely conventional have the same effect? At present, of course, we very often do attempt to impose our morality on other countries. We send armies to Kuwait, we bomb Afghanistan, we impose sanctions on so-called 'rogue states', we send missionaries and engage in human rights dialogues. If we could vindicate the suggestion that morality is *entirely* conventional, all this effort would be irrational. We could continue to embrace our own morality, without trying to impose it upon anyone else.

Now, should these conclusions be an embarrassment for the relativist? Does the fact that embracing relativism would likely lead to some relaxation in the grip our moral standards have upon us make the relativist position less plausible? Some people believe that it does, but we might equally view the same facts in a much more positive light. Indeed, I suspect that once the confusions that typically attend the view that relativism promotes toleration are analysed away, the fact of this relaxation remains as the most plausible buttress for the toleration view. Though the opponents of relativism are perfectly correct in pointing out that it does not entail toleration – or, indeed, any other moral doctrine – nevertheless, if it were widely held that morality is merely conventional, we would lose the motivation, and, most probably, the desire, to impose our views upon other people. We would simply leave them as they are. Thus the recognition that morality is conventional (if, indeed, it is) would reduce moral fanaticism.

However, opponents of relativism continue to fear that it would undermine morality much more radically than I have so far suggested; that we might cease to behave morally at all. Once we know that our morality is not the only one possible, nor indeed the best – that it is incoherent even to speak of better and worse moral systems – we will no longer have any reason to behave morally, the critics of relativism allege. When our interests clash with those of others, when we can steal and get away with it, for instance, why should we not act in this manner if morality is merely conventional? Moreover, if we have more reason to be attached to our moral conventions at home than abroad, why should we respect the rights of other cultures at all? To be sure, the demonstration that morality was conventional through and through would remove the motivation for us to impose our morality on other cultures, but what would prevent us simply invading them when so doing was in our interests?

This fear, that relativism will lead to the undermining of morality, no doubt accounts for much of the opposition to it. Witness John Cook's rather breathless assessment of the consequences of the widespread embracing of the doctrine:

> If the relativist's doctrine is broadcast far and wide, and people come to believe that morality is nothing but a set of arbitrary social conventions, people will cease to feel that they are genuinely *obligated* to do (or forgo) certain things. Or as Henry Veach put it, 'the lid would be off and all hell would break loose'.[21]

Would 'all hell break loose' as Cook suggests? We have seen that the demonstration that a practice is conventional does not strip it of all its power. It does, however, loosen its grip on us somewhat. Moreover, once it is revealed to be conventional, we see that much of the force it has for us derives from the fact that it is in our interests. It is rational for me to obey the conventions of my society, even on occasions when doing so is not in my short-term interests, because it is in my long-term interests that these conventions are maintained. I ought to avoid violating them because my violation could contribute to their being undermined (perhaps because if people see my failure to abide by the rules, they will lose faith in them themselves). But if they are shown to be merely conventional, wouldn't it be rational for me to violate them when these consequences do not attend my so acting (when, for example, I know that no one will ever find out about my violation)? Would it not, also, be rational for me to violate the convention when my pay-off for so doing exceeds the costs of the loss of confidence that might result? Perhaps I could steal so large a sum of money as to be able to insulate myself from the ill-effects of my actions. And finally, would it not be rational for me to act in ways that are contrary to the convention where people who are not parties to it are concerned – that is, members of other cultures? Why should I, indeed all of us, not steal from and cheat them?

How might the relativist reply to these challenges? Perhaps she could attempt to construct a reply somewhat akin to that suggested by rule-utilitarians to the accusations commonly brought against them. Rule-utilitarians contend that we should always act in accordance with those rules, following which usually brings about the best consequences. Thus, their rules are justified by the fact that they generally maximize utility (happiness, welfare, or preference satisfaction, depending upon the version of utilitarianism). The challenge frequently addressed to them is similar to the one that faces the relativist: why act on those rules when doing so will *not*, on this occasion, maximize utility?

Rule-utilitarians reply by pointing out the benefits of rule-following. Rules save us from having to engage in complicated calculations with regard to consequences. Moreover, the disposition to follow rules blindly, as it were, without questioning them, is itself justified by consequentialist considerations. Though the rules get their force from the fact that they maximize utility, this fact need not be known to the people who follow them. Indeed, all things considered, it might be better if most people were unaware of the true justification of the rules, if they regarded them as absolutely binding in themselves.

Can these considerations come to the aid of the relativist? Perhaps they could. The relativist might hold that though our morality is thoroughly conventional, it is rational for us to follow it because it is as good a solution as any other to the co-ordination problems we typically face. We therefore ought to refrain from acting in any way that might undermine the conventions. Given the fact that the conventions usually work to our advantage, we ought to refrain from violating them even in cases where it seems that so doing is in our interests. After all, we could well be mistaken. Moreover, given the fact that blind allegiance to the conventions is in our self-interest, we ought to act in a way calculated to reinforce those conventions. Now, demonstrating that morality is merely conventional will, to some extent at least, tend to undermine the force of the conventions. For this reason, the relativist might think, we ought to refrain from such a demonstration. Perhaps, then, the rational relativist will not endorse relativism, at least in public. Perhaps it would be better for her to align herself with the critics of relativism, and keep her real convictions a secret.

The symmetry argument

From what we have seen so far, relativism seems to have a rather equivocal relationship to toleration. The argument that the truth of relativism *requires* tolerance of us fails utterly: since relativism denies that *any* moral claims are absolutely true, the claim that tolerance is required of us must itself be undermined by the doctrine. On the other hand, we have seen that, in the right circumstances at least, relativism might promote tolerance by removing the motivation for us to impose our morality on other people. Equally, however, acceptance of it removes the restraints that might otherwise prevent us from treating others as mere instruments to our own purposes.

In this section, I want to consider one final argument that might be advanced, to the conclusion that acceptance of moral relativism will, or ought to, promote tolerance: what I shall call the symmetry argument.

The symmetry argument asks us to notice that when we engage in a moral dispute with someone, one of two things is true. Either we share enough in the way of fundamental moral beliefs for us to be able to hope to convince them (or, indeed, them us) or we don't. In the first case, of course, the question of whether or not relativism is true is irrelevant. We are situated in relation to each other in a similar fashion to the way in which two speakers of a single language might be. Most probably, one or other of us (if not both) is making a mistake here: either we are mistaken with regard to some factual question, or we are misinterpreting our own moral principles. For this reason, we can reasonably hope to settle the dispute. In any case, relativism gets no purchase on the matter. There is a difficult question that arises here, with regard to whether each disputant should tolerate the views of the other, if neither can be convinced to alter his or her own, but it is a question that arises for the relativist and the non-relativist alike, and in exactly the same way for each.

It is the second kind of dispute in which we are especially interested, the kind of dispute in which the two sides do not share the relevant fundamental moral principles. If relativism is true, then in cases like this the two sides cannot hope to convince one another. Given that they have nothing significant in common to which they might appeal, the argument is destined to remain unresolved.

Now, let's try to imagine the dispute from the perspective of one of the disputants; it doesn't matter which one (that, in a way, is precisely the point). It also doesn't matter what are his ethical and meta-ethical views: he can be a convinced utilitarian, deontologist, or anything else, and as vociferous an opponent of relativism as you like. Try as he might, he is unable to bring his opponent round to his point of view. She obdurately persists in holding the opposite opinion to him; insisting that an act he regards as impermissible is obligatory, for instance. By hypothesis, this is a conflict that turns on the disputant's *fundamental* moral views. For this very reason, he cannot hope to convince her by adducing non-moral facts (Hume's law – 'no ought from is' – blocks that move). Nor can he hope to move her with moral arguments, because all such arguments beg the question. Since – as we here assume for the sake of the argument – moral relativism is true, it is impossible for him to convince his opponent at all.

It is, of course, equally impossible for *her* to convince *him*. So far as rational argument is concerned, they have reached an impasse. Assume, also, that the conflicting views do not mandate actions that are physically incompatible, in the sense that if one of the parties acts on his or her views, the other will be prevented from acting on theirs (if they are so incompatible, then the matter will have to be settled, one way or another; I cannot tolerate your moral views if they move you to act in a manner that prevents me from acting on mine). Now, the question arises, ought they to tolerate each other's views? Let us suppose that our disputant's first impulse is to attempt to impose his views on his opponent. After all, he is convinced of their truth. His opponent, he believes, is utterly mistaken: why ought he to allow her to persist in her error?

But perhaps a moment's reflection will give him pause. He might, with us, reflect on the dispute as it appears to his opponent. If he does so, he will notice that the position she occupies in the dispute is the mirror image of his. She, too, is utterly convinced of the truth of her position, and frustrated by her inability to convince her opponent of that truth. She, too, sees no reason to respect an error. In other words, each disputant is placed in a position that is, structurally speaking, exactly the same. The positions they occupy are symmetrical.

I suggest that this fact should reduce the brash confidence that each side has in its right to impose its view upon others. Given the symmetry to which we have just pointed, each will realize that whatever is true for one of them is equally true for the other. If it is permissible for him to impose his views upon her, then equally it ought to be permissible for her to impose her views upon him. Moreover, given the enculturation argument, both ought to realize that were they in the position occupied by the other, they would be equally convinced of the truth of the rival view as they now are of their own. This, I suggest, gives each party cause to moderate his or her demands upon the other. Given the symmetry of their positions, both have an equal right to demand that the other embrace their views, which ought to give them pause before making that demand at all. They would both do better to transmute it into a different demand: that each respects the right of the other to maintain his or her views.

Indeed, the symmetry argument is somewhat independent of the relativist thesis. For it to have force, one does not need to think that there is no such thing as absolute truth with regard to morality. It is enough to hold the weaker view that it is impossible to convince other people of the truth of a moral position when the conditions outlined above hold. The great nineteenth-century liberal thinker John Stuart Mill, who was far from being a relativist, relied upon something like the symmetry argument in support of his own appeal for tolerance. For Mill, the intolerant person unthinkingly assumes that the opinions of his or her own 'world' are true. Yet this person ought to be troubled by the fact that

> mere accident has decided which of these numerous worlds is the object of his reliance, and that the same causes which make him a churchman in London, would have made him a Buddhist or a Confucian in Peking.[22]

For Mill, this thought ought to shake our confidence in our views somewhat, at least to the extent to which we relinquish the right to suppress the expression of contrary views. If relativism is true, then Mill's thought is strengthened. Mill's position relies upon the enculturation argument, and the belief that it is difficult to know the truth regarding morality. Relativism transforms that difficulty into an impossibility, leaving enculturation as the whole explanation of our moral views. The truth of moral relativism, of the enculturation argument and of the symmetry of the opposing sides in a moral conflict does, after all, give us some reason to tolerate other views.

The conclusion here is not moral, and therefore does not fall foul of the incoherence that besets the attempted deduction of toleration from moral relativism we examined earlier. It is not that we *ought* to tolerate other views. Instead, the conclusion that Mill and I advance is epistemological: we are not warranted in the confidence we have with regard to our morality. Since the conclusion is epistemological, and not moral, there is no inconsistency in refusing to give it any weight in morality. If someone were to say that though they recognize that their morality is only one among others, no better justified than any, and yet they wish to impose it on everyone, they would not be guilty of a contradiction. Nevertheless, by removing the intellectual support for the claim that we are justified in imposing our views, we greatly reduce the motivation for doing so. Indeed, the conclusion here is not without *moral* force. All systems of morality require that we be able to give *reasons* for our actions, though if relativism is true what counts as a good reason will differ from system to system. By demonstrating the difficulty, indeed, impossibility, of giving reasons that can be fully understood by those who hold moral views very different from our own, the symmetry argument makes it more difficult to justify the refusal tolerance to such people. To that extent, it strengthens the *moral* case for toleration.

Moral relativism: progressive or conservative?

Advocates of moral relativism often accuse their foes of intolerance, witting or not. By continuing to maintain that there is one standard of correctness in morality, the relativists maintain, non-relativists dismiss the rich variety of moral experience as mere error. From what we have seen so far, the evidence for this charge is equivocal. It is far from certain that relativists are better placed than non-relativists to respect the diversity of moral beliefs that exist today. Relativists seem to lack the ability to make the judgements that are a crucial precondition of respect. On the other hand, we have seen that in some ways relativism does promote toleration. On the evidence we have considered, neither relativism nor the opposition to it has the devastating moral implications claimed by the other side. (On the other hand, of course, relativism has no easy way of saying *why* its implications for morality matter at all.)

The opponents of relativism have one more charge to level at the relativist, however, and it is one that, if sustained, will bite deep. Many relativists combine their meta-ethical view, that there is no such thing as absolute moral truth, with a deeply felt commitment to progressive politics. There is here no simple contradiction, so long as the relativist maintains that her political views are merely the expression of local preference (perhaps one that ought to be binding on all those who share her culture). The charge, however, is this: the moral relativism she espouses is incompatible with her left-leaning views. The moral relativist cannot hope to insulate her political views from her relativism by asserting that relativism is a meta-ethical doctrine, whereas her moral views are normative, because, so the argument claims, moral relativism does have normative implications after all. It is, in fact, a politically and morally *conservative* doctrine.

Why think that moral relativism is essentially conservative? The argument runs as follows: according to the relativist, an act is morally permissible if it is in line with the standards of the culture in which it takes place. Similarly, an act is impermissible only if it is condemned by those same standards. The kind of relativism in question here is, of course, *moral-requirement* or *normative* relativism: the view that different people have different obligations in virtue of the culture to which they belong. Now, on the face of it, the view that each of us is required to do whatever our culture thinks is appropriate is a conservative one. It identifies what is right with what is currently thought to be right. On this view, it seems, the best way to discover whether one should act in some particular way is to conduct a survey: ask the members of the culture. The status quo is, by definition, always right.

But now consider the practice of the great social reformers of the past. Think, for example, of the feminist movement. When, at about the time of the end of the nineteenth century, women began to agitate in earnest for the right to participate in political life on equal terms to men, they saw themselves as engaged in a moral crusade. They held that it was right that they be permitted political participation, and that their exclusion was illegitimate and immoral. Now, however, that we have become acquainted with normative relativism, we can see that they were dead wrong. First-wave feminists were *immoral*. Since morality is to be identified with the prevailing standards of the day, and the prevailing standards mandated the exclusion of women, they were advocating a course of action that was morally impermissible. In so far as they acted on their views – for instance, by brazenly entering public spaces from which they were officially excluded – they acted wrongly. We ought to compare them to criminals; indeed, they were criminals of a certain kind. Unlike common criminals, they acted openly, and advocated that other people do the same. But their actions were no better for that.

Surely, however, the view that social reformers are immoral is counter-intuitive. Not just feminists but every great reform movement ought to be seen, on this view, as unethical. Martin Luther King, the men and women who worked to bring the slave-trade to an end, the anti-vivisectionist movement, the animal liberation movement of our own day – in so far as they advocate actions that are not in accordance with the norms of their time, all are acting contrary to the dictates of morality. If relativism has this implication, then surely it is implausible.

In assessing this argument, and therefore discovering to what extent it is true that moral relativism is a profoundly, indeed implausibly, conservative position, we need to ask ourselves two questions:

1. Does meta-ethical relativism imply normative relativism?
2. Does normative relativism really have the counter-intuitive implications we have just sketched?

To the first question, it seems that we must answer in the affirmative. Meta-ethical relativists believe that there is no such thing as absolute truth in morality. However, by itself this is not sufficient to differentiate their views from other possible meta-ethical positions. A sceptic about morality also believes that there is no such thing as absolute truth. What differentiates the relativist from the sceptic is that the relativist holds that there are *relative* moral truths, whereas the sceptic does not. The moral relativist holds, generally, that the truth of moral statements varies from culture to culture. Thus the following statements will be true in one culture and false in another:

> It is permissible to kill one's parents.
> Abortion is wrong.
> Self-sacrifice is morally admirable.

But that just *is* normative relativism. Thus meta-ethical relativism seems to imply normative relativism.

Thus, if normative relativism has the unpalatable implications we have sketched, then a large part of the attraction of meta-ethical relativism will have vanished. Since, as we have seen, many people embrace relativism because they see it as a tolerant, and therefore politically progressive, doctrine, the demonstration that it is in fact politically conservative would cause many people to rethink their allegiance to it. Moral relativism would not, of course, have been shown to be false; nevertheless, it would cease to be attractive to many of its most ardent supporters.

Does relativism have the conservative implications its opponents allege? The answer depends, in important part, on what the truth of moral claims is held to be relative *to*. There are several candidates that, prima facie at least, look plausible: the attitudes of typical members of a culture, the laws of a society, and so on. The accusation that it is conservative hinges upon us holding that whatever it is to which rightness is relative, it is close to the surface, as it were: easily accessible to members of the culture. We need only ask them, or look it up in their laws, and we will know what is right and wrong in their culture. On this view, typical members of a culture cannot be wrong about the morality of acts. Since the answers to moral questions lie close to the surface, they are easily retrieved, and failure to reach the right conclusion is evidence of madness or badness.

If indeed this formulation of moral relativism is correct, then it is the conservative doctrine that its opponents accuse it of being. What is morally right is whatever most people think is morally right, and someone who thinks differently, and urges others to do likewise, is not to be seen as a reformer but as a kind of criminal. Surely, however, it is implausible to think that the answers to moral questions always lie so close to the surface. If this were the case, moral philosophers like me would all be out of a job! In fact, it is frequently a difficult matter to discover if a given action or policy is right. It requires a great deal of work, much of it interpretative. Moreover, the judgements to which we finally come, after having engaged in this work, will very often be subtly nuanced: we will say that the action is right in some respects only, or perhaps right all things considered. Any plausible version of relativism will have to be compatible with these facts.

Fortunately, relativism can be formulated in a manner that is perfectly consistent with the facts concerning the way we go about discovering whether a certain action is or is not right. Typically, moral philosophers proceed using a method called *reflective equilibrium*. We formulate theories that seem to make sense of our moral *intuitions* – our 'gut feelings' about what seems right – and then we test those theories by examining how well they account for our intuitions concerning further cases. Cases that they cannot explain are called *counter-examples* to the theory. When we encounter a counter-example, we are forced to react in one of two ways. If we are very sure that our reaction to the case is correct, we must modify our theory. If, however, we are more sure of the theory – because it does a better job of explaining paradigm cases than any available alternative – than of the rightness of our reaction here, we attempt to modify our intuition, to bring ourselves to feel differently about the case. Often, we need to modify *both* intuition and theory. The intuition with which we begin turns out to be nearly correct, but must be adjusted a little in light of the theory, at the same time as the theory alters under the pressure of the intuition. We continue the process until our intuitions concerning particular cases all match the theory. In fact, in all probability we shall never reach that far-off goal, but the reflective equilibrium it represents nevertheless serves as the object of our striving.

Notice that when we engage in the process of reflective equilibrium, we appeal to more than one *kind* of entity. We discover whether something is right by examining *both* our theories and our intuitions. Ideally, of course, it ought not to matter which we consult: once we achieve reflective equilibrium, the two will be in harmony and either would be adequate by itself. Achievement of that goal is, however, a very long way off (indeed, most philosophers think that we shall never reach it). In the meantime, we can expect our theories and our intuitions to diverge, at least occasionally. Now, what ought our judgements to be relative to, if relativism is true? Our theories or our intuitions? That will depend, of course, on which seems better founded. Sometimes we will want to say that our intuition is most reliable, sometimes the theory, and sometimes we will want to adjust each in the light of the other.

But if this is the case, then relativism need not be conservative, at least, no more conservative than any other ethical view. All plausible ethical theories need to be compatible with the reflective-equilibrium procedure. This procedure commits them all to some degree of conservativeness, since reflective equilibrium represents a process of mutual adjustment of our *present* theories and intuitions. Nevertheless, reflective equilibrium can yield quite radical results. The mutual adjustment of our theories and our intuitions can sometimes take us quite far from where we began.

Let me illustrate the manner in which a plausible relativism can yield quite radical conclusions from starting points that do not appear to suggest them, with two examples. In the first example, we adjust our intuitions in the light of our theoretical commitments; in the second, it is our theories that have to change.

Consider, first, the process by which homosexuality came to be seen as a morally neutral option. At the beginning of the twentieth century, homosexuality was usually seen as either wicked or sick. Indeed, that attitude persisted until quite recently. It was only in 1973 that it was removed from the *Diagnostic and Statistical Manual of Mental Disorders* of the American Psychiatric Association. What led the APA, and society at large, to come to realize that homosexuality was neither immoral nor sick? I suggest it was the pressure exerted by the investigation at a theoretical level. Psychologists who studied homosexuals found that they were no more likely to commit crimes or to suffer from mental illnesses than are other people. Apart from their sexuality, homosexuals were as well adjusted as could be hoped for from a discriminated-against group. They were no more likely than heterosexuals to prey on children, to take drugs, and so on.

In the face of these facts, society as a whole was forced to reconsider its attitude towards homosexuality. It did so, I suggest, in spite of a widespread intuition that homosexuality was wrong. Since we could not back the intuition up with facts, we had to reject it. Indeed, we have been quite successful in modifying our intuitions here. Many of us no longer have the 'gut feeling' that homosexuals are sick.

I suggest that a similar kind of story could be told about the way in which equal political rights came to be extended to women and to members of other races by European societies. Many members of these societies had the intuition that women and non-whites were inferior. But in the face of the empirical evidence that this was not so, and as a consequence of our (hitherto inconsistent) adherence to a principle of equality, we were forced to give up the intuition.

Theories and principles can have greater force for us than intuitions, at least sometimes. They have this power when they account for many of our other, most deeply felt, intuitions. Thus we can be led to modify our intuitions, and consequently our political practices, without it being necessary that we be shown that there is an absolute truth.

Sometimes, however, we will want to modify our theories in the light of our intuitions. I suggest that the manner in which we extended moral concern to animals is a plausible instance of this process. In the seventeenth century, it was widely held that animals were incapable of feeling pain, because they did not have souls. Since they could not experience pain, there was nothing wrong, morally speaking, with acting toward them in a manner that *seemed* to inflict pain. Today, of course, we do not think that animals are incapable of pain. On this score, our theories have changed. Now, it might be that in part this theory change is to be explained by developments *immanent* to theory itself. As our knowledge of anatomy grew, we noted the similarities between the nervous systems of animals and ourselves, and modified our theories accordingly. I suggest, however, that part at least of the explanation will appeal to our intuitions. After all, no one has ever demonstrated that the seventeenth-century vivisectionists were wrong in holding that one must have a soul in order to experience pain. I suspect that part of the reason we abandoned this theory is that it seems so implausible in the face of our intuitions, when we are confronted by an animal that gives every appearance of suffering. If this is correct, then sometimes our views will be modified by the pressure of our intuitions upon our theories, as well as the other way round.

Thus, the process of mutual adjustment of theories (and theory-like entities, such as moral principles) and intuitions can yield conclusions that are very distant from our starting point. It can explain how a culture that was once racist, sexist and homophobic can change so that it is none of those things (or, more accurately, so that it no longer believes it ought to be those things). It explains how the moral domain can expand to include people, and even animals, who were formerly excluded. It can even explain the activity of the moral reformer. On this view, the reformer is someone who points out an inconsistency between our intuitions and our theories. Like the anti-slave crusaders, like Martin Luther King and like feminists, she points out that we are acting in ways incompatible with what we say we believe. She calls for us to bring our actions into line with our norms, our theories, our principles. She demands that we change. But she does all this *without appealing to anything other than the very principles and intuitions we already accept.* She asks us to change in the name of theories or intuitions that are *already* ours. Thus her appeal is entirely consistent with the truth of relativism.

Moral relativism is, therefore, not necessarily conservative. So long as there is any inconsistency between our norms, our principles, our theories and intuitions, and our actual practices, we can alter what we do without needing to appeal to principles that are timeless or transcendent. On this score, there is no reason to abandon relativism.

What conclusions can we draw from this long consideration of the implications that moral relativism might have for morality itself? Can we come down decisively upon one side or the other; are we warranted in saying that relativism is tolerant or intolerant, conservative or progressive? The evidence we have examined is inconclusive. Relativism does not entail toleration, nor is it incompatible with it. It is not, inherently, a conservative doctrine, yet nor is it inherently a progressive one. We have seen, in fact, that the moral implications of relativism give us little reason either to adopt it or to reject it. Its moral implications, such as they are, are neither unacceptable nor compelling. We shall not settle the issue on this score. Considering whether relativism is good or bad has not led us far. We shall have to discover whether relativism is *true.*

4

DESCRIPTIVE RELATIVISM

In the first chapter, we identified three kinds of moral relativism: *descriptive relativism*, *moral-requirement relativism*, and *meta-ethical relativism*. That is, 'relativism is true' can be taken to entail one or more of the following claims:

> *descriptive relativism*: As a matter of fact people (individuals or groups) have different fundamental moral beliefs and principles.

> *moral-requirement relativism*: Different moral requirements actually do apply to different individuals or groups.

> *meta-ethical relativism*: There is no such thing as (absolute) truth in ethics; therefore when people disagree about matters of morality, it is not necessarily the case that either or both is wrong.

In the main, philosophers have concentrated their attention on moral-requirement and meta-ethical relativism; that is, they have not disputed the claim that there are in fact fundamental moral disagreements between people, but have instead confined themselves to showing that when two people disagree about what morality requires of them, one (or both of them) is wrong. At first sight, this seems the only course of action open to them. After all, who could deny that descriptive relativism is true? The moral diversity of the world is just *obvious*. We do not have to look far for the evidence: it is there in the political disputes of every country (between Democrats and Republicans, or Labour and Conservatives, for example). What do parties disagree about, if not their moral vision for their country, their view of what activities should be encouraged and what condemned? In the United States' political context, commentators speak of 'wedge issues'; issues that are certain deeply to divide the electorate, such as abortion, gun control and gay rights. If the electorate is divided over these issues, then clearly it is because it has opposing moral views concerning the permissibility of these things.

Even more striking is the evidence for cross-cultural moral disagreement. We have only to mention a range of exotic foreign practices – the banning of women from working outside the home in Taliban-ruled Afghanistan, the practice of widow-burning in India, and so on – to be persuaded that fundamental moral disagreement is a pervasive fact of life, no matter what the truth of moral-requirement or meta-ethical relativism. Descriptive relativism, it might seem, is uncontroversially true; therefore, if we want to vindicate the notion of absolute truth in ethics, we had better focus our attention elsewhere.

In this chapter, I want to examine this contention. As we shall see, the truth of descriptive relativism is not as obvious as the foregoing suggests. The facts of moral disagreement are complex and open to interpretation; the idea that despite their many differences all people (with some obvious exceptions that need not concern us: sociopaths and the insane, for instance) actually share the same fundamental moral beliefs and principles has at least some evidence in its favour.

Before I turn to the discussion of the truth in descriptive relativism, however, there is an important preliminary question to answer: why does it matter whether or not descriptive relativism is true? What bearing does it have on the issue of moral relativism more generally?

Why does descriptive relativism matter?

Descriptive relativism matters because it offers the most plausible reason for thinking that any sort of moral relativism is true. That is to say, moral relativism (of the threatening kind) typically arises as an *explanation* of observed moral diversity and disagreement. If descriptive relativism is false, there will be little remaining reason to be a moral relativist.

Moral relativism is thus, typically, a response to moral diversity; meta-ethical relativism a response to descriptive relativism. As a matter of historical fact, moral relativism has arisen as a response to apparently intractable moral disputes. Belief in relativism has tended to grow in proportion to knowledge about widely differing moral systems, and the great advocates of relativism have tended to be thinkers who were moved to their position by reflection on cultural difference. Thus, over the past century anthropologists have had an important role in convincing people of the truth of relativism and in promoting its growth. In earlier times, too, the advocates of relativism pointed to the facts of cultural difference in motivating their position. Two names, of thinkers separated by thousands of years yet united by a shared reaction to moral diversity, can represent this great movement of cultural history: Herodotus and Michel de Montaigne.

Herodotus was an ancient Greek historian and traveller, for whom the cultural differences that motivate moral relativism were those between the Greeks and the peoples of the Near East. In his famous *The Histories*, Herodotus recounts an anecdote concerning Darius, King of the Persians:

> When he was king of Persia, he summoned the Greeks who happened to be present at his court, and asked them what they would take to eat the dead bodies of their fathers. They replied that they would not do it for any money in the world. Later, in the presence of the Greeks, and through an interpreter, so that they could understand what was said, he asked some Indians, of the tribe called Callatiae, who do in fact eat their parents' dead bodies, what they would take to burn them. They uttered a cry of horror and forbade him to mention such a dreadful thing.[23]

What are we to make of this story? Herodotus implictly asks us to notice the passion that a culture attaches to its burial customs, the horror with which its members react when it is suggested that they adopt another way of doing things. These are precisely the kinds of horrified reactions we associate with morality. It is in just this way that most of us would react were we asked to sacrifice a human being on top of one of the pyramid temples of the Aztec city, or were it suggested to us that we might abandon our aged parents to die in the snow, as the Inuits traditionally do. We react, that is, as if we had been asked to do something wrong, something absolutely and objectively wrong. Yet in all these cases – Callatian funereal practices, Aztec human sacrifice and Inuit abandonment of the elderly – it is not necessary to postulate the existence of a fact of the matter concerning moral rightness to explain our reaction. Instead, we could explain it more simply and economically by pointing to the way we, and they, have been brought up. We have each *internalized* a set of norms; we now react *as if* there is a fact of the matter here. But there need not *be* any such fact to explain our reactions.

It is precisely this line of thought that Herodotus himself seems to have taken, at least with regard to religious opinions. There is here no fact of the matter; it is custom alone that sets the standards of right and wrong. It is our wont, Herodotus said, for us to take our own customs as those that are (objectively) the best. Thus, he concludes that Pindar was right when he declared that 'custom' is 'king of all'.

Ever since Herodotus, reflection on moral diversity has led many thinkers to the same conclusion. Herodotus wrote at a time when few people travelled far and much of the world remained unknown to those in Europe. Thousands of years later, spurred on by the lure of commerce and exotic treasures, a great age of discovery began in Europe. Explorers set out across the globe: to North and South America; down the coast of Africa and around the Cape of Good Hope; across the Pacific Ocean. In all these places they encountered new cultures, people living in ways hitherto unimagined. They brought back to Europe tales of savage customs and lax morals, tales that found an eager audience in their native countries. More and more evidence flowed in from all parts of the globe that moral opinion was even more diverse than Herodotus had suspected and moral disagreement even more intractable.

Reflecting on this diversity, many European intellectuals came to precisely the same conclusion as had Herodotus before them. Moral disagreements reflect the differences between local customs, no more and no less. Thus, for example, Michel de Montaigne, a great essayist of sixteenth-century France, reacts to reports of widespread cannibalism by just such a relativism:

> I think there is nothing barbarous and savage in that nation, from what I have been told, except that each man calls barbarism whatever is not his own practice; for indeed it seems we have no other test of truth and reason than the example and pattern of the opinions and customs of the country we live in.[24]

Since Montaigne's time, of course, the evidence for moral diversity has increased even more. In every area of life, cultures dispute the standards of right and wrong: with regard to sexual morality, theft, punishment, even the conditions under which it is permissible to kill another human being. In some cultures abortion is considered immoral; in others infanticide is looked upon with equanimity. If meta-ethical or moral-requirement relativism is the rational response to descriptive relativism, then the evidence that we should all be relativists seems by now too great to ignore.

Of course, we do not take the existence of deep disagreement elsewhere to be evidence for the contention that there is no truth of the matter. If some culture asserts that the earth is flat, most of us are quite prepared to conclude that they are wrong, not that there is no truth here. But, as we have seen in previous chapters, we have good reason to think that moral disputes are crucially different to scientific disputes, or disputes over facts generally. The latter are settled, at least in principle, by adducing evidence that is independent of our beliefs and desires. With regard to morality, however, there is an important sense in which our beliefs and desires are all the evidence there is. If this is so, then moral disputes may not be able to be resolved by producing independent evidence. In that case, meta-ethical relativism would seem to follow from descriptive relativism.

Is descriptive relativism true? Some evidence against

Descriptive relativism is doing a lot of work in the derivation of moral-requirement and meta-ethical relativism as we sketched it. An important part of the relativists' argument that moral disagreements are not like scientific disagreements – and therefore that when two people disagree about a moral question, it is not necessarily the case that at least one of them must be wrong – rested on the apparent failure of moral views to converge cross-culturally. If descriptive relativism were false, the argument would lose its main support, and relativism would cease to be tempting. It is therefore important to examine whether descriptive relativism really is true.

As I pointed out earlier, relativists tend to hold that descriptive relativism is *obviously* true. They point to the existence of protracted moral disputes, both within and across cultures, and to the exotic and – to us – savage customs of strange people. But some philosophers question whether this evidence really does support the claim that descriptive relativism is true. If these philosophers are right, relativism cannot even begin to get off the ground: we, all of us, already share the same set of fundamental moral principles.

Of course, if the denial of descriptive relativism is to be persuasive, these anti-relativists will have to find a plausible explanation for the observed moral differences. They must, that is, find a way of accounting for Aztec human sacrifice and American conflicts over abortion rights that is consistent with maintaining that all the parties share the same moral outlook. They attempt this task by introducing an important distinction of levels. Moral principles can clash at the *fundamental* level, or they can clash at some higher level. Now, they argue, only a clash at a fundamental level will be sufficient to establish the claim that descriptive relativism is true.[25] Consider an example to make this clear:

> Sophie and Toby are having a moral disagreement. Sophie thinks that everyone ought to give money to charity, whereas Toby believes that not only is there no such obligation, it is in fact morally *wrong* to give money to charity.

Here is the kind of disagreement that ought to be grist to the relativist's mill. Each disputant holds precisely the opposite view to the other as to what we are morally required to do. Does this disagreement support the relativist's case?

Not necessarily, those who deny descriptive relativism will argue. Further questioning of the disputants might reveal that they are not in *fundamental* moral disagreement. In fact, Toby holds that we ought not to give money to charity because doing so tends to make the poor dependent on welfare. He thus holds that it would be better *for the poor* if money were not given to charity. Sophie, on the other hand, holds that giving to charity will not in fact have the effect of bringing it about that the poor become welfare-dependent. Thus, though they are engaged in what is clearly a moral dispute – they hold conflicting views of what we are morally required to do – their views are both consistent with the same fundamental moral principles. Perhaps they both subscribe to the moral rule that 'people ought to do whatever is in the best interests of the poor'.

We see, therefore, that the fact of moral disagreement is not by itself sufficient to establish that descriptive relativism is true. Despite the existence of such disputes, we might all share the same fundamental moral views. Even the existence of persistent, seemingly intractable, moral disputes is not sufficient to demonstrate the truth of descriptive relativism. For many such disputes, it is plausible to maintain that the disputants hold fundamentally the same moral principles, no matter how heated their disagreements. It might be true, for instance, that people who vote Democrat and those who vote Republican in the United States agree upon the same fundamental moral principles – that everyone should do whatever enhances the life, liberty and happiness of Americans, for instance – and disagree only about the most effective way to implement these principles. Their moral disagreement might reflect a failure to converge on matters of non-moral fact, such as which of the competing economic theories is true, or whether as a matter of fact people's financial rewards tend to reflect their efforts. These disputes have now been raging for centuries, and yet seem no closer to a resolution than ever. Thus, even the existence of intractable moral disputes does not prove that people disagree upon fundamental moral principles.

Let us attempt to explain some of the actual moral diversity we see in the world, both inter-culturally and intra-culturally, using these suggestions. We begin with an example of inter-cultural disagreement:

> Among the Dinka, a tribe living in the southern Sudan, there used to exist the custom of burying alive certain very respected religious and political leaders. These leaders, called the spear-masters, would each be placed in a specially dug hole. He would then have cattle dung heaped upon him until he suffocated to death.[26]

Consider the same act in a different context – in contemporary London or New York, for instance. An aged but otherwise healthy man is killed by slow suffocation. Moreover, adding a final insult to this ultimate injury, he has excrement heaped on him. We have a word for this kind of activity. We call it murder. No wonder the Sudanese authorities banned this savage Dinka practice. Surely, this is incontrovertible evidence that the Dinka do not share our fundamental moral values.

Those philosophers who deny that descriptive relativism is true are not moved, even by examples such as this one. They merely insist that we examine the case more closely, confident that when we do so we will find that the people involved share our values. What do we find upon closer examination of the burial of the spear-masters? We find, first of all, that it was usually the spear-master himself who, toward the end of his natural life, announced that the time had come for him to die. Thus the live burial is more like an assisted suicide than a murder. Already our horror with regard to this practice begins to recede. When we understand the significance of the ritual to the Dinka, it will vanish completely. For the killing of the spear-master is not gratuitous. The Dinka believed that their spear-masters were the repositories of the vital force of the tribe and its cattle. This life was contained in his breath. Now, if the spear-master were allowed to die in the normal way, with his last breath this vital force would leave the tribe. But if he is killed in the prescribed manner, the vital force will pass on to his people and the vigour of the tribe will be maintained. Thus killing the spear-master is not an act of savagery, designed to diminish respect for life. Instead, it is morally required, to enhance the life of everyone. Thus, as John Kekes argues, we should see live burial among the Dinka more as a kind of 'morally commendable sacrifice' made by the spear-masters, and not as akin to murder among us:

> Live burial for them is like donating blood or a kidney is for us [...]. It is true that both blood or kidney donors and spear-masters suffer various degrees of injury, but it is in a good cause, and both the altruistic victims and the beneficiaries see it as such.[27]

The Dinka do not differ from us – or, if the anti-descriptive relativism claim is true, from the Amazonian Indians, Australian Aborigines or Taliban mujahadeen – in their moral values. Instead, they differ only in their factual beliefs. If we shared their beliefs – if we thought that our society would suffer severe damage if our leaders were allowed to die natural deaths, but that this could be prevented by killing them in some prescribed manner – we would feel obligated to act in similar ways. If this analysis is correct, then we can agree with John Kekes that the Dinka share the same moral values we embrace.

Are we to conclude from this example that the Dinka actions are right – perhaps right *for the Dinka*? That is, can we accept the conclusion that (contrary to what the descriptive relativist might have thought) we and the Dinka hold the same fundamental values, and yet continue to believe that the example supports *moral-requirement* relativism? We need to be careful here: on the one hand, we do not want to *blame the Dinka* for their actions. As we saw, if we shared their factual beliefs, we would feel obligated to act in the same way. But though we ought not to blame the *agents*, perhaps we ought to blame the *action*. The Dinka's action is authorized, even made obligatory, by an argument from two premises, one moral and one factual:

> *moral premise*: Everyone is obligated to do whatever enhances human life.

> *factual premise*: Burying the spear-master alive will enhance human life.

> *conclusion*: We are obliged to bury the spear-master alive.

This is a valid line of argument. Moreover, we all share the first premise. But notice that this first premise commits the Dinka to another belief, which I shall call the *derivative moral principle* (DMP):

> Human life should not be taken unnecessarily; that is, unless there is some overriding reason to do so.

They are committed to DMP because it seems to follow from the moral premise of the argument above. Now, burying the spear-master alive was taking a human life. But the Dinka are not blame-worthy for acting as they did because they believed that they had an overriding reason for so acting. They acted as they ought to *given their beliefs*. But because they are committed to DMP, they ought to recognize that whether their act is permissible or not depends upon the truth of their factual belief. That is, *the Dinka themselves* are committed to holding that if their factual belief is false, then their act is impermissible. But, of course, their factual belief is false (though given their belief in it, it might well turn out to be self-fulfilling). Thus the action is wrong, that is, wrong *for the Dinka* as much as anyone else, whether they realize it or not. Though they are not blameworthy for acting as they did, the action itself is morally impermissible, and the Sudanese government was right to ban it. Hence, no relativistic conclusion is supported by the example: neither descriptive nor moral-requirement.

Now let us turn to an example of *intra*-cultural moral disagreement; that is, moral conflicts as they exist internal to particular cultures. One of the most fundamental such conflicts in Western countries today concerns abortion. Some people are so convinced that abortion is wrong – that, in fact, it is murder – that they are prepared to take direct action of the most serious kind to try to prevent it occurring. Many participate in demonstrations against abortion, or picket clinics that provide it. A few go much further; several doctors who were known to provide abortions have been shot and killed. On the other side of the debate, people who believe that banning abortion would constitute an important infringement of fundamental rights, especially the rights of women to choose what happens in and to their bodies, are just as passionate in their defence of abortion. They too are willing to take to the streets in support of their cause; to lobby politicians and commit time and money to pressure groups. Here, it seems, we have a fundamental moral disagreement. Moreover, it is a seemingly intractable one. Twenty-five years after *Roe* v. *Wade*, the famous case in which the United States Supreme Court established that laws prohibiting abortion were unconstitutional, the controversy rages unabated. Is this dispute evidence that descriptive relativism is true? Or is there some way we can show that here, too, the disputants are committed to the same moral principles?

In fact, showing this might be relatively easy. To see this, let's set out the argument that leads some people to oppose abortion. Once again, there is a moral principle and a factual principle leading to the conclusion they support:

▌ *moral premise*: It is wrong to take the life of an innocent person.

▌ *factual premise*: A foetus is an innocent person.

▌ *conclusion*: Abortion, which is the taking of the life of a foetus, is wrong.

This is a valid argument. That is to say, if all the premises are true, then the conclusion must also be true. Now, what do people who support women's rights to abortion argue? Surely they do not disagree with the moral premise above? Surely pro-choice advocates do not think that abortion is the killing of an innocent person, but that there is nothing wrong with killing innocent persons? No, in general they agree with the moral principle that killing innocent persons is wrong. If they come to a different conclusion to those who oppose abortion, then it must be because they disagree with the second premise; that is, they do not believe that the foetus is an innocent person.

And we find that this is in fact the case. What, after all, is a person? Surely it is not anything that is genetically human; if this were the case, then a zygote – a one-celled entity formed by the fusion of a sperm and an egg – would be a person. Clearly it is not a person; instead, we all become persons at some state in our development from zygote to adult. So we will need criteria to identify a person. Such criteria, in order to be satisfactory, will have to distinguish persons from (at least most) animals, since we clearly do not believe that most animals are persons. That is, such criteria will list features that human beings typically have, but (most) animals do not. In a well-known essay, Mary Ann Warren has plausibly suggested that these criteria will refer to our ability to think rationally, to communicate with others, and to have a sense of ourselves as persisting in time.[28] Clearly, most animals do not have all these abilities (though perhaps some higher primates do). Clearly, too, a zygote does not possess them. But nor does a foetus; certainly not a foetus in the first few weeks of pregnancy. Thus, on Warren's criteria, a foetus is not a person.

Of course, if Warren is right then the principle that it is wrong to kill innocent persons is irrelevant to the question of abortion. If the foetus is not a person, then nothing prevents us from killing it. Equally, of course, the question of whether or not the foetus is a person is not itself a moral question. It is a question of fact: either the foetus has the sort of properties that distinguish persons, or it does not (of course, Warren might be wrong about what those properties are; this, too, is a question of fact). Thus the entire dispute between opponents of abortion and those who believe that it is permissible might, at base, be a disagreement about facts, and not a reflection of conflicting fundamental moral principles. Once again we find that an apparently deep and intractable moral dispute can be analysed as a dispute about a matter of fact. Thus, too, the debate over abortion does not necessarily support the claim that descriptive relativism is true.

But this kind of moral conflict – in which the real reason for the dispute is disagreement about a factual claim – is not the only kind. People can agree about all the facts, and yet (apparently, at least) disagree about what is permissible. Does the fact that this kind of disagreement exists prove that descriptive relativism is true? Let us examine one last kind of example, to discover the answer to this question.

The Inuit, the people of the far north of North America commonly called the Eskimos, long engaged in the practice of killing unproductive members of their society. Babies, in particular girls, were exposed to die in the snow, as were the elderly. Now, there is no reason to believe that the Inuit had any false beliefs that led them to do this. They did not believe that killing these people had any supernatural justification. Nor did they doubt that some of them, at least, were persons. Does this show that they, unlike us, were not committed to the fundamental moral principle that it is wrong to kill innocent persons?

Actually, this is far from being the case. On the contrary, the Inuit were reluctant to kill these children and other unproductive members of their society; they regarded it as a terrible necessity. When we examine the Inuit practices, we discover that they had good reason for their actions. Inuits living a traditional life eked out a precarious existence. During the Northern winters, life is harsh and food is scarce. The Inuit were nomadic people, restlessly moving in search of food. Thus they often could not feed an extra mouth, nor could they afford the burden of an extra unproductive person. Hence the need to dispose of excess infants and the unproductive elderly; not because the Inuit did not care for their children or aged parents, nor because they did not respect human life, but because they could only ensure the survival of some by killing others. This explains the practice of infanticide among them; we can go further and explain why it was girls who suffered disproportionately. Among the Inuit, it was the males who did the hunting. Now, this hunting was a dangerous affair and the casualty rates were high. Thus a higher proportion of male children needed to be reared, to maintain approximately equal sex ratios among the adults.[29]

Thus, the fact that people have heated, and apparently intractable, moral disagreements does not show that descriptive relativism is true. Disagreement must concern fundamental moral principles for it to be good evidence for descriptive relativism, but moral disagreements frequently turn out to be the result of different conclusions being drawn from the same fundamental moral principles. In these cases, the real disagreement is about matters of fact (such as what needs to be done to preserve the spiritual health of the tribe, or whether a foetus is a person) and only derivatively a moral disagreement. Nor do cases in which people who share our (relevant) non-moral beliefs nevertheless do things that seem, to us, barbaric necessarily prove that descriptive relativism is true. They may, like the Inuit, be applying the same fundamental moral principles as us, but in circumstances that force terrible choices upon them. We cannot blame the Inuit for their actions, nor can we blame the actions themselves. We might do the same in their situation.

Is descriptive relativism true? Some evidence in favour

We began by thinking that descriptive relativism was obviously true. Now we are beginning to wonder whether it is true at all. Is it possible that all cases of apparent moral disagreement can be analysed in the suggested manner: either by locating false non-moral beliefs, which lead those who hold them to apply their moral principles in odd ways, or by finding facts about the circumstances in which the moral principles are applied that explain and justify the application?

But if descriptive relativism is false, then moral-requirement and meta-ethical relativism will not be tempting. Thus, if descriptive relativism is false we need go no further with our consideration of relativism. The careful analyses and arguments of philosophers with regard to other sorts of moral relativism might be interesting, but they will not bear on a real issue.

However, we cannot dismiss descriptive relativism so easily. Not all cases of moral disagreement can be plausibly analysed as based upon non-moral disagreement, or upon the application of shared fundamental moral principles in unpropitious circumstances. Once again I will illustrate this claim with two cases, one drawn from a culture very different from ours, the other a case of intra-cultural disagreement.

Spartan morality

Consider the ancient Greek city-state of Sparta. At the height of its power, Sparta's political system was entirely subordinated to the aims of the military. Sparta was, essentially, an armed camp, and every citizen's life revolved around the needs of warfare. Unsurprisingly, given this fact, the virtues most prized by the Spartans were those conducive to military success, from physical strength to courage. Spartans therefore encouraged the cultivation of these virtues, most infamously by mandating that infants deemed to be sickly or weak were left in the nearby hills to die of exposure. At the age of seven, Spartan boys began thirteen years of military training, during which they were taught everything from survival skills to how to endure pain (the last taught by subjecting them to various kinds of physical tortures). Upon graduating from this military academy, the young soldier lived for the next ten years of his life in a barracks. It was only at the age of thirty that he was allowed to live in a home of his own. Even then, however, he was expected to remain an active member of the military, up until the age of sixty.

Now consider the moral system of the Spartans. To an extraordinary extent, individual freedoms were subordinated to the needs of the state for a well-disciplined and brave army. Every aspect of the daily life of a Spartan man, from birth up till the age of thirty, was closely supervised and controlled (paradoxically perhaps, in some ways freeborn women had rather more freedom, though they too were expected to display quasi-military virtues). Men were expected to be willing to sacrifice themselves for the state, and the virtues that were prized were those of the warrior: bravery, steadfastness of purpose, strength, indifference to pain. We might call this a morality centred around the notion of honour.

In a wide variety of circumstances, Spartan morality mandates actions that are diametrically opposed to those we could countenance. For instance, it requires that children deemed by the state to be weak should be exposed to die. When we examined infanticide

among the Inuit, we saw that they had a justification for their actions
that we could accept; in their circumstances, we might act in just the
same way. But this does not seem to be the case for the Spartans.
They did not face starvation if they allowed such a child to survive.
Rather, their reasons for their actions seem more directly moral:
such a child seems unlikely to be able to exhibit the virtues they
prized. Worse, allowing its survival would threaten the very foundations of the honour system: it would allow individual preferences to
take precedence over the social good, and introduce luxury and
sentimentality into the austere Spartan lifestyle. Indeed, for the
Spartan there was no good reason to allow the child to live. Life is of
value in so far as it is conducive to the ends of the state; in this case,
therefore, its value is negative.

It is abundantly clear that Spartan life is not one for which most
of us have any sympathy. If ever there was a culture that had different
fundamental moral principles to ours, surely this was it. However,
we need to be careful before we so conclude: appearances have
misled us before. Thus we must ask of Spartan morality the questions we asked of the Inuit, and of the Dinka. Can Spartan morality
be explained as the application of our moral values coupled with
false empirical beliefs, or as the application of those values in unpropitious circumstances?

Do the Spartans suffer from false beliefs that are relevant here? I
think not. It is simply true that valour, military skill and physical
strength are conducive to the values of the morality of honour. This
is a coherent morality, one that is comprehensible to us, and one
that, in a diluted form, survives among the more militaristically
minded of us. They make no mistakes of fact when they praise the
strong and the brave; if they are wrong about anything, it is that
honour and the virtues associated with it are indeed valuable. But
this latter question, of course, is irrelevant to *descriptive* relativism.
We are, for the moment, not concerned whether Spartan morality is
justified, only with the question of whether it expresses different
fundamental moral principles to ours.

If the Spartans are not mistaken about matters of fact, perhaps
they, like the Inuit, apply their moral principles in circumstances so
terrible that their actions are understandable. But we have already

seen that this is not the case. Spartan morality is the morality of the privileged ruling class of a city-state; these are not people who face immediate starvation if they relax their strict vigilance. On this score, too, we cannot demonstrate that their morality is not very different from ours. The Spartans, it seems, did have a moral system that is, in some respects at least, quite alien to ours.

Abortion reconsidered

Even within a single culture we may be able to locate groups of people who subscribe to fundamental moral principles that are significantly different to those held by others. Consider the abortion debate once more. We suggested earlier that disagreements between opponents of abortion rights and those who support such rights could be explained by the failure of the two groups to agree on a factual question: whether or not a foetus is a person. However, it may not be the case that the entire debate is predicated on just this factual question. It may be, for instance, that some opponents of abortion will continue to be so opposed even if they come to be convinced that the foetus is not a person. Or it may be that some advocates of abortion rights will continue to hold this view even if they are persuaded that the foetus is a person. In fact, one well-known defence of the right to choose an abortion takes just this line. Judith Jarvis Thomson asks us to consider a thought experiment:

> Imagine you woke up one morning to find that during the night you had been drugged, kidnapped and transported to a secret medical facility. In the bed next to yours is a famous violinist, who is unconscious. You realize with horror that the series of pipes which lead from his body are attached to yours. In fact, you are plugged into the violinist. The director of the hospital explains to you that the violinist is seriously ill. He is suffering from kidney failure, and needs to remain attached to someone else's circulatory system in order to remain alive. You are the only person with compatible blood. 'Don't worry,' the doctor tells you, 'you only have to remain plugged into the violinist for nine months. After that he'll recover and you can detach yourself.'

Thomson suggests that this situation is analogous to that of the pregnant woman. She, like you, is 'plugged into' another human being, in such a way that if she unplugs herself that human being will die. Now, if it is the case, as Thomson suggests, that you have no obligation to remain attached to the violinist (though it would be a great kindness on your behalf if you did), then it must be true that the pregnant woman has no obligation to bear her child. Notice, however, that the violinist is certainly a person. He has all the features that Warren selects as distinctive of persons: rationality, the ability to communicate, a sense of himself as persisting in time, and so on. Thus the question of the permissibility of abortion does not turn on the factual question of whether or not the foetus is a person. Since you are not obliged to remain attached to the violinist, even though detaching yourself means the certain death of a person, abortion is permissible even if the foetus is a person.[30]

If Thomson is right, then settling the factual question that divides many of the people who disagree about the permissibility of abortion will not suffice to end the debate. At bottom, abortion is not a dispute over matters of fact, but over fundamental moral principles. From this it follows, of course, that descriptive relativism is true: the representative members of some groups really do have different fundamental moral principles to members of other groups.

The coherence of descriptive relativism: the bounds of culture

Thus the strategies to discredit descriptive relativism that we have so far explored do not establish that it is false. They may indeed show that disagreement about fundamental moral principles is less common than many people think, but they do not show that it does not exist. However, the opponents of descriptive relativism have other resources upon which to fall back.

Many such opponents point to a lack of clarity in the kind of language we have hitherto been using. We have been talking about the moral beliefs of other cultures or groups, or, more carefully, the beliefs of representative members of other cultures or groups. But can we identify such cultures or groups with sufficient precision to make this kind of language meaningful? What, for instance, do I mean when I say that *the Aztecs believed that human sacrifice was permissible or even obligatory*? At bottom, does this amount to anything more than the claim that *(some) Aztecs performed human sacrifices*? But this second claim does not show that Aztec culture sanctioned human sacrifices, any more than the fact that some people in England today commit murder shows that murder is sanctioned by English culture. Any culture is a complex entity, the objection continues, not a monolith, and the people who belong to it will have different, often radically divergent, moral views. Since there is no such thing as a bounded culture with homogenous moral views, there is nothing for moral statements to be relative *to* except the moral beliefs of individuals. But we know that the moral beliefs of individuals cannot count as plausible standards of right and wrong (or we could not blame the action of the individual murderer). Now, descriptive relativism requires that there be such well-defined cultures or groups with monolithic views, since its thesis is that such cultures and groups, or their representative members, have different fundamental moral beliefs. Thus, the objector concludes triumphantly, descriptive relativism is false.

This is an objection worth taking seriously. There are several prongs to it.[31] The first concerns the bounds of a culture or group. Can we really speak with confidence about the moral principles of the Inuit, or Spartans, or Christians? Isn't it the case that all these groups are diverse and contain many different moral views? As we all know, some Christians oppose contraception whereas others do not. We are committing the sin of ethnocentrism – that vice against which relativism is designed to immunize us – if we do not realize that Muslims and the Inuit, and so on, also contain moral diversity. As a matter of fact, some Muslims oppose veiling; no doubt some Spartans opposed infanticide as well.

Moreover, it is impossible to draw the boundaries of such groups and cultures. Is a woman born in Paris of Algerian parents a member of Muslim culture, or of French? Very probably, she holds views that stem from both sources. Are we to conclude that her moral views don't count, because she is not an 'authentic' member of either culture? If we so conclude, we are making a rod for our own backs, since it is very likely that all cultures are a blend of elements from heterogenous sources. Cultures just are not fixed entities with stable boundaries. Instead they are fluid, constantly altering and constantly shading off into one another.

Finally, assuming we are able to identify cultures sufficiently well for this question even to make sense, who is to count as a representa tive member of a culture? Up till now, for instance, I have been writing as if there is some Muslim (sub)culture that believes that veiling is mandatory. But the fact that, say, a Taliban official subscribes to this belief does not show that there is such a (sub)culture. Why ought his view to be considered representative, and not that of the woman beaten in the street for daring to appear unveiled?

How are we to reply to these objections? I think we must concede that the empirical case upon which it is built is strong. Cultures are rarely sharply distinct from one another, and perhaps always contain some diversity of moral views. Nevertheless, it is not clear that this is sufficient to establish the falsity of descriptive relativism. That is, the fact that cultures are neither bounded entities nor entities that are completely homogeneous does not show that the truth of moral statements cannot be relative to them.

Let me suggest an analogy to make this claim more plausible. Languages are like cultures in both of the ways mentioned above. They, too, do not have clearly defined boundaries. For instance, we can easily construct a continuum of words that connect two apparently different languages. At one end of the continuum the words will clearly belong to the first language, and at the other end they will clearly belong to the second. In between will be words that each language has borrowed from the other. Here's one such continuum, connecting English and French:

> house, mansion, garage, chauffeur, cliché, gourmand, déjà vu, joie de vivre, computeur, (le) week-end, (le) parking, être cool, maison.

Other such lists could be constructed connecting English and German, French and Italian, and so on.

We can see from the list that everything that the critic of descriptive relativism said with regard to cultures is true of languages as well. With languages, too, there are no sharp boundaries. We might want to say that *enfant terrible* is a French phrase that is now often used in English. But we must recognize that it could become entirely naturalized, as 'garage' has, and 'gourmet'. Need we believe that there is a particular moment in time at which such a word becomes naturalized? Surely there is no such instant. If that is so, then there are likely to be some words that are difficult to classify as either now part of English or not. There is here no fact of the matter. Languages shade off into each other, just as cultures do, and some words will exist on the edges of a language, comprehensible to speakers of that language but heavily marked as foreign.

Languages are analogous to cultures in another way too. Semantically and grammatically, few or no languages are monoliths. That is, speakers of a particular language will not always agree with each other as to what counts as correct in the language. Every language that is large enough has its dialects, its variant versions. Thus different English speakers in different regions will pronounce words differently, will have different vocabularies (*cab* versus *taxi*), differences in grammar (*different than* versus *different from*), and so on. Sometimes these differences will be so great that a particular dialect might be almost incomprehensible to a speaker of another dialect. It is precisely through this kind of process that new languages are sometimes born.

Now, what follows from these two facts; that is, from the fact that languages shade off into one another, and the fact that no language is a monolith? Does it follow that it is nonsensical to speak of particular languages? Surely not. It is a mistake to think that because a concept has indistinct boundaries, it is not appropriate to use it at all. We cannot specify what percentage of a man's head needs to be bereft of hair for him to count as bald. Nevertheless, there is nothing wrong with the concept of baldness. Our failure to specify necessary and sufficient conditions for its application does not prevent us from using it, and nor should it. There are many such concepts with indistinct boundaries: *old*, *tall*, *fast*, and many more besides. They, too, normally give us little trouble.

Thus our failure to locate the precise borders of a language is no reason to think that the notion of, say, English, is not perfectly in place. Nor does this failure prevent us from using the notions of rightness and wrongness with regard to English grammar. Notice that these are *relativized* notions. Something is grammatically wrong relative to English, and not French, or any other language. Thus my English dictionary lists two correct plurals for the word *wunderkind*, borrowed from German. We may say either *wunderkinder*, using the German plural form, or *wunderkinders*, forming the plural in the normal English manner. *Wunderkinds* is grammatically wrong relative to German, but correct relative to English.[32]

What about the fact that there are dialects? Does it prevent us using (relativized) notions of rightness and wrongness? Can we not say that, for example, 'I goes to shop' is grammatically incorrect? Surely not. So long as a group of people (implicitly) agree on what counts as right and wrong in almost all cases, we are able to make relativized judgements of correctness. *'Different than'* is wrong in British English and correct in American English. To be sure, there may be some areas in which there is not sufficient agreement to settle the matter (the question of the wrongness or otherwise of splitting infinitives in English might be one example). But the fact that there are areas of indeterminacy does not imply that there is no such thing as right and wrong at all, any more than the fact that many vague concepts have indistinct borders prevents us from using them.

It would only be true that we could not apply these relativized standards to language if there were no shared agreements about right and wrong at all. That is to say, we could not use predicates like 'wrong in American English' if there was no such dialect, but instead everyone spoke their own idiolect, a version of the language peculiar to them. Of course, everyone has their own linguistic quirks and idiosyncrasies, but it does not follow from this that dialects do not exist. If everyone spoke an idiolect, then we could not have the practice of teaching a language, since teaching a language involves getting someone to use it in a systematic manner. There would be a great deal more mutual incomprehensibility than there is, and neighbours would be no more likely to understand each other than people from different countries. We would not be able to speak of languages at all. Of course, none of this is the case; it is simply not true that languages and dialects do not exist.

What lessons should we draw from all of this? We should see, first of all, that the fact that no language is monolithic should give us pause before we make sweeping pronouncements. That is, when we make statements about what counts as correct in English, we will want to be sure that the feature we are picking out really is generally shared, and not an aspect of the language upon which various dialects conflict. Nevertheless, some sweeping statements *will* be true: there is a great deal of overlap between the various dialects of English, as is evidenced by the fact that these dialects are mutually comprehensible. Moreover, the fact that some general statements are not applicable because dialects conflict on this or that point only shows that we need to make finer-grained judgements. We need to relativize our truth claims to the dialect, and not the language. Though disagreement and conflict are pervasive features of language, we are not prevented from making valid judgements of linguistic correctness, with regard to grammar, semantics, vocabulary and even pronunciation.

But if we are able to make such linguistic judgements, relativized to a language or a dialect, what prevents us from making moral judgements relativized to a culture or a sub-culture? Like languages, cultures are not monoliths. Here too conflict and disagreement are pervasive. But like languages, cultures share a great deal in common: patterns of behaviour, very frequently a religion, a certain style, but above all certain shared manners of interpreting the world, of imputing value to it.[33] Thus we can attribute a great deal to cultures, despite their internal conflicts. And when we locate such conflicts, we will frequently find that they, too, are systematic: that a sub-culture is associated with each of the contending views. Thus we can make judgements relativized to cultures, and, when we can't, we can usually make them relative to sub-cultures. Nothing in the fact that cultures shade into one another, or in the fact that they are not homogenous, prevents descriptive relativism from being true.

Who is a representative individual?

Critics of descriptive relativism have yet another charge to make. Very often, they claim, what we take to be the moral views of a culture are merely the self-serving ideologies of the most powerful elements within it. These groups are the ones most likely to be able to get their voices heard, but what they have to say will not reflect the true views of the great majority of their fellows. Thus, these critics allege, when we ask what are the moral views of a culture – of Muslims, or the Aztecs, and so on – very often the answer we come up with represents nothing more than rationalizations of the *oppressors* of these groups. It is rather as if we had wanted to know what the views of South Africans under apartheid were, and we asked the members of the ruling regime. We would have been told, of course, that South Africans think that apartheid is acceptable or even obligatory. As good cultural relativists we would have left them to it – ignoring the fact that the ruling regime represented only a small proportion of South Africans, and allowing the true feelings of the great majority to go unexpressed. Thus, descriptive relativism is not merely false; it is dangerous. It takes the self-serving views of the powerful to express the morality of a culture; thus siding with the oppressors against the oppressed.

We can appreciate the force of this point by considering an example drawn from the work of Mary Midgley. In a well-known article, Midgley examines the medieval Japanese practice of trying out one's new sword on passers-by. Samurai warriors believed it to be very important that their swords be capable of cutting through the entire human body at one stroke; if they failed to do so in battle, they would be dishonoured, and with them their lord. Hence they could not risk going into battle with an untested sword. Thus arose the practice called *tsujigiri*: testing the sword on the first passer-by one encountered.

Let us note, first of all, that this example resists redescription in such a manner as to render it innocuous. That is, it will be relatively difficult to use the standard anti-descriptive-relativism strategies we have explored to show that the Samurai shared our fundamental moral principles. In the first place, it does not appear as though this practice reflects our shared fundamental principles applied in unpropitious circumstances. If *tsujigiri* were a method of population control, as infanticide among the Inuit might have been, we would expect to see more specific targeting of the people killed. It would be unproductive members of society who would die. But *tsujigiri* selects passers-by at random (thereby ensuring that it will select from among the able-bodied; those able to walk). Moreover, it is difficult to explain *tsujigiri* as the result of false non-moral beliefs. The Samurai warrior's belief that failure to cut through a human body in battle would dishonour him and his lord was true (or, at any rate, it might have been true; only detailed ethnographic and historical work will discover whether it was). Whether or not someone is dishonoured depends solely on the attitudes of the people around him, and what they count as honourable and dishonourable, not on mind-independent facts. If we are to criticize the Samurai's belief that failure to cut through a human body at a single stroke will dishonour him, it will not be on the grounds that it is false, but that it is inappropriate. Honour ought not to be intimately linked to the quality of military equipment or to success on the battlefield. But this is a *moral* criticism. The very fact that we make it shows that we *do* have (at least some) different fundamental moral beliefs to the Samurai warrior.

Thus the standard anti-descriptive-relativism moves will not disarm Midgley's example. Nevertheless, perhaps there is some other way to render it innocuous. This is the suggestion of Michele Moody-Adams. Her proposal is that we take practices such as *tsujigiri* at face value. To us, this practice looks like murder pure and simple. We would have no hesitation in condemning such actions if they took place in any Western city. So why not treat them in exactly the same way when they occur in medieval Japan? It may be true, of course, that medieval Samurai were not punished for their acts. But why should that worry us? We have plenty of experience of people being able to act with impunity because they are too powerful to punish. This does not alter the fact that their actions are wrong.

In fact, Moody-Adams claims, we can be sure that this is the appropriate manner in which to treat *tsujigiri*.[34] We do not have to look to the detailed work of anthropologists and historians to know that medieval Japanese culture did not regard the practice as unobjectionable. Given the facts of human nature, they *must* have rejected it. Thus the example cannot support descriptive relativism.

Moody-Adams holds that this is true, because if medieval Japanese culture really regarded *tsujigiri* as unobjectionable, then it would have to be true 'that endangered passersby would have generally *consented* to be sacrificed to the ritual' (82). But everything we know about human nature leads us to believe that this is extremely unlikely. Human beings just do not willingly give up their lives for no good reason. Hence the claim is implausible. 'Surely at least some potential victims of the practice would have objected to it' (82). But if the peasants who were the victims of it did not consent, then *tsujigiri* is merely an example of an immoral act, imposed upon the suffering peasants of Japan by a military elite against their wishes. The practice does not, therefore, support descriptive relativism any more than the fact that certain people among us would, if they could get away with it, murder and steal shows that murder and theft is not objectionable to us.

Thus, too, we can appreciate the force of the claim that relativism sides with the strong against the weak. If we conclude that *tsujigiri* is permissible in medieval Japan, we are allowing the rapacious Samurai to dictate what counts as morality for everyone. We ignore the more numerous peasants for no other reason than that they are unable to make their voices heard in a feudal society. We enshrine the oppression of the majority by a minority. 'Might makes right' will be our principle if we take this route. But surely morality ought to be independent of political power? In fact, it ought to give us a means of criticizing such power, of siding with the weak against the strong. These are important objections; it is therefore worth examining the line of argument that is offered in support of them in some detail.

Let us begin this examination by setting out Moody-Adams's argument more clearly.

(I)   For it to be true that the existence of a practice like *tsujigiri* supports descriptive relativism, that practice must be generally accepted in the culture.

(II) But it is implausible to think that passers-by would have consented to being the victims of the practice.

(CI) Hence, *tsujigiri* was not generally accepted in medieval Japanese society.

(CII) Therefore the existence of *tsujigiri* does not support descriptive relativism.

How strong is this argument? Premise (I) seems very strong. Since the kind of descriptive relativism we are here concerned with relativizes moral beliefs to cultures, it seems that something like (I) must be the case for descriptive relativism to be true. Premise (II) seems very plausible. It is unlikely, given well-established facts about human beings, that Japanese passers-by would have agreed to be victims of the practice. Moreover, if (CI) follows from these two premises, then so would (CII). Thus if we are to challenge Moody-Adams's argument, it must be by challenging (CI). Does the truth of (CI) follow from the truth of (I) and (II)? In other words, is it true that *tsujigiri* is generally accepted in medieval Japan only if in fact all (or most) passers-by would consent to being the victim of it?

The argument seems valid only if this general rule is true:

> A culture can be said to accept a practice or a principle that potentially reduces the well-being of individual members if and only if all or most of its members would consent to being the object of that practice or principle.

But this general rule is clearly false. Consider the practice of capital punishment. Surely it is plausible to claim that many cultures have accepted this practice. But from the fact that a culture accepts this practice, it most certainly does not follow that any particular member of that culture would consent to being executed.[35] Thus a natural defence of *tsujigiri* against Moody-Adams suggests itself. Though her implicit suggestion, that if we asked each individual victim of the practice whether he or she were willing to be sacrificed in the ritual the answer would emphatically deny willingness, is plausible, this does not suffice to show that the practice was not in fact accepted by medieval Japanese culture. The victim of capital punishment would similarly reject the practice, at the moment he or she is strapped into the chair, yet it is surely plausible to claim that many cultures do in fact accept capital punishment.

Perhaps, however, this counter-example does not show that Moody-Adams's general line is flawed, but merely that she needs to be more careful in stating it. For it seems that she can point to a crucial difference between capital punishment and *tsujigiri*. It is (in principle, at least) up to each of us whether we shall be the victims of capital punishment. So long as we are law-abiding, we are safe from it. Since it is true that some cultures accept capital punishment, but capital punishment does not pass the test of the general rule we suggested, the general rule must be altered. Perhaps it should read something like this:

> A culture can be said to accept a practice or a principle that potentially reduces the well-being of individual members if and only if all or most of its members would consent *now* to being the object of that practice or principle if in the future they act in certain specified ways.

Capital punishment would pass this revised test for acceptance. I can consent to my culture having a rule that murderers should be executed, and therefore implicitly to the idea that I should be executed if I murder someone. But *tsujigiri* does not pass this test. Its victims were selected at random. Hence Japanese peasants could not be said to have consented to it.

Will this revised test establish that *tsujigiri* was not in fact accepted by the medieval Japanese, and that therefore this practice offers no support for descriptive relativism? Unfortunately for Moody-Adams, the answer is no. The revised test is also vulnerable to a counter-example. It is very plausible to believe that the members of a culture can consent to going to war with another. We can, if we like, express this in terms of the beliefs of individual members of that culture. It will sometimes be true of most of the members of culture X that they believe that war with culture Y is just or otherwise appropriate. It can even be the case that the members of the culture consent to do the fighting. Plains Indians seem to have been willing warriors; so were First-World-War volunteers on both sides of the conflict. But notice that when people consent to fighting in a war, they each consent to undertaking the risk of being killed in it. Moreover, they undertake this risk in full awareness that (in broad terms) it will be a matter of luck whether they are killed or not. They consent to the *risk* of death because they believe that it is appropriate that everyone should run this risk.

Thus, rather than think of *tsujigiri* as analogous to crimes committed in our society, why not think of it as analogous to the risks undergone by combatants? Though Moody-Adams is probably right that the Japanese peasant would not consent to being killed by the Samurai, she might consent to *running the risk of being killed*. If she believes that it is better for the society as a whole that *tsujigiri* be practised, she might consent to run this risk. Now, this can be true even if premise (II) above is the case. That is, someone can have consented to take a risk of being killed even in cases in which that person would not consent to being killed. The First-World-War soldier consented to risk his life, even though he presumably does not consent to dying. Similarly, the Japanese peasant might have consented to the risk, even if she now objects to being the victim of *tsujigiri*.[36]

Thus Moody-Adams's argument from facts about human nature to the falsity of descriptive relativism fails. Whether the Japanese peasants actually regarded *tsujigiri* as permissible or not is an empirical question; one that can only be settled by way of detailed historical and anthropological investigation. We cannot show a priori that they could not have accepted it. Thus we cannot know before we investigate whether we are siding with the strong against the weak in saying that *tsujigiri* is permissible.

What ought we to take from our survey of the main arguments against descriptive relativism? We ought, I think, to conclude that we need to be very careful before we attribute fundamental moral principles different to our own to the members of other cultures. Very often we will find that exotic practices that seem to stem from such principles can be interpreted so as to remove this appearance. But not all such practices can be interpreted away in this manner, nor are there conclusive a priori arguments against descriptive relativism.

We have spent much longer on descriptive relativism than is usual in discussions of moral relativism. This extended treatment was necessary because if descriptive relativism turned out to be false, moral-requirement and meta-ethical relativism would not be tempting. However, we have seen that there are grounds to believe that descriptive relativism will, at least sometimes, be true. It is now time to move on. Showing that moral relativism and descriptive relativism are both coherent and possible is far from sufficient to show that moral relativism is true. There are still fundamental objections that it must meet before we can so conclude.

Thus far, the focus has been on the relativist position and the arguments that might be marshalled against it. Let us now turn the spotlight back on to the absolutist. If he is to vindicate his theory, to show that there is a timeless truth regarding what is permissible and what impermissible, he needs to have a plausible story as to what makes our moral judgements true. Now that it is no longer plausible simply to hold that God is the guarantor of this truth, or to postulate an eternal moral law that occupies some Platonic realm, he owes us an account that will take the place of these discredited metaphysical pictures. In other words, he must respond to the Nietzschean challenge.

One way of responding to this challenge that has tempted many people is by way of the examination of human nature. Though we cannot point to transcendental entities that make our moral judgements true or false, nevertheless we can point to our biology. Because of the kind of animal we are, some things are in our interests and some against them. Because of our evolutionary history, some actions are right for us and others wrong. If relativism is to prove itself a plausible moral theory, it must reply to the theorists of human nature.

5

BIOLOGY AND HUMAN INTERESTS

How might an argument from human biology work to discredit relativism? The opponent of relativism might argue as follows: if relativism were true, then there would not be any significant constraints on the contents of morality. It would have to be the case that there are many different ways in which, as a matter of fact, human beings can act toward each other, none of which is better, in any absolute sense, than any other. But this claim is implausible. In fact, there is a significant set of constraints on human action: the constraints represented by our shared biology. In virtue of the kinds of animals we are, we all share a set of interests: in securing food, shelter, sleep, and so on. These are all goods that we must have, no matter what other goods we wish to pursue, for without them we shall not be able to pursue goods, have interests or preferences at all. Now, given their role in human life, these goods will necessarily be valued by all people, everywhere. Thus there will in fact be only one set of goods, valid for everyone. Relativism is thus abolished, or, at worst, relegated to the margins of moral theory.

We have seen that relativism is most plausible when it is advanced as an explanation for the actual differences in the moral systems that we encounter in the world. In other words, it is as an inference from descriptive relativism that meta-ethical relativism is most persuasively advanced. But if the argument from biology succeeds, it will serve to refute relativism at its very root. If it is correct, then descriptive relativism is false, and there is nothing for meta-ethical relativism to explain. If the argument from biology is successful, then as a matter of fact all cultures will overlap on a set of basic goods. There will be no significant differences in the values each upholds, and any observed differences will have to be explained utilizing the various strategies anti-relativists usually deploy against descriptive relativism (application of the same principles in different circumstances, explanation via the possession of false beliefs regarding empirical matters, and so on).

But will the argument from biology, if it is correct, succeed in abolishing any interesting relativism? How might a relativist reply to it? Perhaps she might begin by pointing out that demonstrating that everyone shares some values does not suffice to show that relativism is false. We have seen that descriptive relativism is true if and only if people have different *fundamental* moral beliefs. Now, the evidence we have just reviewed gives us reason to believe that there will be a set of *basic* moral values that all people share. But saying this does not show that they will have the same *fundamental* values. Obviously, I am here relying upon a distinction, between fundamental and basic values, which now needs to be elaborated.

Let us call the values founded on the set of interests that, we have good reason to think, all people will share, *basic* moral values. We so describe them because they are built upon basic facts of our biology, facts about what we all need, regardless of what else we want. Now, these basic moral values are to be distinguished from *fundamental* moral values. When we used the term 'fundamental' in the last chapter to describe moral principles, we meant a principle that did not rest upon any further foundation. There was no further reason to be given in support of such a moral principle. It was acted upon for its own sake, as it were. Thus the principle 'do not kill foetuses' rests upon the fundamental moral principle 'do not kill innocent persons'. But the principle 'do not kill innocent persons' does not rest upon anything else in turn. It is a fundamental principle. Similarly, fundamental moral values will be values that do not rest upon any further foundation.

Now, it might be the case that basic values and fundamental values often coincide. But we have no reason to think that this will *always* be the case. It may happen that some basic values are not fundamental, and that some fundamental values are not basic. Consider the value that having adequate nutrition has for us. It is a paradigm of a basic value, as we have been using the term. It is a value, grounded upon our biology, the satisfaction of which is necessary for us to continue to live, and therefore to have interests and preferences at all. But it is not a fundamental value. That is, we can sensibly ask and answer the question, 'Why does it matter, morally speaking, that we are sufficiently well nourished?' There are a number of answers that might be given: because preserving human life matters morally, because continuing to exist is the condition for having preferences and interests, and so on. Thus this *basic* moral value is not a *fundamental* moral value. On the other hand, some fundamental moral values will not be basic. The principle 'treat everyone equally unless there are relevant differences between them' seems to be a fundamental moral principle. But it is not a basic moral principle in the sense in which we are using the term.

Thus the fact, if indeed it is a fact, that all persons and cultures will share a set of basic values does not suffice to show that they will share the same fundamental values. It therefore will not suffice to show that descriptive relativism is false. But this argument shows only that descriptive relativism *might* be true, regardless of facts about our biology. We need to go much further and show that different human beings do *in fact* have different fundamental moral beliefs; that our shared biology does not, as a matter of fact, lead us all to have the same fundamental beliefs. Perhaps, we might think, our biology and the basic values it founds serve as the base for a more extensive set of fundamental moral principles, which all human beings share. We might think morality was built upon biology in the following way: because of the kind of beings we are, we all need access to certain goods, we all seek pleasure and avoid pain. We all therefore have good reason to value these goods, and to value whatever happens to promote the balance of pleasure over pain. I am, as a matter of fact, motivated to pursue these goods; this is just the kind of thing that moves beings like me to action. We need add only one plausible principle to these facts about each of us to give birth to morality. That principle is *universalizability*.

The principle of moral universalizability states, roughly, that whatever is true of me, morally speaking, is also true of anyone else unless there is some relevant difference between them and me. Thus anything to which I am entitled is an entitlement for anyone similarly situated; anything that is obligatory for me, that I have a right to, that is impermissible for me, and so on, all these apply also to anyone else unless there is a relevant difference between us. This principle seems to lie at the very heart of our idea of morality. It underlies, for instance, our notions of impartiality, of equality and of desert. We believe that moral treatment should be responsive to what people have done: the good rewarded and the bad punished. These are the kinds of differences between people that ought to make a difference, that ought to count, morally. I should be treated differently if I have done something to merit that different treatment, if that treatment is owed to me, or if I have it 'coming to me'. Unless there is such a difference between you and me, however, we ought to be treated in the same way.

There is no doubt that the principle of universalizability is at the heart of *our* conception of ethics. However, we cannot call upon it in an effort to defeat relativism unless we also have good reason to think that every other culture also recognizes it. If we are to use it to build upon the facts of our biology in order to construct a cross-culturally valid morality, we must be sure that in employing it we are not begging the question against different conceptions of morality, arbitrarily imposing upon them something quite foreign to their conceptions. Is universalizability in fact itself cross-culturally valid? Is it, itself, universal?

This seems to be an empirical question. That is, it seems that if we are to answer it, the way to proceed is to examine actual moral systems and see whether as a matter of fact they recognize something akin to the principle of universalizability. But I am not convinced that it is an empirical question. What should we conclude if upon examining some rival system we fail to detect anything analogous to the principle of universalizability? Ought we to think that here is an ethics that lacks the principle? Perhaps, given the centrality of the principle to what we regard as morality, we ought to react in a quite different manner. Perhaps we ought to think, instead, that here is a culture without an ethics at all, or, more weakly, what I took to be the morality of this culture is not its morality but something else. What I am suggesting is that the principle of universalizability is so central to our conception of what an ethical system is that it will serve as one of the criteria by which we identify ethical systems. If something we took to be an ethical system on other grounds – perhaps because it provides a set of rules for conducting one's life – turns out to have no place for universalizability, then we might reasonably conclude that we were mistaken, that we are not dealing with an ethical system at all. Thus the question of whether the principle of universalizability is cross-culturally valid might not be an empirical one after all. It is a constitutive condition of ethical systems, not an optional feature of them. If this is correct, the empirical question we should ask ourselves is not whether such and such a rival ethics recognizes the principle of universalizability but, instead, whether such and such a culture has an ethics at all.

We shall return to the question of the constitutive features of ethical systems in a later chapter. For now, we can say this much: given the fact that universalizability seems to be a core feature of ethics, lacking which we would fail to recognize a system of rules for the conduct of life as an ethical system at all, and given the fact that we do in fact believe that all cultures have ethical systems, we can conclude that all such systems find a place for the principle in some form. Ethics is, in important part, about giving reasons for one's actions, reasons of a particular kind. When we – you or me, Australian or Dinka, Chinese or Amazonian Indian – act morally, or think that someone deserves treatment that falls under the rubric of morality, we are always supposed to be capable of giving some kind of reason that justifies the action, and these reasons mention morally relevant differences between persons. Sophie ought to help Toby *because she has promised to do so*; the fact that she has put herself under this obligation is a morally relevant difference between her and someone who has not so promised. Sam ought to be punished for breaking the law; the fact that he has done so voluntarily is a morally relevant difference between him and other people. And so on. All ethical systems recognize that such reasons must be able to be given to justify the differential treatment of persons. This recognition is encoded in the Golden Rule of Judaism and Christianity ('Love thy neighbour as thyself'), in the so-called Silver Rule of Confucianism ('What you do not wish for yourself, do not do to others'), in the 'all-embracing love' of Taoism, and in every other ethical tradition besides. All ethical systems contain the principle of universalizability, and all cultures have ethical systems.

We now have in hand two significant results that we might hope to use to show that relativism is false. We have established that ethics is founded, in important part at least, on the desires, interests and preferences of human beings, but that these desires, interests and preferences are significantly constituted by the biological nature of human beings, a nature that is shared by everyone everywhere. We also now know that all ethical systems contain (something like) the principle of universalizability. Now, we might reason as follows: given that moral values are significantly constituted by our shared biology, and given the fact that the principle of universalizability constrains us to ascribe to others whatever we recognize as appropriate in our own case, we can expect all cultures to converge on a significant set of moral values. Starting from their own case, the members of every culture will end by recognizing the same universal morality. The process might be expected to run something like this. We each reflect on what, given our biology, we need, what we desire, what is in our interests. We discover that we need adequate nutrition and shelter, and so on, that we desire pleasure and to avoid pain, that it is in our interests to have not merely a life but a meaningful life. Given these interests and desires, we hope to be given the resources to pursue our goals; at minimum, we hope that no one will interfere with us in their pursuit. We hope that our moral right to the things we need will be recognized. But then the principle of universalization constrains us to recognize this same right for everyone else who shares our biology, unless there is some relevant difference between us and them that makes it appropriate to treat them in a different manner. Starting from the bare facts of human biology, then, we might hope to reason to a universal human morality. The failure of other people to recognize this morality, we might think, does not cast doubt on its truth. Rather, it merely casts doubt on the rationality, or the morality, of those who do not recognize it.

Now, something like this strategy might indeed give us reason to expect that the ethical systems of different cultures will have a great deal in common. I noted earlier that all ethical systems seem, as a matter of fact, to contain principles such as an injunction against killing. Indeed, we ought to expect that certain ethical rules are necessary for the continued existence of any society. If human cultures are to subsist and reproduce themselves over time, then some system of rules will have to be in place, a system that prohibits arbitrary killing and that establishes the basis for a degree of co-operation among individuals. Human beings are not especially fast or strong; they cannot hope to live long by themselves. Hobbes's state of nature, a war of all against all, would not merely lead us all to have lives that are 'nasty, brutish and short'; we could expect that very soon there would no longer be human beings at all. But human beings make up for their individual weakness by being social animals; by co-operating we can survive and even flourish. Thus we can expect all cultures, all human societies that are able to persist for many generations, to have rules that facilitate co-operation; moreover, many of these rules will be substantially the same across the world.[37]

Will these considerations suffice to rule out the possibility of a significant relativism? I suspect not. I suspect that though the area of overlap we can expect between the ethical systems of different cultures is substantial, it leaves room enough for important disagreements. It may be true that all ethical systems will have to have certain elements in common simply because these elements are essential to the survival of human cultures. But despite this overlap between them, existing ethical systems mandate quite different actions. Some call for the exclusion of women from public life and from employment, some regard this exclusion as immoral; some permit abortion, some do not. Obviously, all these systems are compatible with our biological nature, since the cultures to which they belong survive and might even be said to flourish. The bare facts of biology do not seem to allow us to rule out these options.

If biology by itself does not accomplish this end, however, can we not employ universalizability to achieve it? Is not the exclusion of women from public life an infringement of the principle? Most of us think that it is. The tides of racism and sexism have slowly retreated over the past century in response to the failure of people in our culture to point to a relevant difference between women and men, between blacks and whites, that would justify differences in treatment. Traditionally, sexist and racist arguments have pointed to alleged intellectual or moral differences in support of their conclusions: to the supposed lesser intelligence of women or of a particular racial group, or their supposed inability to act impartially or their wickedness. When asked to produce evidence for these differences, however, the racist and the sexist have failed to meet the challenge and their positions have been discredited. They have not been able to produce evidence that there is such a relevant difference. Given the kinds of things we generally believe warrant differential treatment, racism and sexism cannot be justified.

However, this is not to say that, for instance, sexism could never be justified. Think of Spartan society, as sketched in the last chapter. This was a social system, and a morality, fundamentally organized around the demands of the military, that valued the military virtues above all else. As a matter of fact, Spartans expected much the same qualities from their women as from their men: physical toughness, athleticism, devotion to the good of the state. But they did not subject women to the same military discipline as their men. Though all attempts to discover systematic mental differences between men and women have failed, there are obvious physical differences, which justify this decision. Most obviously, on average, men are physically stronger than women. Thus, if we value the ability to perform well in warfare above all else, we will tend to think less of women than of men, without making any kind of empirical mistake, and without violating the principle of universalizability. Here, gender is itself a morally relevant difference (or perhaps, more carefully, a marker for a morally relevant difference).

Thus, despite the fact that all ethical systems accept something like the principle of universalizability, and therefore are committed to justifying the differential treatment of people by pointing to relevant differences between them, the notion of what counts as a relevant difference varies widely from culture to culture. We think that intellectual and moral differences alone are appropriate: is the agent a person (capable of deliberation, self-consciousness, and so on); is she a member of our moral community (not psychotic, for instance); has she done something to forfeit her rights? But the principle of universalizability does not dictate this interpretation as the only one that is justifiable. To be sure, to take gender as a relevant difference seems to us to be downright immoral. But it is question-begging to object to a rival morality that, by our standards, is immoral. Before this move is open to us, we must be able to show that our standards are better than theirs.

Notice that this line of thought does give us a ready response to many sexist and racist beliefs. If someone, or some culture, justifies their biased views by reference to supposed facts about women or blacks or Jews, we can challenge their beliefs. As a matter of fact, a great deal of prejudice is predicated on false belief; to the extent that it is, we can demonstrate its irrationality. But, perhaps unfortunately, not all such prejudices are based upon such false beliefs; sometimes, therefore, we cannot convict the prejudiced of irrationality in any simple sense.

Biology and culture

Thus the facts of our shared biology plus the principle of universalizability do not suffice to eliminate moral disagreement, because different cultures can have different standards of what counts as morally relevant. That is, different cultures can take the facts about our shared biology, apply the principle of universalizability and validly draw different conclusions to each other. Moreover, there is another way in which the facts about our biology might lead us to divergent views. Biology provides a natural foundation for many of our values. But we cannot simply read our values off our biology. Instead, it is biology *interpreted*, that is, biology culturally elaborated, that provides such a foundation.

Take a bare biological fact such as the fact that pain is unpleasant. That gives us all a prima-facie reason to avoid pain. But it also makes pain especially ripe for cultural elaboration. The very fact that it is unavoidably unpleasant, that this is a brute fact about human beings, makes pain the kind of thing to which cultures typically attribute significance. It simply is not true that, because it is unpleasant, all cultures seek to avoid or minimize pain. On the contrary, cultures frequently seek to channel pain; they make the experiencing of it, and resistance to it, meaningful. For the American Plains Indian, for example, pain was not something to be avoided at all costs, but something that, under the right conditions at least, was to be sought out for its spiritual power. Consider the famous Sun Dance, practised by many of the tribes of the plains. In this ceremony, young men who wished to receive a vision submitted themselves to a shaman, who would cut slits in their breasts in such a manner as to hold in place a piece of wood, one in each breast, to which

> ropes were tied, with the other end tied to the fork of the center pole. Then each young man leaned back, keeping his ropes taut while he alternately raised himself on his toes and sank back, all the while gazing at the sun. He persisted in his dancing until the skewers finally tore loose under his weight and released him [...]. After this ordeal each participant required several weeks for his wounds to heal and he carried his scars to his grave.[38]

The participant in the Sun Dance went without food and water for several days as well. In this weakened state, it would not be very long before the combination of exhaustion and pain caused him to collapse, and experience the visions he sought. Precisely because pain is unpleasant, because it is something we ordinarily avoid, it is ripe for cultural elaboration. Our biology is shared, but the significance it has for us differs from culture to culture.[39]

Though the Plains Indians took the quest for pain to an extreme that is foreign to our culture, we, too, do not regard pain simply as an evil to be avoided. We too sometimes seek it out, and applaud those who resist it. We have a long tradition of associating the bearing of pain and of deprivation with sanctity. Holy men and women in the Christian tradition have often sought out reminders of Christ's pain on the cross, and have been canonized for the manner in which they have borne their suffering. Consider Saint Catherine of Siena. Catherine

> was an ascetic for whom the humiliation of the flesh provided an indispensable avenue for a direct approach to God. [...] She sees the material world with its vain pleasures as a place of 'venomous thorns' and therefore recommends that the godly – in spurning the thorns of pleasure – should actively seek out suffering through humiliations of the flesh. Such spiritualized suffering, paradoxically, fills them with joy.[40]

Catherine forced herself to vomit her food, until she starved herself to death.

No doubt, this seeking after pain seems as foreign to most readers as do the practices of the Plains Indians. Yet a certain reverence for pain and suffering, and a respect for those who undergo it and seek it out, persists in our culture. Think of the slogan of the gym: 'No pain, no gain'; or the respect accorded to the marathon runner who runs through the 'pain barrier'; or the higher status of 'natural' – that is, free of pain-relieving drugs – childbirth. We continue to believe that pain transforms its sufferer, that it puts us in contact with something higher, if not with God then with the rhythms of the body. Think, finally, of sexualized pain, pain sought after in sado-masochism. Pain is not just something to be avoided, even for us, who reach for the aspirin at the first twinge of a headache. It is, also and at the same time, something to be welcomed, to be experienced, to be sought out and heightened.

Thus, though the fact that we all experience pain, in response to similar stimuli, is biologically based, it does not follow from this that we can build a cross-culturally valid morality on this foundation. Though there is no doubt that biology significantly constrains the content of morality, as it does culture generally (thinking that we do not need to eat will not make it so), a great deal of our biologically based experience must be interpreted before it can play a meaningful role in our lives.

Against this line of argument, it might be objected that we have so far been concerned only with the experience of pain in our own case. From the fact that people might, for cultural reasons, choose to experience pain, it does not follow that refraining from inflicting it, because it is naturally unpleasant, is not a universal moral principle. Morality, after all, is concerned mainly with our treatment of other people, not with our treatment of ourselves. We cannot cheat ourselves, or lie to ourselves. Perhaps if we submit to pain, we act in a manner that does not fall under the heading of morality at all. If this were the case, we might hope to be able to rescue a universal morality that is based on the facts of human biology, despite the evidence I have adduced of the role pain plays in different cultures.

Unfortunately for someone who takes this route, it seems to be false. As a matter of fact, cultures differ not only in the ways they regard it to be permissible and even rational to inflict pain upon ourselves, but also on the kinds of pain it is permissible and even rational to inflict upon others. Many cultures have some kind of initiation ritual that marks those who undergo it as full members. Thus some New Guinea people practised scarification as part of initiations: the skin of the initiate is cut in such a manner as to bear permanent scars in symbolically meaningful patterns. Other cultures have practised circumcision, genital piercing, and so on. All of these involve the infliction of pain by some people on others, not as punishment but as a sign that the person is to be admitted to the full rights of a member of the group. In our culture, such rituals continue to be practised: Muslims and Jews practise circumcision, for instance. Moreover, no one thinks too badly of parents who have their young child's ears pierced.

Human nature and evolution

Since about the 1980s there has been a remarkable resurgence of an approach to understanding morality that was once widespread, but had long been thought to be a dead-end. This approach often goes under the name of *evolutionary ethics*. Proponents of evolutionary ethics hope to show that human morality, like our opposable thumbs and uniquely flexible ability to communicate with one another, is a product of human evolution. Now, if this approach were to be successful, it would seem to be singularly well positioned to meet the relativist challenge. We have, after all, seen that relativism depends for its plausibility in large part on the claim that moral judgements are of an entirely different order to scientific truth-claims. It was this alleged difference between science and morality that was supposed to account for the fact that moral disagreements are evidence for relativism (and not merely evidence that one side or the other – or both – is simply wrong, as in a disagreement concerning scientific matters). But if the evolutionary account of the source and objectivity of ethics is plausible, then the supposed distinction between ethics and science is illusory. Evolutionary ethics provides morality with the backing of hard science.

Very briefly, the claim made by evolutionary ethics is that human morality is the product of evolution; the distinctive claims it makes upon us, and the disposition to follow it, developed as a survival strategy. Members of groups who behave morally toward one another will do better than those who belong to groups whose members act exclusively in their own self-interest. 'Better' here means better in evolutionary terms – roughly, will have more offspring, or pass on more copies of their genes in other ways. Paradoxically, individuals who follow rules that dictate a degree of apparently altruistic behaviour will, on average, do better than those who always act only on their perceived self-interest.

This contention is very well illustrated by an example drawn from Richard Dawkins's famous manifesto of evolution, *The Selfish Gene*.[41] Dawkins asks us to imagine a species of bird that frequently suffers from infestation by a certain kind of tick. The tick carries a disease that will kill the bird if it is not quickly removed. Normally, the bird is able to remove the tick for itself, with its beak. But there are regions of itself – the top of its head, for example – that it cannot reach. If it is to have the tick removed, it will need another bird to do the job for it.

Thus the birds have an incentive to co-operate with one another. However, birds are presumably unable consciously to adopt the strategy of mutual co-operation. They do not have the foresight to understand how it would be in their own long-term interests to aid others. Nor, one might think, do they have a sense of justice. What reason might a bird that grooms another have to think that it will be groomed in return?

Evolutionary theory explains how adaptations come about in a purely mechanical fashion. A strategy is not adopted consciously by a bird or a bacterium; instead, it is the product of the random mutation of a gene, which is then passed on to later generations in greater quantities than are other genes. Imagine, for example, a species of antelope that is the frequent prey of leopards or lions. The predators chase the antelope, bringing down the slower and more unwary animals. Now, suppose that purely as a chance result of a random mutation, one antelope is able to run slightly faster than the others. Its extra speed gives this antelope an advantage over the other members of the herd. It is less likely to fall prey to the big cats, and therefore more likely to live long enough to reproduce, perhaps many times. The offspring of this lucky animal are likely to inherit the gene for running faster, and so they too will have an advantage over their slower fellows. Gradually, we can expect those animals that lack the gene for extra speed to die out, to be replaced by those who possess copies of it. Through an entirely mechanical process, a process no one intended or controlled, a survival strategy has been adopted and has flourished.

Evolutionary ethicists hope to explain the rise of ethical behaviour in a closely analogous fashion. They accept that birds cannot have sufficient foresight consciously to adopt a strategy of mutual grooming. Indeed, such abilities, intelligence itself, would themselves stand in need of an evolutionary explanation. We are intelligent animals, evolutionary theorists hold, because being able to make calculated decisions has survival value for us. We need to be able to give a purely mechanical explanation of the manner in which intelligence arose, structurally similar to the one we just told concerning how the ability to run fast arose among members of the antelope species. Similarly, we need to be able to give a purely mechanical explanation of the manner in which ethics arose among us. In short, we need to show how ethical behaviour might have a survival value that would lead to those animals who possess the genes for it out-reproducing those who do not possess these genes.

Now that we know what kind of explanation we are looking for, let us return to our birds. What will happen to this population if, as a result of a random genetic mutation, some birds begin to groom others? Remember, when the antelope developed the ability to run faster, it benefited. But when a bird begins to groom other birds, those *other birds* benefit. In fact, the grooming bird suffers in two ways. First, it suffers because the energy it puts into grooming is wasted. This is energy it might have used in foraging for food, or some other activity. Second, it suffers because it is at a comparative disadvantage. The birds it grooms are relieved of their parasites, but do not relieve it of its own.

Dawkins labels birds that groom other birds indiscriminately 'suckers', and those that do not groom anyone he calls 'cheats'. In a population of birds in which these two strategies are both employed, he points out, the cheats will always do better than the suckers. Cheats get all the benefits of being groomed and pay none of the costs. They will therefore be fitter, in evolutionary terms, which is to say that they will tend to have more offspring than suckers. As a result, the genes for cheating will come to dominate the population. Eventually, there will be no more suckers left.[42]

This may seem to be a bad result for the evolutionary ethicist. Remember, her aim was to demonstrate that morality could arise through the processes of evolution as a survival strategy. But, as we have seen, the simulacrum of morality in which suckers engage is not a good survival strategy. Suckers are less fit, from the standpoint of evolution, than are the 'selfish' cheats. Thus far, the evolutionary ethicist seems to have done nothing more than confirm the frequently voiced suspicion that morality is a mug's game.

However, there are other strategies that might arise spontaneously among the bird population, apart from 'sucker' and 'cheat'. One promising strategy is that adopted by the 'grudger'. The grudger will groom any bird once. However, if the groomed bird fails to reciprocate, the grudger will recall this fact and will refuse to groom it again. It will, as it were, bear a grudge against it. How well will grudgers perform in the bird population?

The answer to this question depends upon the proportion of grudgers in the population. In a population that consists very largely of cheats, the grudger will not do well. It will expend a great deal of energy in grooming birds – since it will try every bird that has not previously cheated it – and will get little grooming in return (since there are few grudgers to return the favour). Under the right conditions, however, the grudger will flourish. Once they are numerous enough to be able to meet each other fairly frequently, their grooming will be reciprocated often enough for them to begin to outperform the cheats. Eventually, cheats will die out altogether, and the population will consist only of grudgers.

The grudger strategy has an important advantage over the sucker strategy. A cheat can take advantage of a grudger only once, whereas suckers can always be exploited. The random appearance of genes for cheating among a population of suckers quickly leads to the demise of the suckers altogether. But though a few cheats could survive in a population of grudgers – since they will meet the same birds only infrequently – the population as a whole is not vulnerable to what Dawkins calls 'subversion from within'. It is, in fact, an evolutionary stable strategy, one that is likely to persist no matter what random mutations occur within the population.

When we are concerned with explaining the evolution of behaviour, there is very little evidence to which we can point to confirm or falsify our hypotheses. There are no fossil traces left by strategies such as those employed by suckers and cheats, for instance. Thus the evolutionary ethicist cannot hope to prove that the story she tells is a faithful representation of what actually occurred. All she has done is put forward a plausible account of how morality *might* have developed. In the right circumstances, the disposition to help others could arise and become dominant in a population purely because such behaviour might be in the interests of the helper as much as the helped. If this account, or one like it, is correct, morality is given a scientific foundation of sorts. It is shown to be in the interests of the organism (or, perhaps more correctly, of the organism's genes).

Now, what role might this explanation of the origins of ethics play in defeating relativism? We suggested earlier that it might serve to show that descriptive relativism is false, thereby preventing the relativist argument from clearing even the first hurdle. Descriptive relativism, of course, is the thesis that different cultures accept different fundamental moral principles. But if the evolutionary ethicist's account is right, we have good reason to think the descriptive relativist thesis is false. If it is true that 'grudger' genes – that is, genes for mutual aid – could be expected to replace 'cheat' and 'sucker' genes, then it will be likely that most human beings possess copies of these genes. As a result, each of us would have the disposition to engage in the appropriate form of behaviour. Thus, human beings everywhere would tend to engage in mutual aid, and, to that extent at least, the thesis of descriptive relativism would be false.

Intuitively, this is a plausible idea. The disposition to engage in mutual aid is one of several that we would expect to find in any society that is capable of reproducing itself over many generations. In the absence of this disposition, the society could be expected to be unstable, and out-competed and overcome by other, more harmonious, groups. Similarly, the disposition to keep promises might well be necessary to group survival, as well as the disposition to refrain from violence towards group members. In the absence of these, life would resemble that in Hobbes's state of nature: it would be 'nasty, brutish and short'. Groups that are characterized by relations of mutual distrust and antipathy would, in fact, probably not survive long.

Do these considerations serve to defeat descriptive relativism, and therefore any interesting meta-ethical relativism? I suggest that they do not. I think we ought to accept that the evolutionary-ethical account of the origin of morality, and the role it plays in human life, do constrain morality. They set limits on the possible contents of human morality. It seems very plausible to maintain that any and all moral systems must contain prohibitions against killing members of one's own group, for precisely the reasons mentioned. A group that did not have such a rule could not be expected to survive long. It is equally plausible to think that all human beings everywhere will share dispositions to mutual aid. Both of these facts constrain descriptive relativism: they set limits on the degree to which different moral systems can diverge from one another. Because they are true, there will be some systems of 'morality', some rules for governing the interaction of members of a social group, that will be ruled out straight away. Not every society imaginable is in fact possible, given these facts about human beings. But these constraints are very broad. Within the boundaries they set, there remains a great deal of room for an interesting descriptive relativism, for an endless variety of human moral systems, each of which fulfils the evolutionary function of morality well enough. Thus descriptive relativism might be true, in spite of the evolutionary ethicist's account of the origin of morality.

Let me illustrate this contention by examining some of the cases we have already used to explore descriptive relativism. Is *tsujigiri*, for example, or Aztec human sacrifice, compatible with the evolutionary ethicist's account? Do not these practices weaken the group as a whole, thereby reducing its chances of long-term survival? After all, doesn't each rob the group of some of its fit members? There may be something to this accusation. But the practices will have many effects besides this one. If they reduce the average fitness of members of the group in one way, they might increase it in another, perhaps by promoting group cohesion. Indeed, each of these practices might be seen as an effective survival strategy, justifiable in evolutionary terms. Perhaps the number of Aztecs killed in the 'flowery wars' was so low that the benefits of Aztec domination over surrounding peoples more than offset them. After all, these wars were one of the mechanisms whereby the flow of tribute to Mexica was maintained. Similarly, *tsujigiri* might have helped maintain the power of the Samurai class, at little cost to them, and thereby offered the peasantry a degree of political stability and security.

But what of the dispositions that, the evolutionary ethicist claims, are likely to be inculcated in all human beings? We saw that it was likely that the disposition to mutual aid – to adopt the grudger strategy – was likely eventually to spread throughout the human population. Now, surely the acts performed by the Samurai warrior or the Aztec priest on the killing stone are contrary to the dictates of this disposition? Doesn't this show that these acts ought to be condemned? Doesn't it offer us a non-question-begging standard to which we can appeal – indeed, a standard in some sense accepted by the perpetrators of these actions, as much as their victims – to demonstrate they are contrary to the standards of universal morality?

We need to be careful here. To say that the disposition to mutual aid will be universal is not to say that everyone will have a disposition universally to offer aid. In fact, according to the evolutionary story as it is usually understood, the disposition is likely to be far more restricted: we would each have a disposition to aid only members of our group, especially close kin (who carry copies of our own genes). The evolutionary account does not, it seems, provide a foundation for what most of us regard as morality, merely for a circumscribed version of it. For this reason, there may be no evolved disposition to refrain from the kind of killing with which we are here concerned. The Aztec priest kills someone from outside his group, and the Samurai someone who does not belong to his social class. Moreover, even if there is a disposition to refrain from this killing, it is only one disposition among others. It might well be true to say that human beings have such a disposition, a natural tendency to sympathy, but we also have competing dispositions – a disposition to violence, for instance. What makes it more rational, or natural, to follow the first, and not the second, disposition? We differ from the birds in Dawkins's imagined scenario in one crucial respect. Whereas they simply follow the dictates of instinct, we assess our actions in the light of our goals and aims. Thus, if the evolutionary story is true, and the birds possess an innate disposition to mutual aid, we can expect them always to engage in it on every occasion that the opportunity to do so presents itself. But human beings have the ability and the motivation to reflect each time such an opportunity comes up, to ask themselves whether, on a given occasion, it really is in their best interests to help. Though it may often be in their interest, sometimes it will not. Given our competing dispositions, and our ability to reflect upon what we do, we have the ability to discover when it is in our interests to engage in helping behaviour and when not, and to refrain from obeying our helping urge when we so desire. Indeed, we may be able to choose to suppress this urge altogether if we so wish: history affords many examples of people who seem to have done so.

The fact that we have these conflicting dispositions is one important obstacle to attempting to base morality on the scientific foundation offered by evolutionary ethics. Why ought we to obey one set of dispositions and not another? The answer to this question simply seems beyond the competence of science. Indeed, the claim that evolutionary ethics can provide foundations for morality seems a paradigm of an error known in philosophy as *the naturalistic fallacy*. An argument is guilty of this fallacy when the attempt is made to define moral value in terms of some natural property. The gap between empirical facts and moral values remains unbridgeable, just as Hume claimed.

The prestige of evolutionary ethics, and of other approaches that claim to found morality on nature, human or otherwise, is a result, I suggest, of our tendency to forget the fact-value gap. We are especially prone to so doing in the case of arguments that invoke nature, because we all feel, obscurely, that nature is as much a normative category as a descriptive one. We cannot help but think that if something is natural, it is, *ipso facto*, good, and if it is unnatural, it is necessarily bad. This is exactly how the appeal to human nature functions in political discourse. Consider, for example, the manner in which it is appealed to by George Will, a conservative American political commentator. Feminism, according to Will, asserts not merely the equality of women with men, but their sameness, and, as a consequence, degrades traditionally female activities, such as child-rearing and maintaining a household. Yet these are not merely *traditional* activities for women, they are *natural*. And ignoring our nature has consequences: it causes unhappiness. If women are to be happy, they must obey the dictates of their nature. Follow Danielle Crittenden's advice, Will counsels: marry early and have children young. Only by so doing will you live the life that nature intended for you, and reap the rewards that natural behaviour inevitably carries with it.[43]

Thus, Will implies, what is natural is good for us – will make us happy, or at least happier than we would otherwise be. Sometimes, those who would invoke nature for political purposes make a stronger claim, that what is natural *cannot* be changed. This version sometimes makes an appearance in arguments against socialism. In this form, the speaker concedes that doing what is supposedly unnatural – living in a socialist society, in this case – might make us happier, but laments that it is simply impossible.

The facts of human nature prevent us from realizing this dream. 'Human beings are simply too selfish', such a critic might argue. 'It's in our nature to be greedy.'

The problem with both these lines of argument is that, even if it could be established that the recommended behaviours were indeed natural, this fact would not have the political implications its proponents claim for it. Unfortunately for those people who invoke this argument, there is a whole range of cases in which doing what is unnatural is neither impossible nor likely to make us unhappy. For instance, I am naturally short-sighted. That is to say, unless we 'interfere' with my physiological processes, I will not see clearly. Yet it neither follows that it is impossible so to interfere, nor that it is inadvisable so to interfere. Indeed, it is very plausible to believe that I am much better off for having interfered with this natural characteristic: for having had a pair of glasses made for me. Thus the mere fact that something is natural does not suffice to show that it is normative for us, in any sense. It does not set standards by which we ought to live.[44]

There is such a thing as human nature. There really are biological constraints on what we can do and on what we can hope for. However, they do not seem to play any role beyond that of *constraining* our moral systems. They cannot dictate its *content*. It is a mistake to think we can read what we ought to do from what we are; indeed, even to think we can get a very determinate picture of what we are. Moreover, the constraints placed upon morality by our nature are few and broad. Within these bounds, there is room for a very large number of moral systems. Those we actually see around us, and the examples of exotic practices brought to our attention by anthropologists and historians, are just a few of the vast range entirely compatible with human nature.

6

THE PROBLEM OF FALSE CONSCIOUSNESS

If the moral theory which I have been sketching, in the course of my examination of arguments against relativism, is correct, then morality is very different from science. Scientific facts are facts about the world, independent of us, whereas moral facts are in some way importantly dependent upon us, upon our beliefs and our interests. I have been arguing that critics of relativism ought to take this very plausible view of morality seriously, and that doing so will force all of us to recognize that the differences between ethics and science are greater than most of us want to admit. It might, in fact, force us all the way to some version of relativism.

However, some critics of relativism accept the value theory I have sketched, or something like it. They argue that despite the fact that values are importantly dependent upon us, our beliefs, practices, and so on, relativism is false. Moreover, the critics I have in mind do not engage in the (now, I hope, discredited) project of attempting to found morality upon our shared human nature. They accept, as they should, that our values are largely the product of processes of enculturation. The fact that our values are a product of our enculturation does not, they argue, prevent us from being able to assess the relative superiority of competing moral views. There are independent and non-question-begging criteria to which we can appeal in order to break deadlocks and demonstrate that some moralities are better than others.

Such criteria, if there are any, could be either *substantive* or *procedural*. Substantive criteria will refer to the *content* of the beliefs in question, whereas procedural criteria will be concerned only with the *processes* that lead to their formation. Thus any approach that criticizes moral views on the basis of their content – that they do not recognize the value of autonomy, for instance – is substantive, whereas approaches that criticize moral views on more formal grounds – that they are not consistent, for instance – are procedural. Obviously many substantive criticisms of rival moral views would be question-begging. Take the example I just used to illustrate a substantive approach. If we were to criticize a certain rival moral system on the grounds that it does not recognize, or give sufficient weight to, the value of autonomy, the question would immediately arise: why think autonomy is an important value at all? A substantive answer to this question, that is one that mentions a further supposed good, merely provokes the same question with regard to the new good. A non-question-begging vindication of the superiority of one value or moral system over another must find a way to stop this regress. Some of the objections we examined in the previous chapter were, broadly speaking, substantive; the approaches to which we shall now turn are largely procedural.

Adaptive preference formation

Those critics of relativism who concede, rightly in my view, that our values are a product of socialization, continue to maintain that we need some means of distinguishing better and worse values from each other. These critics point to the problem of what is sometimes called *false consciousness*: the failure of people to perceive the realities of their own situation. This is especially pressing with regard to what I shall call, following Jon Elster, *adaptive preference formation*. Elster points out that very frequently the preferences that people have are a result of their adaptation to their circumstances. Elster's book on the topic is called *Sour Grapes*, and the 'sour grapes' phenomenon well illustrates the notion of adaptive preference formation.[45] In Aesop's fable, the fox initially desires the grapes, but when he is convinced that he will be unable to reach them, his desire vanishes as he concludes that they are probably sour anyway. In general, our desires are adaptive when they come about as a reaction to the limitations of our situations. Because it would be painful, psychologically, to yearn after things we know we cannot have, we trim our desires to our circumstances. We desire only what we might achieve, and learn to be contented with what we have.

Why should this phenomenon represent a difficulty for moral theory? The problem is this: if adaptive preference formation is widespread, and people can be counted on to trim their desires to their circumstances, then it looks as though a large range of unjust actions and situations cannot be condemned on the grounds that they frustrate people's desires. We might have thought, for instance, that one of the main reasons why slavery is wrong is that it frustrates the desire of slaves to be free and that therefore they will be unhappy. But if, as is likely, the slaves adapt their preferences to their circumstances – especially those born to slavery – they will not in fact desire freedom.

Empirical studies of people's actual desires seem to confirm the hypothesis that adaptive preference formation is a pervasive phenomenon. Martha Nussbaum provides one example; a study of the health of Indians and their attitudes to their health. Widows included in the study rarely rated their health as bad, whereas widowers frequently did. In actual fact, the health of the widows tended to be much poorer than that of the widowers.[46] It is plausible to maintain that the widows had adjusted their expectations, and with them their preferences, to what they believed they could realistically hope for. They had, as it were, got used to their ill-health, to the extent that not only did they no longer complain about it, they did not even think they had anything to complain about. The widows had internalized the norms of a deeply sexist society to such an extent that they regarded women's health – their own included – as unimportant.

This is a problem for any moral theory that gives some weight to preferences. But it is particularly troubling for any theory that holds that values are importantly constituted by our desires and preferences. Since these desires and preferences are themselves susceptible to formation by the mechanisms to which Elster points, such a theory seems to commit us to identifying the deformed preferences with moral values. If the kind of theory I have been defending is correct, then, it looks as though moral values can be the product of what, on the face of it, seems a history of oppression and injustice. But if this is the case, then the slave might well value her slavery! Surely any ethical theory that reaches that conclusion must be false. It is not so much an ethics as merely a psychology, and an apology for the status quo. It tells us that people will value whatever their circumstances force upon them, and insists that we have no way of criticizing these values.

We therefore urgently need some way of distinguishing among people's preferences, between those that are mere reactions to injustice, and so ought to be ignored or overriden, and those that ought to be taken seriously and given full weight in our deliberations. The need to make this distinction seems as pressing in our own case as in that of others. Marxists and feminists have long argued that we are all victims of false consciousness. We are all manipulated by advertising, brought to think we need things that are in fact completely superfluous; we have systematically distorted perceptions of our social world, brought about by our class-position and its illusions, or by gender-stereotyping. If we could discover some way of making the necessary distinctions, some method we could employ to sort our desires into the ideological and the authentic, then we would have made a contribution to political and moral thought of the highest importance. We might also, *inter alia*, have defeated relativism. We would be able to show that some preferences are just better than others, and therefore that there is some, non-question-begging, way of choosing between different values and competing ethical systems. I will therefore devote this chapter to examining ways in which we might hope to make this distinction.

Eliminating false consciousness?

Anti-relativists have employed a variety of strategies to make the distinction between those preferences that ought to be ignored and those that we ought to take seriously. Many of the arguments they employ are fascinating in their own right. Some of them might even have some success in making the required distinction. As we shall see, however, we would do well not to place too much faith in them in this regard. There seems to be no general way of making the distinction. In order to establish this, I will set out and explore the arguments for each of the major strategies employed by anti-relativists.

Human nature

In the course of this book, we have examined anti-relativist appeals to human nature in several different contexts. It is very tempting to think that we could simply read an adequate and universal moral system off from our biology. As we have seen, however, these attempts fail. Since I have already examined these appeals from several angles, I will make my consideration of human nature in the context of adaptive preference formation brief.

Some political philosophers base their theories of justice upon some kind of theory of human nature. Aristotelians – followers of the great ancient Greek philosopher Aristotle – for instance appeal to the idea of what is characteristic of human beings and what would contribute to their 'flourishing'. But flourishing, in this context, is a highly *normative* notion, which is to say that it has built into it a morally loaded conception of what counts as a good human life. To say that someone is flourishing is not simply to say that they are happy. We can, in fact, imagine a variety of situations in which someone was happy but in which they were very far from flourishing, in the Aristotelian sense. A happy drug addict, who is perpetually high, would be one example; so would be the inhabitants of Aldous Huxley's *Brave New World*, who are fed a constant diet of drugs and entertainment designed to numb their minds and keep them content with a merely animal existence. In any case, any theory that identified flourishing with happiness would be vulnerable to the problem of adaptive preference formation. Take the example of an unhappy slave. There are two ways in which we might make her happier. The first is by freeing her, and the second is by making her embrace her fate. In order to distinguish these two responses, which are *subjectively* on a par, we need a normatively-loaded notion of flourishing, not one that simply refers to the satisfactions of the individual.

If this is the case, however, then we are unable simply to read off the normative notion of human nature the Aristotelian requires from the facts about human biology, or even human psychology. We cannot, for instance, identify flourishing with the exercise of a full range of normal human capacities. No merely descriptive account of human nature will give us the means of distinguishing between those things that human beings do and want that are morally considerable, and those things that human beings do and want that are of no moral weight at all. A conception of human nature must be *normatively constrained* before it can play the role it is here called upon to perform, which is to say that we must *already* have a way of making the required distinction. As one prominent contemporary Aristotelian, Martha Nussbaum, points out:

> any concept of the human being (or person) that is useful for settling ethical questions must be evaluative and, in the broad sense, ethical: for among the many things we do and are, it will have to single out some as particularly central, as so important that without those we don't think that a human life exists any longer.[47]

Why can't we appeal directly to a mere description of human beings in order to discover a basis for our values? We cannot do so because human nature contains many different kinds of elements. Some of those elements are the kinds of capacities that Aristotelians (and many other people) value: the capacity to form intimate relationships with one another, to choose a conception of the good life and shape one's life with reference to it, and so on. But other elements of ourselves, equally part of our nature, are objectionable. Nussbaum herself gives the example of aggression. In order to select which elements of our nature ought to be cultivated and which suppressed, we must appeal to normative considerations. We cannot, therefore, appeal to our nature in order to derive those same normative considerations. It would be circular to reject elements of human nature in the name of norms and values that we then justify by saying that they are based on our human nature. Hence the appeal to human nature cannot help us distinguish merely ideological preferences from those that ought to be identified with our authentic values.

Pure proceduralism

Is there some purely procedural approach we can use to winnow our desire and preferences in order to make the required distinction among them? A purely procedural approach might, for instance, examine our preferences for consistency, or examine the manner in which we acquired them. If such approaches could succeed, then we would have the non-question-begging, non-circular method we need to solve the problem of adaptive preference formation.

Pure proceduralism must surely be a part of the story we require here. It will allow us to make some *necessary* distinctions between preferences and desires, even if it turns out not to be *sufficient* by itself. We certainly have good reason to discount preferences that do not meet some minimum procedural standards. Preferences ought to be consistent, for instance, or they will not serve as a guide to values and actions at all. We might also justifiably insist that preferences be suitably informed. Consider the person who prefers to live on a diet of crisps and soda, in the mistaken belief that these are nutritious foods that fully meet all the needs of their body. We might discount this preference very heavily on the grounds that it rests upon false beliefs and that therefore allowing it to be satisfied would frustrate other preferences of the agent.

These apparently unobjectionable procedural constraints will allow us to begin making necessary distinctions between our preferences. But it is very far from clear that this will be sufficient to solve the problem of adaptive preference formation. There is no reason to believe that people's adaptive preferences must be inconsistent. Nor is there any reason to think that these preferences must be misinformed. The preferences of the happy slave we have been considering are not misinformed. By hypothesis, her preferences are an adaptation to her real circumstances; to the fact that she is a slave and has little chance of ceasing to be one. If a purely procedural account of preference formation is to play the role envisaged, it will be by some other means than merely examining our preference structure for consistency or ensuring that our desires are suitably informed.

In *Sour Grapes* Jon Elster proposes one such procedural account. For Elster, a preference is to be discounted or ignored if it has the sour-grapes structure – if we have come to possess it only as the result of adaptation to the limitations of our circumstances. The fact that it comes about as a result of such adaptation is, for him, enough to disqualify it from being taken seriously. It is not an authentic expression of our wants but a preference imposed on us from outside. As Martha Nussbaum points out, however, some of the preferences that count as adaptive on this view are in no way objectionable. It is a normal part of growing up and becoming more mature that we adjust our aspirations to what we can realistically hope to achieve:

> We get used to having the bodies we do have, and even if, as children, we wanted to fly like birds, we simply drop that after a while and are probably the better for it.[48]

It is, Nussbaum argues, often a good thing that we trim our expectations to our circumstances. Short people are better off for giving up the desire to be basketball players. Yet this change in their preference is clearly adaptive, and therefore counts as objectionable on Elster's view. Since this is implausible, Elster's procedural account fails to provide us with what we sought: it does not distinguish objectionable preferences from those that we ought to take seriously in our moral deliberations.

The resources of pure proceduralism are not yet exhausted, however. Some philosophers have suggested that only those preferences are to be taken seriously that pass some kind of test, in which we reflect critically upon them. Several have suggested a winnowing strategy in which we reflect upon the *processes* that brought us to embrace the preferences we now possess. If we can endorse the process of preference-acquisition, then the preference counts as authentically ours. If, however, we cannot endorse the process by which we came to embrace that preference, then we have good reason to reject the preference itself:

> If I look back on my past and see that much of my character
> was formed by educational and parental practices that I would
> not want to have been molded by, or if my conditioning has
> been so manipulative that I cannot even reflect clearly on these
> events and processes at all, then I am not autonomous relative
> to those aspects of my character.[49]

Thus, for example, if I were to discover that my preference for expen-
sive cars is the result of subliminal advertising, or of brainwashing
drugs placed in my breakfast cereal, then I would have good reason
to reject the preference as inauthentic. Proponents of this approach
to the testing of our preferences believe this will give us a means of
making the distinction we need, between our autonomous preferences and those we ought to reject. It will allow us to distinguish
between preferences brought about by processes of indoctrination,
such as the preference of fundamentalist Muslims that women be
housebound, and the authentic, morally considerable, preferences
with which we ought to identify ourselves.

   Will this test succeed in making the required distinction? I have
serious doubts that it will. If the enculturation theory is correct, then
we all typically come to embrace our values in the same way: as a
result of our socialization. That is to say, we all have our most fundamental values as the result of a process over which we had no
control. We can confidently say that there is no clear difference
between socialization, the indispensable process by which all human
beings come to hold values (indeed, come to be fully human beings
at all) and the kind of manipulation that Christman and other
proponents of pure proceduralism reject. Perhaps an example will
make this clearer.

> Imagine the education of any person brought up in a religious
> community. As a child, this person was made to engage in regular
> prayer, in attendance at a place of worship, in rituals that mark the
> fact of that child's belonging to the community. She is taught that
> her religion expresses a timeless truth, the most fundamental truth
> there is, that the salvation of her immortal soul is bound up with her
> recognizing this truth. Has she been manipulated into her belief?
> Ought she to reject it on the basis that it is not autonomous?

Christman requires us to examine the process of our value formation and ask ourselves whether we would want to be formed by this
process. Very well, let us conduct the experiment for this person. She
reflects on her education and sees that she was brought up as a
believer. She was not asked to reflect upon theological questions and
make up her own mind. Nevertheless, she neither rejects her faith
nor believes that she ought to reject her faith. Why should she? She
believes that the tenets of her faith are *true*, and we do not object to
being taught the truth. You, presumably, do not object to having
been taught that the world is round, nor do you believe that you
ought to object on the basis that you were simply taught that the
world is round (rather than being asked to reflect on the evidence
and come to a considered judgement yourself). In fact, we object to
the conditioning of beliefs only when it is used to bring about beliefs
that are false, or very unusual, not when the beliefs in question are
true, or at least widely held. Thus we frequently talk about the way in
which people who join minority sects such as the Moonies are the
victims of 'brainwashing' or 'mind-control' whereas people who are
born into a mainstream religion are respected for their beliefs. There
may in fact be no difference in the processes that in each case
brought them to embrace their views. Both are equally the product
of conditioning. In neither are the adherents in a position independently to verify the content of the teaching, but nor are you in a position to verify your belief that the world is round. If we are to have less
confidence in beliefs or desires when we are brought to possess them
as a result of processes over which we had no control, and in which
we had no independent access to the objects of the beliefs, then few
beliefs will survive unscathed.

We need to ask ourselves whether the kind of ideal that
Christman and the other friends of proceduralism implicitly suggest
we ought to aim for is even possible. If it is true that beliefs we are
brought to embrace as a result of processes that deny us the opportunity independently to verify their truth are objectionable, then it
must be the case that belief can be brought about in some other
manner. Is there some autonomy-enhancing education, which gives
its subjects greater control over what they believe so as to ensure that
they will only believe things that they have good independent

grounds for holding to be true? In other words, can we educate people in such a manner as to allow them to make up their own minds about what they believe, and if this can be done, will the beliefs that they come to possess be better justified than otherwise? To some extent, it seems that this might be the case. Consider the Amish, a religious community who live mainly in Pennsylvania in the United States. Old Order Amish are distinguished by their dress and their rejection of modern technology, from cars to electricity. More controversially, the Amish have been granted a special exemption from American laws requiring attendance at schools. In a 1972 decision, the Supreme Court of the United States ruled that Amish children could leave the school system two years earlier than other children. The express purpose of the decision was to allow Amish children to be brought up in a manner that would ensure that they would embrace the beliefs and lifestyle of their parents, and thus to ensure the survival of the community:

> Formal high school education beyond the eighth grade is contrary to Amish beliefs, not only because it places Amish children in an environment hostile to Amish beliefs with increasing emphasis on competition in class work and sports and with pressure to conform to the styles, manners, and ways of the peer group, but also because it takes them away from their community, physically and emotionally, during the crucial and formative adolescent period of life. During this period, the children must acquire Amish attitudes favoring manual work and self-reliance and the specific skills needed to perform the adult role of an Amish farmer or housewife.[50]

If the Amish were to continue to survive and resist the pressures of an increasingly secularized society, they had to be able to limit their children's exposure to that society. By exposing them only to Amish beliefs and the Amish way of life, they could virtually ensure that their children would embrace the faith and remain in the community.

Now, it seems hard to avoid thinking that this kind of education is more manipulative than that given to other children. It aims to limit the range of options open to its subjects and therefore to bring about a certain result. It thus seems to limit the autonomy of Amish children. If this is correct, then the kind of contrast for which we were seeking, between autonomy-enhancing and autonomy-limiting education, would be vindicated.

However, I'm not convinced that this is the correct view. Rather than thinking that expanding the range of influences upon the child expands its options, and therefore gives it a greater role in deciding what beliefs it will adopt, we might instead think that beliefs are always caused by social pressures. Thus, when we act so as to ensure that the social pressures are always of a particular sort, we can ensure that the outcome is the one sought. This is what the Amish demanded and got from the Supreme Court. But when the range of social pressures is much greater, the outcome is much more unpredictable. This is not because the decision to adopt a belief is more autonomous, but simply because there are so many conflicting forces acting on the child. Given that the forces are so many, the results of their interaction will be unpredictable; as some conflict while others reinforce each other, in ways we do not fully understand, we cannot know in advance what beliefs the child will finish up with. But she is no freer or more autonomous for that.

To drive home the point, let us try to construct a contrast case. If we think that Amish education undermines the autonomy of Amish children, then what kind of education might enhance it? Let us try the experiment:

> Imagine a child very similar to the one we considered before. She, too, is born to religious parents. But this time her parents wish to bring her up in a way that enhances her autonomy. They want her to decide for herself whether or not she embraces their faith. How should they act so as to maximize her freedom?

Parents who face this dilemma might act in one of several different ways. The first and major decision confronting them is whether they will give the child a religious education. Do they, on the one hand, bring the child up as Catholic (Jewish, Amish...), giving her a Catholic education, having her baptized and confirmed, and so on, until such time as she is mature enough to make her own decision, fully comprehending its implications and the alternatives open to her? If they decide to act in this manner, however, there is every likelihood that she will simply endorse her parents' decision to raise her in the faith. Like the Amish child, she will have been brought up to grasp what she cannot help but believe is an important truth. The decision will not truly be hers, but will have been made for her, by her parents.

Perhaps, then, her parents ought to act in some other manner. Rather than raise her in the faith, perhaps they ought to raise her with no faith at all, or perhaps by teaching her the doctrines of a multiplicity of faiths, allowing her to choose among them. Will this enhance the autonomy of her decision, ensuring that the beliefs she comes to embrace are more authentically hers? I doubt it. Isn't it more likely that by refraining from bringing her up within a faith, they communicate to her their belief that religion is unimportant or false? Don't they as effectively choose for her a non-religious life, as before they chose a life in the faith?

Perhaps we might think that nevertheless there is some middle way open to them. Perhaps the parents of the baby girl could bring her up belonging to a faith – taking her to services, baptizing her, and so on – but nevertheless teach her the importance of questioning her beliefs, and respecting those of others. What would be the result of such an education? Would it be an adult who holds beliefs that are better justified than those she might otherwise have had? Isn't it more likely that instead her parents will have brought her up as a half-hearted believer, someone who formally subscribes to a faith yet whose life is little shaped by their belief? In all these cases, her parents decide for her, and when they do not, it is because the pressure they exert upon her beliefs is so light as to ensure that some other influence – equally external and therefore heteronomous – is decisive.

Even with regard to empirical, as opposed to religious, beliefs, it is difficult to sustain the distinction between autonomous and heteronomous processes of belief formation. What is the alternative to simply teaching a child that the world is round? Allowing him to make his own mind up? On what evidence? Most of the relevant evidence he simply will not have access to. It might be suggested that rather than *teach* him geography, he should instead be directed to the books that examine the evidence. But which books? Which ones ought to be taken seriously, and which ones ignored? If we direct him to the books by members of the Flat Earth Society, we shall be dictating the outcome of his research. Of course, he might evaluate the evidence for himself. But how is he to acquire the mathematical tools to do so and the physical theories that he will need?

None of this is meant to cast doubt on the belief that the world is round, or to suggest that it is an irrational prejudice. It is, in fact, a well-established truth. Instead, my point is that acquiring the information and tools necessary to be able rationally to evaluate such theories cannot itself be a process open to rational evaluation. We acquire these fundamental beliefs and these tools simply as a result of a process of education. It is only after we have been taught how to apply them that we can undertake rational evaluation at all. This fact does not cast doubt on our physical theories or these tools, because they are so well confirmed in a number of ways – explanatory fertility, predictive success, convergence, and so on. But with regard to theories of morality, in which there is no independent reality against which to test our fundamental beliefs and our basic tools, we do not have and cannot hope for any such means of confirmation. We value what we are socialized into valuing, and pure proceduralism offers us no way of assessing these values or this socialization.

The transition argument

The failures of pure proceduralism that I have outlined so far have not deterred philosophers from seeking some other kind of procedural justification for their views. One potentially promising approach, which has been suggested by several people, I call the *transition argument*. The transition argument aims not at showing that some beliefs or values are the best, or the best justified, but is instead essentially comparative. It aims to show that one belief (value) is better than another, by appeal to the views of people who have held both.

Briefly, the transition argument proposes the following test for measuring the superiority of one belief over another:

> A belief, X, is superior to another, incompatible, belief, Y, if the *transition* from believing Y to believing X is experienced (for whatever reason) as an improvement but a transition in the reverse direction would or could not be experienced in this manner.

Thus, for example, the belief that the world is round is superior to the belief that the world is flat if the transition from the second to the first is experienced as an improvement but a transition from the first to the second is not so experienced.

The transition argument is meant to provide us with an independent criterion for assessing moral beliefs and values, and therefore to circumvent the problems that arise from the fact that we cannot compare these beliefs to something independent of them. We can't compare moral beliefs to moral reality but we can compare one moral belief to another to see if it is (or would be) vindicated by the transition from one to the other. Once again, a concrete example will help bring home the force of this argument.

> Almost all of us, it is plausible to think, believe that we live in a better society today for the fact that slavery is now illegal. The transition from a slave-owning society to one in which slavery is condemned is unequivocally a moral improvement. But, we might think, it just could not happen in reverse. That is, we cannot imagine a society that went from condemning slavery to condoning it *and experienced that transition as a moral improvement*. Because the story can only be plausibly told with the transition occurring in one direction, its content is vindicated. We therefore have a reason, independent of what we happen to value and what our society teaches us, to think that condoning slavery is morally worse than condemning it.

The transition argument has been used by philosophers to vindicate a number of alterations in people's lives. Martha Nussbaum appeals to it to show that literacy is better than illiteracy.[51] Alasdair MacIntyre appeals to it to show that the transition from Aristotelian science to Galilean was objectively an improvement.[52] It has even been called upon to demonstrate that fine Brie is better than processed Cheddar![53] We are here concerned with it only in its application to moral beliefs or systems. Can we appeal to it to show that one such belief or system is superior to another?

Certainly when we look back upon our own history, we cannot help but see it as a story of progress (at least in part). Our past, even our recent past, contains many elements we now repudiate. We used to discriminate against women, against people of different races or religions, we were unconcerned about animal suffering, or with basic human rights. When we read about our own history, we can barely recognize ourselves in it. We are appalled by the unthinking moral blindness of our grandparents, even of our parents. Surely, we think, we have made progress. Surely the moral changes we have experienced since the end of the Second World War represent the kind of transition that must be experienced as improvement, that is unidirectional precisely in the manner required by the transition argument?

However, when we ask ourselves *why* we experience these changes as moral progress, we see that there are good reasons to be sceptical of the transition argument. Why do we identify the alterations in our moral landscape as improvements, and not decline (or even just sheer change)? When we examine these transformations, we are engaged in a comparative exercise. We compare our current values with those that we, or our ancestors, held in the past. Now, as we saw in the preceding chapter, we *identify* with our values. They form the horizon of our moral world; the point of view from which we view ethics. Thus *whatever* values we now have will be the standard of comparison against which others will be measured. If our values have changed, then we will say that we have made moral progress. The alternative is inconceivable and incoherent, as we can see when we try to imagine it. Consider what would have to be the case for someone to look back on the moral changes they had undergone and experience them as decline. This person would have to say something like this:

> I used to value X and now I value Y (where Y is incompatible with X). But X is actually better, more valuable, than Y. So I have declined morally.

This is incoherent. If I believe that X is better than Y, then I do not in fact value Y, I value X. I am deluded in my belief that I value Y (perhaps because I suffer from weakness of will). Or perhaps I really do value Y, in which case I am deluded in thinking that I believe that X is more valuable. Perhaps, most probably and commonly, I have inconsistent values. In that case, I can attempt to order them and make them consistent by testing them, by constructing thought-experiments and counter-examples, until I identify my deepest values. When I do this, I will be led to jettison X or Y, or perhaps to discover that they are not really incompatible after all. Whatever I do, I will not be able, rationally, to conclude that I suffered moral decline. Perhaps I no longer live up to my values as well as I once did, but my values themselves have not, indeed cannot (from my perspective) decline. The idea is just incoherent. I cannot even experience moral change as *merely* change. Given that my current values are constitutive of my moral identity, change is always, necessarily, experienced as change for the better.

Thus whenever I experience an alteration in my values, I experience (what I take to be) moral progress. We have experienced the expansion of our sphere of moral concern over the last fifty years, our greater compassion toward the suffering and our recognition of the rights of all human beings, as great progress. But if moral change had occurred in a different direction, we would have experienced that change, too, as an improvement. Consider, for example, how the triumph of fascism might have been viewed by a Nietzschean culture. For Nietzsche, as we saw in an earlier chapter, compassion for the suffering of others was a symptom of an illness, the sign of a sick people living in a sick culture. Securing the basic human rights of the masses, creating for them a life secure from suffering, is mere pandering to the mob, and ensures the spiritual degeneration of a society. It ensures that the weak survive and enslave the strong, it ensures that the highest values of a culture will not be allowed to flourish, it substitutes mediocrity for greatness. Now, if these sentiments, ugly as they seem to us, were to become widespread, then a whole society could look upon the triumph of fascism as moral improvement. We used to be compassionate, they would say. We opposed slavery and sought to eliminate suffering. Now, however, we see that we were wrong to do so. Now we recognize the true values, of hardness and iron discipline. The philosophers of this culture might write books on the moral improvement their society had undergone. Perhaps they would even seek to utilize the transition argument to prove that it was improvement. Perhaps, seeing things from the perspective of their values, they would not be able to conceive of anyone adopting the now despised values of compassion and experiencing the change as progress. They might, therefore, think that the transition they had undergone was unidirectional. A transition in the opposite direction just could not be experienced as progress, they might argue. But, as we now see, they would be wrong. The transition argument fails for them, just as it does for us.

The pragmatic contradiction argument

If the transition argument fails, perhaps the anti-relativist proceduralist can appeal to the *pragmatic contradiction argument*. What I have in mind here is this. We saw in earlier chapters that in order to identify our values, we had to do some work. We had to test our preferences against each other, to discover which were most authentically ours. Now, what we were doing when we undertook this process was testing *beliefs* and *desires* against each other, in order to identify inconsistencies. The pragmatic contradiction argument asks us to do the same thing, but this time casting the net wider. In addition to the conflicts between our beliefs and our desires, perhaps there are contradictions between our practices, or our beliefs and our practices, or our desires and our practices. If so, then we might be able to interpret these practices and discover the contradiction. So doing will give us reason either to make a change in our practices or, if we find that we cannot do so for whatever reason, alter our values. Thus the interpretation of what we do offers us a potential perspective from which to criticize what we believe.

Now, this will only offer the anti-relativist a valuable aid in his quest for an objective morality on condition that people's actions are more universally similar than their beliefs. Perhaps we can hope that whatever the fundamental moral values of the Aztecs and the Nazis, pro-life and pro-choice advocates, and so on, all behave in a manner that implicitly commits them to moral beliefs. Perhaps, then, the interpretation of practices offers us an Archimedean point from which we will be able to refute entire ethical systems without engaging in question-begging moves.

Why might it be thought that our practices are more universal than our beliefs? Perhaps because, though there is a great deal of diversity in what people believe, there is nevertheless a shared human *condition*. We all need to eat, to find shelter, perhaps we all share psychological needs as well; there may well be certain elements that all societies must possess if they are successfully to reproduce themselves, generation after generation. Given this shared condition, perhaps what we all do is more similar than what we think. Perhaps, then, we can use our shared practices as a weapon of criticism of our divergent beliefs.

Once again, examples will demonstrate the power of the pragmatic contradiction argument much better than could any amount of exposition of it. The following examples come from the work of Martha Nussbaum:

> in certain specific argumentative contexts, we may point out that our interlocutor's very behavior shows that she grants the centrality of the element on whose centrality we are insisting. There would be a pragmatic self-contradiction were she to reply by denying its importance. Thus, it would be self-contradictory to engage in philosophical argument about the ends of human life and then deny that reason and argument have any importance. It would be similarly peculiar to attend the dramatic festival of Athens looking for illumination about matters of human significance and then to deny that community with others has any importance at all.[54]

People contradict themselves when they argue (as some people sometimes do) that rationality is not important. The moment they engage in argument they implicitly acknowledge that it is important (as, indeed, it had to be, given the human condition and the characteristic means whereby humans cope with their environment). Whatever our beliefs might be, no matter how coherent they are, there is a contradiction between what we believe, if we believe that reason is unimportant, and what we do. One or the other must go. Thus the pragmatic contradiction argument might provide us with the means of criticizing people's beliefs, and therefore give us some way of standing outside desires, preferences and so on. We might thereby be provided with a means of criticizing the content of people's preferences that is not question-begging. When we utilize the pragmatic contradiction argument, we do not impose upon our interlocutors views foreign to them. We do not criticize them in the name of views that they do not hold. Instead, we point to values and beliefs to which they themselves are committed, albeit implicitly.

The pragmatic contradiction might be a powerful way of convincing certain people, when, coincidentally as it were, these people explicitly deny something upon which they implicitly rely. If someone claims that the lives and welfare of animals are of no importance but is always careful to avoid stepping on the cat's tail, we might be able to convict him of pragmatic contradiction. His acts belie his beliefs. But do we have any reason to believe that such contradiction is general? In particular, can we hope that whenever people sincerely affirm that certain ways of treating human beings that to us are abhorrent (human sacrifice, *tsujigiri*, and so on) are permissible or even obligatory, aspects of their actual practices will belie these views, thus opening the way for the use of the pragmatic contradiction argument?

For this to be the case, the value that is denied by the people in question would have to be presupposed by central aspects of human life – the human condition – in such a manner that people who denied it were nevertheless always necessarily committed to it. Demonstrating that this is the case will be difficult. Consider what might seem a likely candidate for this role: the denial that it is necessarily wrong to inflict pain on other people. Of course, people who deny that pain is unpleasant are almost certainly involved in a pragmatic contradiction. We will have no difficulty in finding evidence in their behaviour that contradicts their assertion. They will take care that their fingers are not in the way when they close doors, they will be circumspect around sharp knives, and so on. By being so careful to avoid pain, they give a clear sign that they do not really believe what they so confidently assert. However, people who engage in behaviour that inflicts pain on others do not have to believe that pain is not unpleasant. Indeed, as we have seen, cultures may endow pain with all kinds of significance precisely *because* it is so unpleasant. If we are to find behavioural evidence that will the convict the person who believes that human sacrifice is permissible of a pragmatic contradiction, we must look elsewhere.

Perhaps, however, this evidence will not be difficult to find. Surely this person is committed to – that is, in this context, gives behavioural evidence of commitment to – at least one proposition that contradicts his actions? Surely at very least he is committed to the proposition that human life is important? After all, he takes care of his own health; he avoids situations that are life threatening, sleeps and eats when he needs to, and so on. All of this is good evidence that he wants to avoid a premature death. Now, we saw earlier that as a matter of fact the members of all cultures of which we are aware are committed to something like the principle of universalizability, which is to say that they believe that whatever is true of them is also true of other people unless there is some morally relevant difference between them. Thus, it would seem, the person who is committed to the belief that his own life is important ought to be committed to the value of human life more generally. Does this give us grounds for convicting the person who approves of human sacrifice of a pragmatic contradiction?

Unfortunately, standards of what counts as a morally relevant difference between persons themselves differ from culture to culture. Consider Aztec human sacrifice. The most prized sacrifices, especially sought after for the consecration of new temples and for major feast days, were enemy warriors captured in battle. Now these battles, the so-called 'flowery wars', were held for the specific purpose of obtaining captives. Each warrior therefore entered the fray seeking captives, and in order to do so risked capture himself. He knew that if he were taken in battle, he would die on the altar in front of an alien people's temple. When, therefore, he brought a prisoner to the temple, he did not make an exception of him, he did not treat him in a manner different to the way he would be treated if he were captured. For the Aztec and for the prisoner alike, the very fact of having been taken in battle was itself the morally relevant difference that justified the treatment dished out to them. Much the same could be said of some groups of American Indians and the way they slowly killed their prisoners. The prisoner shared the values of his captors, including the values that dictated that he should die. He therefore determined to die a brave death, in accordance with the values he shared with those who killed him.

Thus, though the pragmatic contradiction argument might be effective against some views, there is little reason to hope that it will allow us to criticize the great majority of moral systems that are or have actually been espoused by other cultures. There is no reason to think that these moral systems should not be coherent, nor to believe that there will necessarily be a contradiction between what people who accept them believe, and what they do.

If none of these procedural arguments work, however, if all our attempts to show that rival moral systems *must* be incoherent at some level fail, then it might be that we simply cannot argue that those who hold them have any good reason to give them up; that is, reasons accessible to them, and not imposed upon them from without. If this is the case, however, then it seems as though there are no non-question-begging arguments we can use against them. If their beliefs do not rest upon empirical claims that are false, if they cohere with one another, if they were brought about through socialization processes we cannot fault, and if the behaviour of those who hold them does not belie them, then we have no arguments to use against them that they are bound to accept, on pain of lapsing into irrationality. We are, in fact, no better placed with regard to convincing them of the wrongness of their values than they are with regard to us and ours.

Substantive arguments, however – those that criticize the content of someone's morality on the grounds that it overlooks some element of morality, or includes an element that is itself immoral – seem inevitably to beg the question against the moral views they oppose. Since such criticisms are, by definition, made in the name of some value that the rival view does not accept, the criticism will have no purchase on the person criticized. He will not be irrational if he simply dismisses it. We may wish to continue to insist that he is immoral, but we have no means whereby to show that it is he, and not us, who is wrong. When it comes to the content of our morality, false consciousness, if indeed there is such a thing, seems insurmountable. Indeed, on those occasions when we feel inclined to think that someone suffers from it, that person may well feel equally inclined to believe the same of us.

7

INCOMMENSURABILITY AND THE SHARED CORE OF MORALITY

In the course of this book, we have examined many different arguments against moral relativism, the most powerful, I believe, that the anti-relativist has available to him. None of them has succeeded in convincing us that relativism is not a coherent and plausible position. Does this imply that in ethics anything goes; that any set of beliefs might be adopted as the moral outlook of a culture? Does it leave us unable to criticize those who appeal to moral systems radically different from our own, in justification of what seem (to us) frankly immoral practices? The answer to both these questions is, I believe, no. Nothing in the considerations I have advanced implies that any set of beliefs whatsoever can constitute a moral system. In fact, there are significant constraints upon the contents of any adequate morality. Moreover, we are at least sometimes able to criticize the proponents of moralities at odds with ours, on rational grounds. Sometimes, at least, these people are just plain wrong.

Why moral systems cannot diverge widely from each other

Many of the anti-relativist arguments we have examined purported to identify features of morality that all moral systems had to share. Moral systems have to include as a central feature the requirement of universalizability; they have to play a distinctive role in human life; they have to facilitate the settlement of interpersonal conflicts and allow the reproduction of social groups over time; there are distinctive characteristics of human beings, as evolved rational animals, that constitute the human condition and that set powerful constraints on the contents of moral systems. We have seen that these constraints are not powerful or substantive enough to limit the number of viable and coherent moral systems to just one, and that therefore they do not suffice to show that relativism is not a plausible position. In fact, all, or nearly all, actually or formerly existing moral systems pass these tests, just as we should expect. That said, however, these arguments do establish that not just any set of rules or principles can constitute a moral system. They do succeed in constraining the contents of morality in ways that matter. Thus, for instance, some rules just could not be rules of anything we could call a moral system. For example, any purported morality must include rules against wanton killing or the group that regulates its life by this system will not long survive. Similarly, given the human condition, we should expect moral systems to emphasize those aspects of human life that are essential for survival – to pay special attention to primary goods, such as shelter and nutrition; goods in the absence of which life cannot continue. These goods will always be among those that will count as significant on any plausible moral view. Thus, though the considerations adduced do not defeat relativism, because they allow for a plurality of adequate moral systems, they do set constraints on what the content of such moral systems may be.

Some philosophers have gone further than this and argued that there are a priori reasons to believe that all moral systems must be *very* much like our own. The claims I have in mind here are frequently advanced in an attempt to refute relativism; as considerations that limit the number of viable ethical systems to just one. Once again, we shall see that this claim exaggerates the force of the argument. Nevertheless, it is very powerful, serving to further limit the divergence between our morality and other possible moral systems. All moral systems *must* be much like our own. This set of considerations I shall call the *argument from incommensurability*.

This argument has its provenance in the intellectual ferment that surrounded the publication of Thomas Kuhn's *The Structure of Scientific Revolutions*. Kuhn claimed – or, perhaps more accurately, Kuhn was widely taken to claim – that the transition from pre-scientific to scientific ways of understanding the natural world should not be understood on the model of progress. The idea of progress presupposes a fixed scale against which we can measure the various positions. If we advance further along the scale over time, we can say that we have progressed. But, Kuhn claimed, there was no such scale by reference to which we could compare our science to Aristotle's. So different are the methods used, so different the goals and the approaches, that it is misleading to think that modern scientists are even engaged in the same kind of enterprise as their Aristotelian predecessors. Modern science is not medieval science only better; it is simply a different kind of activity. Far from it being the case that modern scientists now see the same world as did the Aristotelians, only more clearly, the two groups of thinkers engaged in the activity of trying to understand nature inhabit different worlds: 'when [scientific] paradigms change, the world itself changes with them', Kuhn says.[55]

These claims were taken by many people to be evidence for a kind of relativism that we have not explored previously: *conceptual* relativism. Conceptual relativism combines two claims. Its first, descriptive, claim is that different cultures use different systems of concepts to understand the world; its second claim is that there is no (non-question-begging) way of showing which set of concepts is best (true, most accurate, and so on). If the first claim is true, then the second claim seems to be on strong ground since any argument must necessarily utilize some system of concepts. Thus it seems as though a defence of a system of concepts is condemned to be circular. We shall examine the plausibility of this claim later in the chapter but for now let us focus on the first claim. Is it indeed true that different cultures use different systems of concepts?

Evidence that conceptual relativism might be true comes from many sources. Apart from Kuhn's work on the history of science, the most influential such source was probably the so-called Sapir-Whorf hypothesis. Edward Sapir and Benjamin Lee Whorf were American linguists and anthropologists who argued that our conception of reality – our notions of space and time, of causality, and so on – is strongly structured by the language we speak. Their evidence for this was mainly drawn from Whorf's studies conducted upon the Hopi language. Hopi, Whorf claims, has a different tense structure to that with which we are familiar; it does not distinguish as we do between past, present and future. This Whorf took to be evidence that the Hopi had a different sense of time from the sense shared by people who speak a language such as ours. Since we all think (largely) in language, the languages we have available to us will shape the world in which we live. Thus, speakers of English live in a world in which time flows from distant past to far future, in a straight line, whereas the Hopi speaker lives in a world that is timeless, or in which time is circular. The claim that our language determines the concepts available to us, and these determine our world in turn, can be generalized, Whorf claimed:

> We dissect nature along the lines laid down by our native language. The categories and types that we isolate from the world of phenomena we do not find there because they stare every observer in the face; on the contrary, the world is presented in a kaleidoscope flux of impressions which has to be organized by our minds – and this means largely by the linguistic systems in our minds [...]. We are thus introduced to a new principle of relativity, which holds that all observers are not led by the same physical evidence, unless their linguistic backgrounds are similar, or in some way can be calibrated.[56]

We each live in a world that has a structure determined by the language we speak. Thus, speakers of different first languages inhabit different worlds. Moreover, there can be no question which world is the one closest to the truth, for we have no access to the world *except* through our linguistically determined concepts. We cannot step outside our language to compare the world 'as it really is' with the world as it is seen from within this or that language.

We cannot even attempt to discover which system of concepts is best. In fact, supporters of conceptual relativism often argue, the very idea that one could be better than another is incoherent. As we saw, the idea of progress presupposes a common scale against which to measure ourselves. Similarly, the idea that one system of concepts is better than another presupposes a shared standard that each accepts. But the standards that each system of concepts regards as appropriate are themselves determined by that system. If I appeal to my standards in criticizing your system of concepts, I am begging the question against you; unless I can give you some independent reason why you ought to accept my standards, my invoking them is inappropriate. The standards themselves are as much in dispute as is anything else. But I cannot give you independent reasons for, as we saw, there is nothing independent of our system of concepts, no reality as it *really* is to which we can appeal. Strictly speaking, we cannot even compare two systems of concepts. They are not merely different and incompatible; they are *incommensurable*.

To say that two systems (or standards, concepts, and so on) are incommensurable is to claim that they cannot be compared. Two systems of concepts are incommensurable when some or all of the major terms within each cannot even be expressed fully in the language of the other. Each presupposes so much that is alien to the other that they do not exist in the same logical space. Incommensurability is a difficult concept upon which to get a grip in the abstract; perhaps an example will drive home what is meant by it better than any amount of exposition of the concept.

The Azande are an African people who were studied by E.E. Evans-Pritchard, an English anthropologist, in the 1920s and 1930s. Evans-Pritchard's reflections upon Azande culture, and especially upon their beliefs concerning witchcraft, sparked off a debate about 'primitive' rationality. According to Evans-Pritchard, the Azande seem to possess all the common-sense beliefs and the practical rationality they need to explain the world and the events that occur in it, yet they habitually have recourse to supernatural explanations as well. For instance (to use one of Evans-Pritchard's own examples) the Azande know about the existence of termites and their propensity to eat wood. They know that a termite-riddled wooden structure will likely collapse. Yet when a granary supported by wooden legs collapses while people are sheltering from the summer sun beneath it, and they are injured as a consequence, the Azande immediately suspect witchcraft. They simultaneously believe the natural account that fully explains the event and a supernatural account as well. Why postulate the existence of supernatural forces that are unverifiable to explain an event, when everyday forces are all that is needed? For Evans-Pritchard, the belief in witchcraft was fundamentally irrational, albeit a logical consequence of the Azande belief system.

Other thinkers took a different view of Azande beliefs. Peter Winch argues that if we compare Azande beliefs to our scientific beliefs, then they will indeed appear irrational. But this is an artefact of the comparison, not a fact about the belief system. Azande witchcraft is not failed or primitive science; it is a fundamentally different activity, with its own methods and criteria of success. For instance, whereas a Western doctor practises her craft with the intention of curing her patient, the Azande witchdoctor may have no intention of trying to bring about any such result by way of her ceremonies. It is a religious practice, not one designed to reach a goal. Thus Azande thought is more appropriately compared to our religion than to our sciences. When we pray, we express our devotion to God; even if we ask for specific things, we do not judge the value of prayer by its ability to bring about those ends. Prayer is more an expressive activity than an instrumental one; thus we cannot fault it on the grounds that it is not the most effective means of reaching concrete goals. The same goes for the Azande ceremony. It cannot be judged by the criteria of our sciences, since it does not seek the same ends as our sciences. It is, in short, *incommensurable* with science, which is to say that it is so different that it cannot even be compared with science.[57] Evans-Pritchard was wrong to convict the Azande of irrationality because their practices do not achieve the goals of science; they are not *intended* to achieve those goals.

Thus when we say that a practice, a belief or a concept is incommensurable with one of ours, we mean to point to a radical difference. Two incommensurable concepts can be incompatible without either of them being false. Naturally, if incommensurability is real and widespread, its existence would be a powerful support for relativists. Indeed, most friends of incommensurability have utilized it to relativistic ends. They typically aim to show that when two cultures differ, it is at least sometimes the case that questions of relative superiority are inappropriate. If they are incommensurable, it is impossible to judge their relative merit. More to the point, as far as we are concerned, the idea that two systems of concepts might be incommensurable could be and indeed has been transferred to the domain of ethics. Mightn't it be the case that two moral systems are incommensurable? And if it is, then won't we have incontrovertible evidence that moral relativism is true?

We are finally in a position to begin examining the arguments against incommensurability. The best-known such argument is due to Donald Davidson, an important contemporary philosopher. In his article 'On the Very Idea of a Conceptual Scheme', Davidson argues that the idea that there could be two incommensurable languages or conceptual systems is incoherent. Davidson's argument is dense and opaque. It is best understood by considering a thought-experiment developed by Davidson's mentor W.V. Quine:

> Imagine that you are an anthropologist who comes across a group of people who are entirely unknown to you and whose language is utterly foreign. Their speech is as incomprehensible to you as yours is to them. But if you are to make any progress studying them, you need to understand what they are saying. Thus you set about learning the language as quickly as possible. How are you to accomplish this?

Quine suggests, plausibly enough, that we will engage in this task by attempting to correlate what these people say with their actions. Thus, to use his example, if upon seeing a rabbit run past, the natives excitedly exclaim 'gavigai', we will probably conclude that 'gavigai' is their word for 'rabbit'. Of course, this is as yet fairly weak evidence. 'Gavigai' might not mean 'rabbit' at all. Perhaps it means 'small animal', or 'dinner!'. Perhaps the word does not refer to the animal at all, and was only coincidentally uttered at the moment it appeared.

However, these problems are easily solved, at least in principle. We test our hypothesis that 'gavigai' means 'rabbit' by making further observations. Do the natives exclaim 'gavigai' every time a rabbit runs past? Do they exclaim it on other occasions? As our evidence accumulates, our translations get more and more certain. Ideally, if we were able to devote enough time to the task, we could provide an English equivalent for every word in the native language.[58]

All this presupposes that their language is commensurable with ours, however. If it is incommensurable, then we will not be able to provide such translations, for no such translations will be possible. If two languages are incommensurable, in the manner suggested by the Sapir-Whorf hypothesis, then there will be at least some terms in each for which there are no equivalents in the other. Since Hopi is incommensurable with English, it cannot be translated into English. Thus the question of whether or not there are incommensurable conceptual systems is equivalent to the question of whether or not there are untranslatable languages. Davidson hopes that by examining the latter question he can answer the former.

Now, Davidson asks, what exactly do we do when we engage in this process of interpreting a foreign language? More particularly, what do we presuppose when we engage in the enterprise of correlating what the natives say with what they do? We assume, Davidson points out, that what the natives say will be *true*. If it were not – if, for instance, they were fundamentally deluded – then we could not engage in the exercise he calls radical interpretation at all. For instance, if they shout 'gavigai' whenever they see something they take to be a rabbit, but they are confused about what a rabbit is, so sometimes they use the word upon seeing a lion, and sometimes upon seeing a tree, we could never discover that they meant 'rabbit' by the word. Moreover, they must react in ways fundamentally similar to ours. They must cry out when they are in pain, laugh to express humour, and so on. How could we discover the meaning of their word for 'funny' if we did not share their reaction to humour? We just cannot engage in radical interpretation unless people are consistent in the ways they use language, and their language use agrees with ours. Thus radical interpretation presupposes the exercise of the *principle of charity*: the assumption that what the natives say will be very largely true and rational. Moreover, when we assume that what they say will be true and rational, we mean true and rational *by our standards*. They must utilize our notion of causality, have our concepts of space and time, and so on. If they do not, we could not even begin to interpret their speech.

We can now spell out Davidson's first argument against the existence of incommensurable conceptual schemes. Since rival conceptual schemes are embedded in a language, if they exist the languages that contain them ought to be untranslatable into ours. But as a matter of fact we have never encountered an untranslatable language. Whorf tells us that Hopi concepts are unexpressible in English, but he also tells us – in English – what these concepts express. Similarly,

> Kuhn is brilliant at saying what things were like before the revolution using – what else? – our post-revolutionary idiom.[59]

There is, if you like, a pragmatic contradiction between what these philosophers claim and what their own examples show. Their very success at conveying the content of supposedly untranslatable schemes belies their doctrine. We have never encountered an untranslatable language or an alien conceptual scheme; even the best examples the proponents of untranslatability can muster have contents that are expressible in English (or any other natural language).

However, Davidson is not content to stop here. He is after much bigger game. He believes that he can show that not only have we never encountered an untranslatable language, but that the very notion that we *could* encounter one is incoherent. Imagine what it would be like to encounter such a language. We come across a group of people who are emitting sounds as they go about their daily business, but all our attempts to correlate these sounds with their activities, and with the world around them, fail. We cannot detect a consistent pattern in their vocalizations, which we could take as evidence that they are words referring to what we see. Ought we to conclude that we have discovered an untranslatable language? Davidson suggests not. Rather than think that these people have an untranslatable language, we should conclude that they do not have a language *at all*:

If we cannot find a way to interpret the utterances and other behaviour of a creature as revealing a set of beliefs largely consistent and true by our own standards, we have no reason to count that creature as rational, as having beliefs, or as saying anything.[60]

Any time we encounter a group of people who are apparently speaking a language, one of two things must be the case. Either the language they speak can be translated into ours, in which case the people who speak it do not have an alien conceptual scheme, or the language cannot be translated into ours, in which case we have no reason to think that it is a language at all. It is merely a sequence of meaningless sounds. Thus we can rule out the possibility that we might ever encounter a language, or a conceptual scheme, that is incommensurable with ours. Davidson believes that once this is established, we can go further and jettison the idea of a conceptual scheme altogether.

Now, Davidson's argument is relevant to us because it seems as though we can transfer it to the domain of morality. If it is impossible to conceive of, or encounter, a radically different conceptual scheme, then perhaps it is also impossible to conceive of, or encounter, a radically different morality. Place yourself in the position of the anthropologist once more. This time, you are studying the moral practices and judgements of an alien people. You are beginning to suspect that these people have a radically different morality to yours: they think that things you take to be paradigms of moral virtue (sharing your food with a starving person, caring for the helpless) are vices for them, whereas the things they take to be good (kicking children, letting excess food rot rather than share it) you regard as vicious. Ought you to think that they have a radically different moral system? In answering this question, we need to bear in mind the centrality of the principle of charity to the enterprise of radical interpretation. In order to interpret an alien language, we need to assume that its speakers are rational and that their utterances are largely true. Now, it seems to follow that in order to interpret the morality of an alien people, we need to make an analogous assumption: that their moral judgements are, for the most part, correct (that is, the same as ours). We need to share a great deal in the way of moral judgements even to be able to identify their moral beliefs. Thus it simply isn't conceivable that we could identify a system of morality that was *radically* different from our own. As David Cooper puts it, if we were to encounter such a strange tribe:

> we should shortly decide their beliefs are not moral ones at all – or that we had misunderstood what they were moral beliefs about. We can only identify another's beliefs as moral beliefs about X if there is a massive degree of agreement between his and our beliefs. Hence there is no chance of radical moral diversity.[61]

Just as there can be no rival conceptual schemes, so there can be no rival moral systems. Without the need for further investigation moral relativism is defeated. We know, a priori, that it is false.

Assessing Davidson's argument

At least, this is the case if Davidson's argument is correct. However, we have good reason to doubt that it really proves anything like as much as it is commonly taken to prove. Does Davidson's argument achieve his goal, of demonstrating that the very idea of an incommensurable conceptual scheme (indeed, of a conceptual scheme *tout court*) is incoherent? I do not believe it does. Instead, I think it demonstrates only that the idea of an *entirely* incommensurable scheme, an entirely untranslatable language, is incoherent.

Davidson seems to be correct about this much: if our field linguist is ever to be able to begin compiling a translation manual, she needs to be able to assume that her informants share with her a core of true beliefs. That is, she needs to be able to identify a core of sentences asserted by them that express propositions she would assent to. Almost certainly these sentences will refer to the everyday objects of the world that surrounds them: trees and animals, sky and rain, houses and people. If she cannot translate sentences about these everyday objects, it is difficult to imagine how the translation enterprise could ever get off the ground.

But once agreement on these core sentences has been established – once, that is, the linguist and her informants are able to talk to one another, however haltingly – Davidson's argument is no longer effective. The linguist will have established what several philosophers have called a 'bridgehead', an overlap between the languages, which allows the interpreter to begin to enter into the world of the interpreted, and thus to begin to understand their less familiar ideas. The bridgehead once established, failure to translate an utterance of our informant is not evidence for his irrationality, his failing to have beliefs or to speak a language. It is, instead, evidence that we need to deepen our understanding.

Davidson's argument thus refutes only *global* incommensurability. It does not show that difference between conceptual schemes is impossible; it just shows that the differences cannot be radical. Two cultures cannot disagree unless there is a shared subject matter concerning which they differ. We cannot identify the beliefs of an alien culture unless we share a great deal with that culture. We must possess much the same set of concepts concerning middle-sized physical objects, much the same notions of causality, and the same logic. Without these, we could not communicate. However, once the bridgehead is in place, there is plenty of room left for substantive difference.

Thus, while the argument from incommensurability does not, as its supporters sometimes claim, disprove relativism, it does suffice to place significant constraints upon the contents of anything that purports to be a moral system. Unless such a system was very like ours, in a number of important ways, we would have no reason to think it a system of morality at all. It was this kind of consideration to which I appealed when I claimed that any morality must have something like a principle of universalizability, must be committed to treating like cases alike. As I argued then, an alleged morality that lacked this feature is not a morality at all. But, as I also pointed out, this fact leaves plenty of room for disagreement, since nothing prevents different moralities from selecting different features to count as relevant differences between cases. Similarly, any supposed morality had better play a similar role in the lives of the people who espouse it to that played by our own. It had better set limits upon acceptable actions for them, regulate their interpersonal conflicts, and have some significant weight in their deliberations. If it lacks these features, and perhaps many others as well, we shall have no reason to believe that it is a morality at all. In that case, most likely we are making a mistake: we are misidentifying a local set of regulations – the rules of a game, for instance – as a moral system, or we are mistranslating the utterances of our informants.

Are these considerations merely abstract speculations, of interest only to philosophers? Or might they play a concrete role in ethical enquiry? In other words, will the argument from incommensurability ever come into play when we are actually engaged in the process of attempting to understand or translate another culture, when we try to delineate its ethical beliefs and moral concepts? Occasionally, at least, these considerations really will be relevant, I believe. Occasionally, that is, we might be tempted to attribute to the members of another culture moral beliefs that are very strange. When we do so, we would do well to remember the argument from incommensurability.

Consider, for example, this account by Colin Turnbull of the language of the Ik, a notoriously immoral African people:

> [Food] is the one standard by which they measure right and wrong, goodness and badness. The very word for 'good,' *marang*, is defined in terms of 'food,' or, if you press, this will be clarified as 'the possession of food' […] if you try the word as an adjective and attempt to discover what their concept is of a 'good man,' *iakw anamarang* […] you get the truly Icien answer: a good man is one who *has* a full stomach.[62]

At first sight, we may wonder at the strangeness of the Ik concept of goodness. After all, if the Ik are anything like the picture Turnbull paints, they are indeed an alien people. But I suspect we have at least as much reason to wonder at the proffered definition. If the Icien *marang* is really defined solely or primarily in terms of the possession of food, then the word simply does not play the role in their language that 'good' plays in ours. It is, in fact, not the Icien word for good. On the other hand, if it is the Icien word for good, then it is probably not defined primarily in terms of food. More likely, what

Turnbull took to be definitions were intended to be examples. Thus, to say that *marang* is defined for the Ik in terms of food is probably as sensible as saying that for English speakers 'good' is defined in terms of money. I suspect, therefore, that the mistake lies not with the Ik, but with their ethnographer.

Davidson, and those philosophers who have seen in his arguments a way of avoiding confronting the problem of relativism, are right at least to this extent: incommensurability cannot be global. But we can take little comfort from this conclusion. *On the contrary*: the very fact that incommensurability is never global, but always local, is what makes it so disturbing. Very simply, if two conceptual schemes, world-views or ethical systems *were* globally incommensurable, they would never conflict with each other on any issue. Global incommensurability is consistent with compatibility. But local incommensurability requires a shared subject matter, a shared background of agreements against which the disagreement can appear. It is *because* incommensurability is local that it is troubling. Nevertheless, if we can take nothing else from the argument from incommensurability, we can at least take comfort in the knowledge that the differences between moral systems cannot be global or radical.

Can we criticize proponents of actual moral systems without begging the question?

The conclusion to which we have come, at the end of our consideration of the argument from incommensurability, is that though we can rule out the possibility of global incommensurability upon a priori grounds, we have no reason to believe that local differences between ethical systems are not possible, and that these differences might not be troubling and significant. Put another way, the argument from incommensurability does nothing to disprove the possibility of descriptive relativism. It is one thing, however, to say that different and conflicting ethical systems might, indeed do, exist, and quite another thing to say that we have no grounds for asserting that one such system is superior to another. It is to this question that I now turn.

Of course, almost everything that we have examined so far, almost all the conclusions we have reached, is of direct relevance to this question. After all, ever since we established that descriptive relativism is possible, we have been concerned with discovering whether there are non-question-begging arguments available to us that show that one ethical system is superior or inferior to another. As we have seen, there are few such arguments, and none that promises always to resolve the dispute. However, this conclusion does not suffice to settle the question with which we are now concerned. In those earlier chapters, we dealt mainly with the *possibility* of there being ethical systems that conflict with ours, without us being able to prove which is better. The examples we examined, of actual ethical systems past and present, served an illustrative purpose only. We were not much concerned with their details, nor with discovering whether there are in fact any such ethical systems that meet the conditions we laid down. We showed that descriptive relativism is possible and that moral relativism is coherent. We did not show that *in fact* there are ethical systems that conflict with ours, the relative superiority or inferiority of which we are not able to assess. We now turn to the exploration of an actual moral system, whose confrontation with our own is all too practical.

I have neither the space nor the expertise for a really thorough examination of rival ethical systems. For that, we need to turn to the work of anthropologists and historians. Nevertheless, I hope that even a cursory examination of the workings of such a system will give us reason to believe that though a thoroughgoing relativism is *possible*, the conditions in which it will occur are rather uncommon. Very often, I suspect, when two actual moral systems clash, one (and sometimes both) is simply wrong.

For the purposes of this examination, I will return to the example with which we began: the moral system to which the Taliban and their supporters appeal. That this moral system clashes with ours is, I take it, simply obvious. It is this moral system that motivated the actions of the terrorists who destroyed the World Trade Center in New York, at the cost of more than three thousand lives. This same morality has sanctioned the execution of hundreds, perhaps thousands, of members of the minority Hazaras, an ethnic group that espouses a variety of Islam somewhat at variance with that of the Taliban. It mandates the amputation of the right hand of men convicted of theft, as well as the execution of homosexuals. It also places enormous limitations upon the range of options available to women. According to the strict interpretation of Islam upheld by the Taliban, women must be veiled at all times, cannot go out in public unless they are accompanied by a male relative, and are barred from education and paid employment. Women have had their thumbs amputated as punishment for the crime of wearing nail polish, and have been flogged for walking with a man who is not a relative. It is primarily these restrictions upon women that I wish to examine.

I assume that the Taliban's motivation in so restricting women is the same as that behind similar practices in some other Muslim countries. Across the Arab world, the amount of personal liberty allowed to women is severely limited, whether by law or by custom. Proponents of these laws often claim Qur'anic sanction for them, but at least as important as religion seems the role played by notions of shame and honour in these cultures. A great deal of what, to us, seems to be oppression of women in the Arab world and beyond (in non-Arab Iran, Turkey and Afghanistan, for instance) is explicable in terms of the importance of honour in these societies. In examining this characteristic, I will, for the most part, ignore differences between these societies, considerable though they sometimes are, and instead draw a kind of ideal-type picture of the notion of honour as it interacts with Islam in the countries of the Middle East.

Honour is a central concept in the cultures of the Middle East, as indeed it is in many others. The identity of members of these cultures is intrinsically bound up with their sense of honour. Indeed, for these cultures honour is *essentially* a social concept. Someone's honour is inseparable from the way in which they are perceived; it is impossible to be honourable despite the negative opinion everyone has of one. As the renowned French sociologist Pierre Bourdieu says in his study of the Arabs of Algeria:

> The point of honour is the basis of the ethic appropriate to an individual who always sees himself through the eyes of others, who has need of others in order to exist, because his self-image

is inseparable from the image of himself that he receives back from others. [...] Respectability, the obverse of shame, is essentially defined by its social dimension, and so it must be won and defended in the face of everyone.[63]

To be honoured and honourable is to occupy a worthy position in the social world, whereas to be shamed is to suffer what anthropologists call social death, to be banished from the world with which one's sense of self is inextricably bound. 'Honor is what makes life worthwhile: shame is a living death, not to be endured.'[64]

Honour is a social concept; moreover, it is one that is at stake in almost every social exchange. Every act in public space is, at least potentially, an occasion for honour to be challenged and defended. Even the apparently simple and innocent act of giving someone a gift is understood as a challenge, the opening gambit in the game of honour. To give someone a gift is to challenge that person to respond. The gift requires a counter-gift; if the recipient is not able to respond with a suitable offering, he is dishonoured. Bourdieu has analysed the subtleties of the gift-giving game at length, but we need not concern ourselves with them here. What matters, from our perspective, is just the point that honour is central to the social life of these cultures, and that its calculation and the exchanges it requires pervade every aspect of that life.

Importantly, too, honour is never an entirely individual affair. Instead, it always concerns a larger group, especially the family to which the individual belongs. 'Because an Arab represents his kin group, his behaviour must be honourable so that the group are not disgraced.'[65] The social standing of all members of the family are at stake in the actions of each of its members. Thus, every individual's behaviour is the legitimate concern of all his or her relatives. An honour culture is strongly community-oriented, and the needs of the group are regarded as outweighing those of the individual:

there is a strong correlation between honor and group cohesion and group survival. Honorable behaviour is that 'which strengthens the group...while shameful is that which tends to disrupt, endanger, impair or weaken...'[66]

Thus, the shameful or respectable behaviour of their relatives concerns each person, in two distinct ways. It concerns him or her as an individual, in so far as this behaviour reflects upon all members of the family. Dishonourable conduct by one member of the family can adversely affect the marriage prospects of another, for example. But it also concerns him or her as a member of the group. Dishonourable conduct weakens the group by disrupting social life and transgressing the norms of expected behaviour. Even beyond the family, then, dishonourable behaviour is condemned, and regarded as the legitimate concern of the entire community.

Thus every person is entitled and expected to police the behaviour of all others. Dishonourable behaviour is noticed and reported; social surveillance is not intrusion or spying, but the appropriate means of ensuring that life is well regulated. However, the targets of this surveillance are disproportionately women, for reasons connected to prevalent views on female sexuality. One of the most highly prized virtues in the cultures of the Middle East is self-control. The honourable man is master of himself; he does not act without thinking, or give in to his emotions. But women are widely regarded as lacking in this requisite self-control. Women are unable to restrain their powerful sexuality, and lack the moral and cognitive judgement that would enable them to make correct choices concerning it. Moreover, their great seductiveness represents a threat to *male* self-control. It is the one force that can overcome it. At the same time, female sexuality also carries with it great dangers for the honour of the family. Nothing dishonours a family so much as the suggestion that one of its female members has engaged in illicit sexual activity:

> The failure of women to remain chaste – including cases of rape – is a social catastrophe of the highest order as it brings shame to the whole family.[67]

Thus female sexuality is dangerous because it is powerful, and seductive, and women themselves are incapable of controlling it. Women therefore represent a constant danger to the members of an honour culture: a danger to themselves, to their families and to their community. Since they cannot govern themselves, they must be governed. As Bourdieu puts it:

a woman, evil by nature, must be placed as soon as possible under the beneficent protection of a man [...]. The Algerian Arabs sometimes call women 'Satan's cows' or 'the Devil's nets', meaning that they are the initiators of evil. 'Even the straightest of them', says a proverb, 'is twisted as a sickle.' Like a plant which tends to the left, woman can never be straight, only straightened by the beneficent protection of man.[68]

We are now in a position to understand the network of prohibitions and restrictions with which women are surrounded in the Arab world and beyond. Since women are almost irresistibly seductive, they must be kept secluded. They are best kept confined to the home of the male who is their guardian: their father until they are married, and thereafter their husband. When they must go out, they must be kept covered; hence the need for the wearing of the veil. Even veiled, women must be prevented from extended exposure to the outside world; hence their exclusion from education, and especially from paid employment, in which they would inevitably mingle with men. The same considerations help explain the practice of female circumcision, which is practised in only a few Muslim countries (predominantly Egypt and the Sudan). Removing the clitoris reduces or eliminates female sexual pleasure, thus lessening the power of female sexuality over the woman herself and reducing the risk that she will engage in illicit sexual activity. For the good of the community, of the family, and of the woman herself, she must be controlled, dominated and ruled over by men.

Against this background, the honour killing of women, too, becomes explicable. If, despite the regime imposed upon her, a woman does engage in illicit sexual activity, pre- or extra-marital sex, for instance, she brings great shame to her entire family. This shame can be expunged only through the death of the woman. Moreover, this killing must be carried out by the men who ought to have prevented her from transgressing: her brothers, her father or her husband. The killing is, therefore, not morally wrong; it is morally *required*.

Thus, men who engage in honour killings are not at all ashamed of the fact. Some examples will illustrate the point:

Sirhan, a 35-year-old murderer, is cheerful and relaxed and happy to tell his story. He's especially proud to describe the efficiency with which he shot his young sister Suzanne in the head four times last March. 'She came to the house at 8:15' he relates, 'and by 8:20 she was dead.' Three days before, the 16-year-old girl had reported to police that she had been raped. 'She committed a mistake, even if it was against her will,' says Sirhan. 'Anyway, it's better to have one person die than to have the whole family die from shame.'[69]

'We do not consider this murder,' said Wafik Abu Abseh, a 22-year-old Jordanian woodcutter, as his mother, brother and sisters nodded in agreement. 'It was like cutting off a finger.' Last June, Abu Abseh killed his sister, bashing her over the head with a paving stone when he found her with a man. He spent just four months in prison.

Marzouk Abdel Rahim, a Cairo tile maker, stabbed his 25-year-old daughter to death at her boyfriend's house in 1997, then chopped off her head. He also said he had no regrets. 'Honor is more precious than my own flesh and blood,' said Abdel Rahim, who was released after two months.[70]

These men, and their families, see the acts they have committed as entirely justifiable. They have restored honour to themselves and their families by killing someone whose life was, in any case, no longer worth living.

Now that we have grasped the background against which honour killings occur and are understood by their participants, it is time to turn to the central issue that concerns us here. Given that the cultural significance of these practices, the manner in which they fit into the way of life of the cultures of the Middle East, is reasonably coherent, can we criticize the treatment of women in these cases without begging the question against the members of these cultures? Are they making a mistake to which we can point, and which they ought to be able to grasp?

Let us begin exploring this question by examining the concept that is central to the entire network of significances informing these cultures, the concept of honour. Are these cultures making a mistake in so installing honour at the centre of their lives and their identities? Aristotle, in his discussion of the highest good at which we can aim, considers and dismisses the idea that this good can consist in honour. Honour, he says, depends on those who bestow it rather than on those who receive it, 'but the good we divine to be something of one's own and not easily taken from one'.[71] Further, wise people wish to be honoured for the right reasons, on account of their excellence; it is therefore excellence, and not honour, that ought to be at stake. Honour, as an end in itself, is therefore incoherent, Aristotle seems to suggest.

Can we therefore condemn the honour system on these Aristotelian grounds, and with it the oppression of women that it licenses? Notice that in appealing to these considerations, we seem not to be begging the question against the cultures we condemn. It appears that both these arguments are likely to have at least some force for the members of these cultures. They are likely to agree that, other things being equal, a good that depends on yourself alone, and which is for that reason more secure, is preferable to a good that is vulnerable to the vagaries of other people's caprices. And indeed, female honour, as it is understood by these cultures, seems peculiarly susceptible to destruction by the merest hint of suspicion. Several writers find it odd that the victims of honour killings are sometimes known *by their killers* to be innocent of any 'wrongdoing', yet on the logic of the honour system, this is not so strange. Reputation is as easily destroyed by false innuendo and rumour as by gossip with a basis in fact. Though the victim might not have done anything wrong by the lights of her killer, nevertheless her death is the only way in which the honour of the family can be restored.

Thus, members of Middle Eastern honour cultures might agree that the good of honour is fragile. Though constant vigilance and upright action will help preserve it, nothing can ensure that it will not be undermined by chance, by actions outside the control of the family, or by malicious gossip. They would also, I suspect, agree that it is preferable to be honoured for the right reasons. They would, I suppose, agree that the family that manages to preserve its honour by presenting an honourable face to the world at the very same time as it is engaged in dishonourable activities is, to that extent, worse than one that, equally honoured by the world at large, does not hide any such shameful secrets. Do these two points of agreement provide us with the means of criticizing the honour-shame cultures?

I suspect that they will not. The first point – that honour depends on chance and upon others, over whom we have little control – is too general to count as a mark against the identification of the highest good with honour in particular. *All worthwhile goods* are so vulnerable, as Aristotle himself points out elsewhere. No matter what good we select as the highest – pleasure, or wealth, or excellence, or even virtue, which according to Aristotle is most immune from the reversals of fortune – we are at least somewhat dependent on chance and upon the opinions and actions of others. For Aristotle himself, unless we have been brought up in good habits, we shall not be capable of understanding virtue. Such an upbringing, however, is obviously not under our control, but depends on chance and the actions of others. Furthermore, we require leisure, and therefore wealth, in order to inculcate the virtues. To the effects of fortune that Aristotle recognizes, we can add others. Surely our happiness is dependent, to some extent at least, on the opinions of others? Few of us, indeed, I suspect, none, could be truly happy so long as we were despised by everyone. Thus, it is vulnerable to the same reversals as honour. Virtue might, perhaps, be more stable, as Aristotle thinks, but it too can be undermined by chance. In a famous series of experiments, Stanley Milgram showed that very ordinary, apparently quite virtuous, individuals could quite easily be brought to engage in activities that can only be described as torture.[72] Perhaps the difference between us and the subjects of these experiments is mere chance. Indeed, some philosophers have argued that the Milgram experiments, and others designed to show the influence of situation on behaviour, demonstrate that there is no such thing as character; no stable set of traits that are consistent across situations.[73] Aristotle's virtues are supposed to be character traits; thus if character is dependent upon situation, virtue is as vulnerable as honour to the effects of chance and of other people's actions.

What about Aristotle's second criticism of any conception of the good centred around honour? He held that wise people do not wish merely to be honoured; instead, they want to be honoured *for the right reasons*. But this seems to suggest that it is not honour at all that is held to be the highest good. Instead, it is the characteristics or actions for which these people wish to be honoured that are really valued by them.

As we saw, it seems plausible to think that something like this is at least minimally true of the members of honour cultures. They will, most likely, prefer to be honourable as well as honoured to merely being honoured because they have succeeded in *appearing* to be honourable. But this just shows that they prefer that they, their families and their communities possess the virtues and act in the ways that *they* consider honourable. They prefer, that is, that the female members of their family are chaste, that the men behave courageously, and so on. Now, if it is really true that their conception of the good centres upon honour, and not upon the possession of these traits, then it might be that if we ask them why they value these traits, they will reply that it is because they are honourable. But there is no vicious circularity here, it seems. They value honour, and because they do value it, they prefer to be honoured for the possession of traits and the performance of actions that are really honourable. We can criticize them for this preference only by showing that honour is not an appropriate focus for a conception of the good, or by showing that these traits and actions are not in fact honourable. But, as we have seen, the attempt to show that honour is not an appropriate focus for a conception of the good fails, and it begs the question against this conception to hold that these traits and actions are not in fact honourable. By what alternative conception of honour will we show this, and how will we justify it? I simply cannot see a viable way to proceed in this direction.

Perhaps we can criticize the oppression of women in these cultures by invoking the victim's perspective. That is, we could hold, as Michele Moody-Adams does, that when the practices of a culture oppress one group, and not another, we can expect members of that group not to share the values that justify it. In this case, we might hope that the women, who suffer disproportionately from the culturally entrenched practices of many honour societies, would reject the values that justify their treatment. They might resent the veil, and the restrictions that limit almost every one of their actions. They might long for the opportunity to participate in the wider life of their society, and to pursue careers. For them, therefore, these values will be alien impositions, not the authentic expression of their identity.

Unfortunately for those who are tempted to take this line, it is very far from true that the victims of these practices do not share the values that justify them. Women internalize these values just as much as men do. Mothers and sisters are often as – or more – eager to punish wayward girls as are brothers and fathers.[74] Indeed, the victims themselves, those who are condemned to die because of some real or perceived transgression of sexual morality, sometimes applaud the actions of their killers:

> Even some victims of the attacks said they deserved their fate. 'He shouldn't have let me live,' said Roweida, 17, who was shot three times by her father after she confessed to an adulterous affair, and, along with dozens of girls with similar stories, is being held for her own protection in a Jordanian prison. 'A girl who commits a sin deserves to die.'[75]

Indeed, at least some women positively *demand* their own punishment for dishonourable behaviour. In one extreme case, a woman who had committed adultery killed her husband because he did not punish her adequately for her fault. When her husband did not show signs of wanting to take revenge,

> the woman became desperate. To not be punished for what she had done was a greater shame for her than punishment. The only way her husband could regain his honour in his society was that he would die. She killed him.[76]

Women can internalize this system of values as well as can men, and on its basis demand their own deaths.

Thus, we cannot confidently assert, with Moody-Adams, that the fact that women are, overwhelmingly, the victims of the honour-shame society and the practices it sanctions will inevitably lead to their rejecting its values. Nor, as we have seen in earlier chapters, can we confidently assert that any such identification with their society can be shown to be false consciousness. These women are not, necessarily, making a mistake: in affirming the importance of honour, and in holding that sexual impropriety is a dishonourable act that can be expunged only with blood, they believe something that is *true*, for them. It just is the case that illicit sex dishonours the entire family, for honour and dishonour depend crucially upon what people believe.

Criticizing the honour system

Thus far, I have been stressing the many difficulties that confront those who wish to criticize the oppression of women in the Middle East. Cultures that regulate their lives by the values of an honour system are not making any kind of obvious mistake in doing so; non-question-begging grounds for criticizing them are hard to come by. Thus, it is extremely difficult to present them with reasons for changing their views and their practices that ought to have weight for them. Difficult, but not necessarily impossible. Though I suspect that the honour system that is immune to rational criticism is a logical possibility, the actual cultures of the Middle East, and everywhere else the honour system justifies the oppression of women, are not so immune. At least some of the pillars of this world-view can be brought down by reason.

Though we cannot criticize the centrality of the notion of honour to this moral system, we can ask its members to justify the form it takes; in particular, why there is this obsessive concentration upon female sexuality. To be sure, gender is not arbitrarily chosen as a fundamental feature of honour-cultures. These cultures are strongly focused around family unity, and this unity is strengthened by the closeness of blood-ties.[77] This is almost certainly part of the explanation for the surveillance of women's sexuality: illicit sexual activity might result in children whose paternity is in doubt. However, the facts about the role women play in reproduction only go some little part of the way to explaining the obsession with female sexuality. For one thing, it is no longer true that extra-marital sex carries with it a significant risk of producing children. Even if it did, it is very far from obvious that reducing this risk requires so many restrictions upon female liberty. Finally, the emphasis upon legitimate children itself requires explanation. Why think that family solidarity requires that each child can identify its biological father as a member of that family? In fact, the members of this culture do offer reasons for the focus on women, and it is these reasons to which we now turn.

One set of justifications often offered in defence of the differential treatment of men and women refers to women's nature. Women have two characteristics that make them dangerous, it is often said. They have a sexuality that is more powerful than that of men; needs that are stronger. But at the same time they have weaker powers of self-control than men. Thus, they have fewer resources with which to overcome a more powerful drive. Hence the need for men to take over the task of controlling their sexuality for them. Defenders of traditional sex-roles who take this line justify their views by reference to the different 'natural physical, physiological, psychological and emotional disposition' of women, as compared to men.[78] Men and women have different rights, different duties, different tasks and restrictions placed upon them, each justified by their different capacities and dispositions. As we saw in earlier chapters, anything that counts for us as a morality will need to justify differential treatment of people and cases by pointing to relevant differences: here we are presented with just those relevant differences needed to explain the roles of men and women.

And just what are these differences between men and women? According to Afzular Rahman, beyond the obvious physical and anatomical differences, they concern the role of intellect and emotion:

> Man differs from the woman to a large extent from a psychological viewpoint. Women are normally more emotional, while in man, the intellect dominates the emotions. This difference is directly related to their nervous systems. [...] Physiologists have proved that the male's brain is anatomically distinguished from the female's, showing signs of superior intelligence and mental growth.[79]

These differences explain the different roles assigned to men and women. Since men are more intelligent than women, and better able to control their emotions, 'jobs demanding more intellect and where emotions are impediments should go to man, as per the natural order'.[80] Women, on the other hand, can best utilize their emotional sensitivity in caring for children and for their husbands. These differences also explain why men ought to guide women. Since the latter are easily misled by their emotions, they must not be allowed too much leeway to act upon them. The right to divorce, for instance, should rest largely with the man: since women are so emotional, and 'quick to take offence', if she has this right, she is likely to misuse it. The proof of this, Rahman tells us, comes from Western countries in which the right to divorce is easily accessed by women; there, 'eight percent of the appeals for divorce come from women, on petty excuse'.[81]

Rahman does not give a source for the figures he cites, nor for the scientific evidence he puts forward. This is not surprising, for I suspect that there are no reputable sources for most of his supposedly scientific contentions. There is, in fact, very little evidence of significant differences between the mental capacities of men and women in the scientific literature, and what there is is hotly contested. Most, if not all, of the observed gender differences are better explained by socialization than by postulating innate dispositions. Nor is there evidence that the consequences Rahman fears would follow from the lifting of the restrictions upon women are at all likely: promiscuity, the breakdown of families, the deprivation of maternal love. Why think for one moment that 'illegitimate offspring [...] are denied motherly affection during their growth'?[82] What shred of evidence is there for this contention? In any case, even if it were the case that lifting the restrictions upon women lead inevitably to the destruction of the family, why should we think this a cause for regret? Once again, Rahman has scientific evidence to show that this would be an evil:

> researchers have proved beyond all doubt, that a society based on the family system is the most natural and genuine of societies [...]. Any law contravening this natural order will therefore be inhuman, detrimental to society and repressive to the woman and the whole of mankind.[83]

Once again, however, he does not provide a source. Who are these researchers? In fact, they don't exist: no one has shown any such thing. There has indeed been a great deal of work on the value of the family, and upon the question of whether it is inevitable. What most of it seems to suggest is that human social formations are historically variable to an enormous extent, and the extent to which the formation we call the family is best is hotly debated.

Thus the supposed empirical evidence upon which the case for differential treatment of men and women rests is very weak or absent. The facts as we know them do not support Rahman's contentions. We might note, too, that there are conceptual confusions, as well as empirical mistakes, in the arguments presented. Women, he has told us, are less able to control their emotions than men. That is why they are to be excluded from occupations in which emotions are impediments. However, a quite different explanation is offered of why they should be kept sequestered to the greatest extent possible, and why they must be veiled when they cannot be confined. Women's charms, too freely displayed, present an irresistible temptation to men:

> women's coquettish and licentious display of their beauty plays havoc with the feelings and emotions of men [...]. The fact is that the free and unrestricted display of woman's beautification and ornaments can break any man's resistance.[84]

Now, suddenly, it is men who are overcome by emotion, who cannot control themselves. Perhaps, then, it is men who ought to be excluded from those tasks in which emotions are impediments.

Much the same kind of supposed empirical evidence is cited by defenders of female circumcision. According to Loretta Kopelman, its advocates advance five arguments in support of the practice:

1. It meets a religious requirement;
2. It preserves group identity and cohesion;
3. It helps to maintain cleanliness and good health;
4. It preserves family honour and prevents immorality; and
5. It increases the sexual pleasure of men without incurring any loss of pleasure by women.[85]

Once again, however, there is little empirical evidence for these claims. Claim 3. is especially weak. Far from maintaining cleanliness and good health, female circumcision causes a great variety of health problems, some of which stem directly from the frequent infections to which many circumcised women are subject. Some girls die from loss of blood or shock at the time of circumcision. Those who survive frequently experience life-long health problems, such as infertility, chronic urinary tract infections and pelvic infections.

Claim 5. is also easily refuted. Any increased pleasure experienced by men is almost certainly a function of their socialization; their preference for circumcised women is not due to any intrinsic characteristic of the latter, but simply because circumcision is a culturally endorsed practice. Thus it is unable to function as an *independent* justification of the practice. Moreover, it is simply false to believe that the practice does not involve any loss of sexual pleasure by women. Almost all circumcised women are unable to experience orgasm. Members of the cultures in which female circumcision is practised do not believe this involves any loss of pleasure to women, but only because they falsely believe that women cannot have orgasms in any case.

These claims are clearly false. Claims 1., 2. and 4. are slightly better founded. The evidence for 1. is equivocal. It is false to think that female circumcision is required by Islam. Indeed, it is not practised in many Muslim countries, including Saudi Arabia, the spiritual home of Islam. It is true, however, that the Qur'an endorses the practice as 'an embellishment to women'. Claim 2., that female circumcision helps preserve group identity and unity, is no doubt true. However, we must be careful not to place too great a weight on this fact. When Kenya, then under British rule, outlawed circumcision in the 1930s, Kenyatta, the future prime minister of an independent Kenya, argued for its retention on the grounds of its importance in maintaining the traditional culture:

> The abolition of irua [the ritual operation] will destroy the tribal symbol which identifies the age group and prevent the Kikuyu from perpetuating that spirit of collectivism and national solidarity which they have been able to maintain from time immemorial.[86]

In fact, however, cultures are complex totalities, and they contain few elements that, taken individually, are essential for their continuation. There is no reason at all to believe that female circumcision plays so central a role in the life of any culture that it could not die out without taking the culture with it. In all cases it could be replaced by a symbolic equivalent, without any significant alteration to the culture as a whole. Defenders of traditional cultures would do well to avoid insisting on the necessity of every traditional practice to the identity of a culture; cultures are living entities, and they reject old practices and adopt new ones as a natural part of their evolution.

Claim 4. is a variant of the contention we have already examined at length; that measures must be taken to control women's sexuality because it is so powerful. No doubt circumcising women does discourage illicit sexual activity, if for no other reason than that it makes intercourse painful. Nevertheless, the further claim, that women have a powerful sexual drive that cannot be regulated without external aid, is itself false.

Thus, the empirical arguments advanced by defenders of the traditional practices that restrict the lives of many Muslim women are largely false. At best, they are too weak to bear the weight they are asked to support; at worst, they are myths and superstitions. If these are the relevant differences that are supposed to justify the honour ethic and the practices it mandates, then this ethic is unjustified.

However, for all that we have said so far, there is one path still open to defenders of differential treatment. Seeing that the reasons advanced so far are weak, they can simply cease advancing justifications for their position, and just insist that the mere fact of gender differences – whatever that consists in – is sufficient by itself. They might say that gender is *itself* the relevant difference that justifies differential treatment, regardless of the facts about gender or what consequences it might have. After all, reason-giving has to come to an end somewhere, they might insist, and here we take our stand.

If they do take this line, will we be left where we started, presented with rival ethical systems that are immune to criticism and each of which is as coherent and as plausible as every other? I doubt that this will be the result. It is no accident, I suspect, that the defenders of differential treatment typically do advance reasons in support of their claims; that they don't rest content with simply adducing the fact of gender difference, but point to the alleged implications and consequences of that difference. It is true enough that reason giving has to stop somewhere, but reason has its own internal dynamic, its own impulse to seek deeper and further justifications. Once the possibility of giving further reasons for a claim has been opened up and looks coherent, it is very difficult to go back and rest content with less fundamental considerations. Instead, we are almost compelled to go further, to seek better reasons. Thus it is that the defenders of differential treatment for women – like those who support racism or homophobia – seek scientific support for their views. When the competing views go deeper and demonstrate the possibility of giving further reasons, any that halts too soon does so on pain of losing its plausibility.

So long as we could plausibly invoke the Bible, or the Qur'an, or some other transcendent law in support of our views, we did not need to investigate their subjects in too much detail. Now that our ethics has lost its cosmic supports, our views had better be well founded empirically. We will need to go at least as far in justifying them as do our competitors, or we will lose out to them. At the beginning of the twenty-first century, we live in a much more globalized world than at any other stage in human history, for good and for ill. One of the many consequences of this globalization is the awareness that our ethical views compete on the world stage. For the first time, each is required to show itself to be plausible before an audience that is familiar with all the others. Though once we could point to mere group membership as a fact of the greatest moral significance, increased mobility has reduced its importance. Once we could rely upon our audience sharing our prejudices and assumptions; now we must argue for more and more of them. Once we occupied relatively homogenous cultures; now the opposition to our way of going on comes from home as well as abroad. Now the justifications that we offer for our ethical systems had better be as broad and as deep as our science, our psychology and our philosophy allow.

Thus, it is false to think that reason is powerless against competing moral views. There are powerful constraints upon the content of any adequate moral system, which ensure that none can be radically different from our own. Every actual moral system, past and present, therefore looks, at bottom, quite similar to our own. Moreover, what differences there are and have been are often vulnerable to criticism. They rest upon empirical foundations that are false, or they refuse to give reasons where the demand for reasons is powerful. Despite the failure of all attempts decisively to defeat relativism, we have available to us powerful weapons of moral criticism, which can be levelled against other moralities by us – and which they can utilize against us in their turn.

8

BEYOND RELATIVISM AND ABSOLUTISM

Where do we stand, after this detailed examination of the arguments for and against moral relativism? We have seen that none of the attempts to refute relativism, powerful though some of them are, succeed in showing that it is not a coherent and plausible position. We have seen, too, that though it does not have the moral implications sometimes claimed for it by its supporters – it does not entail the toleration of others, for instance – it is nevertheless in some ways attractive on purely moral grounds. We have seen its explanatory power, and grasped why so many people have adopted it.

We have also seen, however, that though the arguments against relativism do not refute it, they do powerfully constrain it. For a number of interlocking reasons, any adequate morality will have to look a great deal like our own. It will have to play a similar role in human life to ours, and enshrine goods that we endorse. It will endorse rules similar to those we live by, and motivate its adherent as ours does us. Failing all this, we shall not recognize it as a morality at all.

Perhaps something emerges from all this that is not relativism *per se*, but that we cannot call absolutism either. To illustrate what I mean here, it might be useful to return to our consideration of the moral implications of relativism in chapter 3. There, we examined the extent to which relativism or absolutism was better placed, not merely to *tolerate* other cultures, but, more substantially, to accord them *respect* and *recognition*. When we did, we came to something of an impasse. Each position seemed flawed in some important way. If it is true, as the non-relativist asserts, that the relativist notion of toleration is thin gruel, too thin to satisfy the members of the tolerated culture, it is also the case that the more substantive recognition that the non-relativist can grant seems a mere prelude to the assimilation or fusion of cultures. Neither the relativist nor her opponent seems to have the resources to affirm and celebrate a diversity of cultures. But perhaps there is a middle way between the two positions, as we sketched them. Perhaps between relativism and absolutism there is a principled moral view that has the resources really to celebrate cultural diversity. The position I have in mind is known as *pluralism*.

The problems we saw with the absolutist picture stem, in important part, from its view that all values are commensurable; that each can be measured upon a common scale of value in terms of which they can be compared (this is a different notion of commensurability to that we examined in the last chapter). For example, hedonic utilitarians hold that all moral goods can be cashed out in terms of happiness. Thus, whenever we are faced with a choice between two incompatible courses of action, we should do whichever one maximizes happiness. Value pluralists, however, deny that when two values conflict one must always be better than the other. Instead, they hold that it might be the case that the conflicting goods are *both* valuable. Just because they clash does not show that one or the other is not really a good. Even if it can be shown that they are completely incompatible, this does not show that they cannot both be real goods. Consider an analogy:

> Anna is gifted cellist, as well as an outstanding mathematician. She receives scholarship offers from the Julliard School of Music as well as the Massachusetts Institute of Technology. She can only accept one. She knows she is faced with a choice. If she accepts the scholarship from Julliard, she might reasonably hope to become a professional

> musician, but she will only be an amateur mathematician. Conversely,
> if she goes to MIT, she will likely only ever be an amateur cellist.
> There just are not enough hours in the day to devote sufficient time
> to both cello practice and maths.

For Anna, the goods of excelling in mathematics and music are
contingently incompatible. Because of the limitations of the human
body, the length of human life and the hours available to her, she
cannot hope to achieve excellence in both. Instead she must choose
between them. But the fact that these goods clash here is no evidence
that they are not both real or important. On the contrary, it is
because they are both great goods that she experiences a conflict. If
one or the other was not really valuable, she would not be faced with
the dilemma in which she now finds herself.

Now, a value pluralist can agree with the relativist that when two
values conflict, there may be no fact of the matter which is better.
The achievement of personal autonomy and the enhancement of
community cohesion might, for instance, be incompatible; it doesn't
follow from this incompatibility that one is better than the other.
Perhaps there are many such values, which are contingently or
necessarily incompatible with one another, yet which remain valuable for all that. But from the fact that of two conflicting values
neither is better, the value pluralist need not draw strong relativist
conclusions; she need not think that because values are plural and
conflicting, there is *never* any fact of the matter which of two judgements or practices is better. Very often values can be ranked; pluralism is entirely compatible with the rejection of radical relativism.

The value pluralist is much better placed to accord respect and
recognition to other cultures than is a non-relativist who denies
pluralism. The latter, as we saw, will have a tendency to proceed from
his judgement of other cultures to assimilation or fusion; thus his
recognition will be (at best) provisional. But the value pluralist can
recognize the value of aspects of other cultures without feeling
compelled to adopt those values. Imagine, for example, that she is
the representative of a culture much like our own, which places a
high value on individuality and autonomy. She is engaged in the
process of assessing an alien culture; one in which autonomy and

individuality are accorded little weight. Instead, this culture values community cohesion, harmony between its members and respect for tradition. Our autonomous judge might admire these qualities in the alien culture, thinking that they are the realization of values that are real. She might regret the lack of community in the life of her own society. Nevertheless, since she also thinks that autonomy is a real value, and that it is incompatible with robust community, she will not feel compelled to adopt the lifestyle of the alien culture. Their way of life realizes a set of real values and is therefore worthwhile, she might think, but my way of life realizes a different set and is therefore also worthwhile. Thus the value pluralist can affirm the value of many different ways of life. If recognition requires that judgement be substantive and not merely formal, as Charles Taylor suggests, it is she, and not the radical relativist, who is best placed to exhibit respect for cultural diversity.

Pluralism also has other moral implications that recommend it to us. The relativist held that her doctrine taught us humility; accepting its truth would make us slow to impose our values on others, and would therefore make less likely a repetition of the disasters of colonialism. But pluralism is also capable of motivating this humility. If it is true, then other cultures can be worthy of real respect, even when they differ from us. So long as the goods they enshrine are real, they do not have to be ours for us to acknowledge their power.

Moreover, pluralism seems capable of explaining much of the evidence that motivated the relativist's view – the fact that moral disagreement often seems intractable and the historical and anthropological evidence of great cultural diversity. This is just what we should expect, in a world of plural and conflicting values. No one morality will be capable of giving full expression to all such values; instead, we can expect each to emphasize different goods to different extents.

Finally, pluralism seems fully compatible with those considerations we have examined that powerfully constrain the contents of an adequate moral system. As we stressed, any such morality must play a distinctive role in human life, contain rules in the absence of which cultural survival is unlikely, such as a prohibition upon arbitrary killing, and, most importantly here, enshrine goods that we all recognize. It seems as though any adequate moral system can differ from others only in the emphasis it places upon goods that we all recognize (though, as we shall see, this leaves ample room for real and substantive disagreements). But this just *is* pluralism. Moreover, pluralism accomplishes all these tasks without the risks that the absolutist worried about: without undermining respect for morality *per se*, or of endorsing sadistic fantasies as moralities worthy of respect.

But how ought we to characterize the pluralist view? Is it itself a variety of relativism, as some people claim? Or is it a non-relativist position?

Let us explore the pluralist position by way of an example. According to one of its defenders, we should understand the differences between (at least some) Asian countries and the liberal democracies of the West in terms of value pluralism.[87] David Wong believes that Eastern and Western conceptions of morality, though overlapping on a great many things, differ systematically in the emphasis each places on the value of individuality and of community. These are both real values, Wong believes, but they are values that frequently clash. In the West, we have resolved the tension between them largely, though not exclusively, in favour of individual rights. Thus, we believe that each person has the right to express (almost) any opinion, no matter how false, stupid or vindictive. We allow people to exercise their right of free speech at the risk of endangering community solidarity, even of promoting violence. To be sure, there are limits on this right. Several countries have laws banning public discourse calculated to incite racial hatred, for instance. Nevertheless, in general we believe that the threat to community solidarity, the risk of real violence, must be high before we are willing to countenance restrictions upon free speech. Our attitude is encapsulated by the test developed by Oliver Wendell Holmes and other justices of the United States Supreme Court, for assessing whether particular acts of speaking or publishing were protected by the constitution: unless there is a 'clear and present danger' that the speech will bring about 'substantive evils', it should be protected. Individual rights take precedence over those of the community, unless there are very strong reasons why they should not.

However, at least some Asian countries have taken almost exactly the opposite view: holding that language that represents *any* risk to community cohesion ought to be restricted unless there are very strong reasons to allow it. In other words, these countries have decided to settle the conflict between community and the individual largely in the favour of community. Indeed, they believe that their economic success – the manner in which the so-called Asian Tigers have been able to transform themselves from some of the poorest nations in the world to having standards of living comparable to, in some cases even better than, many Western nations – is in large part attributable to this choice. Thus, for instance, Goh Chok Tong, the Prime Minister of Singapore, claims that his country's economic success is due to the emphasis Singapore places on social cohesion:

> For success to continue, correct economic policies alone are not enough. Equally important are the noneconomic factors – a sense of community and nationhood, a disciplined and hard-working people, strong moral values and family ties. The type of society determines how we perform. It is not simply materialism and individual rewards which drive Singapore forward. More important, it is the sense of idealism and service born out of a feeling of social solidarity and national identification. Without these crucial factors, we cannot be a happy or dynamic society.[88]

Singapore, like some other Asian nations, has chosen community cohesion over individual rights, and reaped the rewards that come from so doing. Thus, for instance, its laws regarding freedom of speech are much more restrictive than those to which we are used. It censors internet access, sometimes restricts the circulation of the international media and does not tolerate any speech that threatens to disrupt religious harmony.

The claim that Wong, and other value pluralists, make is that the two values in question here, community cohesion and individual rights, are both real goods, but goods that inevitably conflict. Since they are real goods, any adequate morality must find a place for both. A morality that does not find a place for individual rights at all is mistaken; but at the same time so is a morality that always allows such rights to trump social goods. However, though all viable moralities must find a place for both, the precise point at which each draws the boundary between them, the weight it gives to each in cases of conflict, is somewhat arbitrary. It is up to each society to decide whether it wishes to give greater emphasis to one or the other (or to attempt to balance them evenly). So long as it finds some significant place for each, there are no grounds upon which we can criticize it. When real goods clash, hard decisions must be made, decisions concerning which there is no one definitive answer. Just as we cannot criticize Anna for deciding to pursue mathematics rather than music, or vice versa, so we cannot criticize Singapore for choosing to place rather greater weight on community cohesion, and correspondingly less on individual freedoms, than we do.

Opponents of Asian values disagree with the foregoing analysis. According to them, there are no such things as 'Asian values'. There is only one set of real values, and they are universal. They hold that the invocation of Asian values by politicians in Singapore, Malaysia, China and elsewhere is no more than a cynical attempt to justify their own authoritarian powers. Asians value freedom as much as Americans do; they too want to elect their own governments in free and fair elections, they too want access to as much information as possible and the opportunity to express themselves as they please. Human rights are universal, and take the same form everywhere.

Now, for these opponents of Asian values to be right, one of two things must be true. Either it must be true that, in fact, the people who live in the Asian countries in question actually have the same set of values we do, or, if they turn out to have a different set of values, that they are wrong to do so. Either human rights (as we, and not the proponents of Asian values, understand them) are in fact universal, or they are objective (or, possibly, both).

Is there any evidence that Asians do in fact value community solidarity more highly than do Westerners? In fact, there is quite a lot of evidence that this is the case, ranging from the findings of psychologists in controlled experiments, to the more impressionistic accounts of journalists.[89] It is not just the elites, those with the most to gain from the continuation of the current regimes, who report satisfaction with the choice these nations have made to emphasize the social over the individual. It is, apparently, the majority of ordinary people who think that their system is preferable to what they see as the over-emphasis on individuality in the West. Indeed, even some members of opposition groups who have campaigned for greater rights and freedoms in Asian countries believe that their governments should not go as far as, say, the Americans. Yao Chia-wen, for instance, a Taiwanese politician who was jailed for seven years after participating in a pro-human-rights rally, still 'would not advocate as many rights' for the Taiwanese as for Americans. 'Harmony is more important in our society, so people do not put so much value on equality or personal freedom.'[90]

It seems clear, then, that the first line of attack will not work. In all probability, Asians (or, more carefully, the populations of at least some Asian countries) do value social goods more highly than Westerners typically do, and place correspondingly less emphasis on individual rights and freedom (though it may well be the case that the leaders of these countries exaggerate their population's commitment to these values for their own political ends). Thus, opponents of Asian values will have to take the second option: they will have to show that these people are making a mistake in holding the views that they do.

But are there non-question-begging grounds upon which this can be shown? This, of course, is a variant of a question that we have been concerned with throughout this book: can we find grounds for criticizing people's moral beliefs? In this context, however, we are concerned with a much more specific matter. Here, it seems, we can only succeed in showing that the people in question are mistaken in their values if we can refute value pluralism, either in general or as far as these specific values are concerned. But neither task looks promising. Value pluralism does seem to be true, as the example of Anna and her career choices showed. Moreover, it seems that the two values with which we are here concerned are both real values, yet inevitably conflicting. Of course, it might be the case that there is a unique point at which the boundary between them ought to be drawn. But this seems very unlikely. Indeed, even different Western countries have drawn the boundary between individualism and the community somewhat differently. Upon many issues of personal freedom, the United States represents an extreme, in which individual freedom is given the most weight. But on some matters, other countries are more, not less, permissive. Thus, for instance, some European countries have legalized prostitution, and have decriminalized drugs that remain illegal in America. On these matters, the United States has chosen to give greater weight to (perceived) social benefits, at the expense of individual freedoms. Indeed, we could multiply examples of the ways in which different countries have chosen to resolve the conflict between freedoms and the social good in different ways on different issues. (Think of the language laws in Quebec, or for that matter in France, or the laws in the United States on flag burning, all of which represent decisions to emphasize the social good at the expense of personal freedoms.) Isn't it very plausible to think that on at least some of these issues, these different decisions represent reasonable disagreements; that here there is no answer that is uniquely justified? Unless the opponent of value pluralism can convince us that upon every one of these matters there is a unique fact of the matter, we will be justified in thinking that value pluralism is true, and that here there is ample room for reasonable disagreement.

Value pluralism is a powerful and plausible position. Moreover, it is one that holds out the promise of satisfying both sides in the relativism debate. It offers the relativist many of the perceived advantages that attracted her to relativism in the first place. It vindicates the tolerance of, and respect for, at least some cultures with moralities that differ from our own, by showing that the values they pursue are real values, and the decisions they have made regarding them are comprehensible to us. It counsels humility for us in the face of difference, since if it is true we are forced to acknowledge that our morality is just one reasonable system among others. It therefore opens our eyes to difference, and liberates us from the constraints of excessive ethnocentrism. At the same time, however, it promises to avoid at least some of what relativism's opponents see as its worst excesses. It does not advocate respect for all moralities, no matter what, but places constraints on what counts as a moral system worthy of such respect. It therefore leaves open the possibility that we will be able to condemn some moral systems, on non-question-begging grounds –

when the values they enshrine are not in fact real goods, or when they place so much emphasis on one or another good that they leave no place at all for another important value. Given this fact, there is the real possibility that any particular morality could, upon examination, turn out not to be worthy of respect. For this very reason, if, after such an examination, we declare that it is in fact worthy of recognition, our recognition will be substantive, and not purely formal. Because the culture in question might have failed the test, passing it will be meaningful to it and its members. Of all the positions we have so far examined, the pluralist one therefore seems best equipped to recognize cultural differences, and therefore to enshrine substantive toleration of, and respect for, such differences.

Is value pluralism a kind of relativism?

David Wong thinks that value pluralism is a kind of moral relativism. Other philosophers disagree.[91] What are we to think?

The best way to answer this question is by referring to the definition of relativism we developed earlier. As you will recall, we settled on the following definition:

Moral relativism is true just in case both the following theses are true:

a.   Moral claims are true only relative to some standard or framework; and
b.   This standard or framework is not itself uniquely justified.

Now, how does pluralism stack up against this definition? It depends on how we interpret it. If we interpret a. as holding that *all* moral claims are true only relative to some standard, then pluralism is not relativism. At least some moral claims are non-relativistically true, according to pluralism. For instance, given what we have said before, at very least this claim is true:

❚ Individual freedom matters morally.

I have phrased the claim in this vague manner on purpose, in order for it to be compatible with both Asian collectivism (if indeed there is such a thing) and Western individualism. If pluralism, as Wong formulates it, is true, then different moral systems can legitimately emphasize individual freedom to different degrees, but all adequate moral systems must find some significant place for it. Exactly the same claim can be made for community cohesion, and for every other real value. Adequate moral systems must find a place for them, and therefore the claim that they matter, morally speaking, is (non-relativistically) true.

However, if we interpret a. as claiming only that *some* moral claims are true only relative to some framework (which is not itself uniquely justified), then pluralism is a form of relativism. For, according to pluralism, some moral claims are true only within particular cultures. Though everyone ought to admit, for instance, that individual freedom matters morally, only the members of particular cultures must agree that individual autonomy ought to take precedence over the claims of community in particular circumstances. Since different cultures can legitimately weight the claims of conflicting values differently, there will be many specific moral claims that will be true only within particular cultures. For example, this claim might be true in some cultures, and false in others:

> Individuals ought not to criticize their government in situations where their criticisms risk undermining confidence in the institutions of the state, unless there is an overwhelming public interest in so doing.

Thus, according to pluralism, at least some moral claims will be true only relative to a framework (constituted, in all likelihood, by an ongoing way of life), and that framework itself will not be uniquely correct (since other legitimate weightings of these same values are entirely possible).

To be sure, value pluralism does hold that some moral claims are non-relativistically true (and, correlatively, that others are non-relativistically false). It also rules out some moral systems as inadequate. However, as we seen in earlier chapters, any plausible relativism must do the same. Pluralism is not a *radical* relativism, but radical relativism is false. There really are significant constraints on the contents of adequate moral systems, constraints we have explored. I therefore see no reason not to conclude that pluralism is a kind of relativism. Indeed, it might be the most plausible kind of relativism.

Pluralism thus offers us everything that is attractive about relativism, while avoiding the pitfalls, intellectual and moral, that threaten more radical versions. It, and it alone, can give us a plausible foundation for the intuition that cultures that differ from our own deserve our respect, and explain the moral diversity of the world, all without threatening to countenance the thought that, morally speaking, anything goes. The most plausible moral theory will therefore be pluralist in nature. Of course, saying that is not the end of moral enquiry; rather, it is the beginning of a more difficult and constructive task. We need to discover just what goods all adequate moralities must enshrine, and explore the links between these goods, so as to be able confidently to distinguish between moral systems that deserve our respect and those that ought to be condemned or altered. That, however, is a task for another book.

SUGGESTIONS FOR FURTHER READING

This bibliography lists the books and articles on moral relativism I have found most helpful or insightful, including the majority of those cited in the text. They range in difficulty, in outlook and in focus; I comment briefly on each to help the student find his or her way into the thicket of writings on this topic.

Anthologies

☞ Martin Hollis and Steven Lukes (eds), *Rationality and Relativism* (Cambridge, Mass.: The MIT Press, 1982).

This collection of articles has two primary focuses: the incommensurability thesis, and the extent to which rationality can vary across cultures. My discussion of Davidson's attempted refutation of the incommensurability thesis has been strongly influenced by the essays of the two editors included here.

☞ Michael Krausz (ed.), *Relativism: Interpretation and Confrontation* (Notre Dame: University of Notre Dame Press, 1989).

An interesting collection of recent writings across the relativism debate, including contributions from such big-name philosophers as Hilary Putnam, Nelson Goodman, Donald Davidson and Richard Rorty. Clifford Geertz, perhaps the best-known anthropologist alive today, sets out the reasons why he doesn't so much support relativism as oppose its opponents, and Alasdair MacIntyre contributes fascinating reflections on incommensurability, history and language. The essays range from quite approachable to fairly difficult.

☞ Jack W. Meiland and Michael Krausz (eds), *Relativism: Cognitive and Moral* (Notre Dame: University of Notre Dame Press, 1982).

An excellent collection of articles on moral relativism, drawn from scholarly books and journals. It contains several classics on the topic, including Donald Davidson's influential attempt to refute the incommensurability thesis, Bernard Williams's demonstration of the failure of the standard attempts by relativists to show that their position entails toleration and important articles by Philippa Foot and Gilbert Harman. Some of the articles will prove difficult for the beginner.

☞ Paul K. Moser and Thomas L. Carson (eds), *Moral Relativism: A Reader* (New York: Oxford University Press, 2001).

This is the most recent, and probably the most useful, anthology of (mainly) philosophical writings on moral relativism. It includes Richard Brandt's 'Ethical Relativism', which distinguishes usefully between different kinds of relativism, James Rachels's challenge to descriptive relativism, Gilbert Harman's defence of relativism and Loretta Kopelman's discussion of the extent to which the practice of female circumcision is based upon false empirical beliefs. Though none of these texts is easy, this is a suitable place for someone with some philosophical background to begin exploring the topic.

☞ Susan Moller Okin and others, *Is Multiculturalism Bad for Women?* (Princeton: Princeton University Press, 1999).

Susan Moller Okin believes that multiculturalism is too often taken to entail a version of cultural relativism that is detrimental to women's interests; since cultural relativism requires us to refrain from interfering with the practices of sub-groups, it reinforces a patriarchal status quo. This is a powerful challenge to relativism and multiculturalism, a challenge that is taken up and discussed by the series of essays which follow Okin's, by such big names in the liberalism and culture debate as Will Kymlicka, Yael Tamir and Martha Nussbaum.

☞ Ellen Frankel Paul, Fred D. Miller Jr and Jeffrey Paul (eds), *Cultural Pluralism and Moral Knowledge* (Cambridge University Press: 1994).

A collection of articles originally published as invited contributions to the journal *Social Philosophy and Policy*. The articles focus on the problems for morality that arise from the fact that different cultures (apparently) have different moralities. All are relevant, though some are quite difficult. John Kekes's contribution to the collection is a good introduction to the pluralistic approach to morality I advocate.

Books

☞ John W. Cook, *Morality and Cultural Differences* (New York: Oxford University Press, 1999).

In his attack on relativism, Cook draws together philosophical and anthropological discussions of the topic. His aim is to demonstrate that the anthropological evidence for descriptive relativism is weak and confused, and that relativism has unacceptable implications for morality. A lively and accessible discussion of these issues.

☞ Gilbert Harman and Judith Jarvis Thomson, *Moral Relativism and Moral Objectivity* (Blackwell, 1996).

Gilbert Harman is one of the few analytic philosophers of any note to defend moral relativism. This book involves him in a debate with the equally well-known Thomson, who rejects relativism. This book presents itself as an introduction to the debate, but it most definitely is not; even those with a background in meta-ethics will find it hard going at times. It also tends to get sidetracked by issues that are somewhat peripheral to the main questions. Nevertheless, this is high-quality philosophy.

☞ Rom Harré and Michael Krausz, *Varieties of Relativism* (Blackwell, 1996).

This book is worth reading as background to the moral relativism debate, for the manner in which it places moral relativism in a wider context. Harré, a well-known philosopher of science, and Krausz, who is primarily interested in relativism and interpretation, discuss relativism as the issue arises in the philosophy of language, metaphysics, epistemology and science, as well as morality. Their writing is approachable and lively. Inevitably, however, in a book of this length dealing with so many topics, many avenues remain unexplored.

☞ Elvin Hatch, *Culture and Morality: The Relativity of Values in Anthropology* (New York: Columbia University Press, 1983).

The best evidence for relativism comes to us from anthropology, and anthropologists have been very influential in propagating the idea that morality varies from culture to culture. Hatch usefully summarizes the history of the relativism thesis within anthropology, and the evidence for and against cultural relativism. An ideal introduction to the anthropological literature.

☞ Benjamin Lee Whorf, *Language, Thought and Reality* (Cambridge Mass.: The MIT Press, 1964).

This book collects Whorf's classic papers, in which the so-called Sapir-Whorf hypothesis is expounded and defended. The hypothesis has it that what we can think is shaped by what we can say, and that, further, what we can say differs according to what language we speak. Thus, speakers of different languages live in (what is for them) quite different worlds. The suggestion is almost certainly overstated by Whorf, but some weaker version of the thesis might be defensible. For a good recent discussion of the limitations of the Sapir-Whorf hypothesis, see Steven Pinker, *The Language Instinct: How the Mind Creates Language* (New York: HarperPerennial, 1995). For Pinker, the mind creates language, rather than language creating the mind. The truth probably lies somewhere between these two radical positions.

☞ Thomas S. Kuhn, *The Structure of Scientific Revolutions* (Second Edition), (University of Chicago Press, 1970).

This is Kuhn's classic statement of the incommensurability thesis: the notion that science as it is practised today cannot be said to be better than the science of earlier periods in our history, because it just is not a comparable kind of enterprise. Whether this thesis is rightly taken to have relativistic implications is still a hotly contested issue.

☞ Michele M. Moody-Adams, *Fieldwork in Familiar Places: Morality, Culture, and Philosophy* (Cambridge, Mass.: Harvard University Press, 1997).

This is a spirited attack on the very idea of cultural relativism. For Moody-Adams, relativism is incoherent. She attacks cultural relativism by attacking the notion of culture she takes to underly it: cultures are not the closed, monolithic entities they would need to be for cultural relativism to be true; and human beings everywhere have a shared nature. Though I think Moody-Adams's work fails to establish that no interesting form of cultural relativism can be true, it represents an important challenge to all relativists. The book is fairly accessible to the student.

☞ David Wong, *Moral Relativity* (Berkeley: University of California Press, 1984).

Along with Gil Harman, David Wong keeps the flag of relativism flying in respectable analytic philosophy. Wong defends the idea that morality is intended to perform a certain function in human life – to regulate interpersonal conflicts – and that there are many systems of rules and principles that perform this function equally well. There is therefore a plurality of adequate moral systems. This is a scholarly work; nevertheless, it is quite accessible for anyone with a little background in philosophy.

Articles

☞ David E. Cooper, 'Moral Relativism', in *Midwest Studies in Philosophy* III (1978).

Cooper attempts to apply Davidson's attack on the incommensurability thesis directly to moral relativism.

☞ Mary Midgley, 'On Trying Out One's New Sword', in her *Heart and Mind: The Varieties of Moral Experience* (The Harvester Press, 1981).

The first, and influential, discussion of the medieval Japanese practice of *tsujigiri*, or trying out one's new sword on a passer-by.

☞ Charles Taylor, 'The Politics of Recognition', in Amy Gutmann (ed.), *Multiculturalism: Examining the Politics of Recognition* (Princeton University Press, 1994).

Taylor's claim that undiscriminating cultural relativism cannot provide for the need we all feel to have our culture recognized for its intrinsic qualities, not merely tolerated, has important implications for multiculturalism and its relation to relativism.

☞ David B. Wong, 'Pluralistic Relativism', in *Midwest Studies in Philosophy* XX (1995).

Wong's position seems to have become more nuanced and subtle since *Moral Relativity*. In this article, he defends a version of relativism that recognizes the existence of absolute values; since these values sometimes conflict, different cultures can make systematic choices to prefer one or another without making any kind of mistake. Wong's views have influenced my conclusions.

NOTES

1. 'Bin Laden: Yes, I did it', the *Sunday Telegraph*, 11 November 2001.
2. 'Muslims have the right to attack America', *The Guardian*, 11 November 2001.
3. Liz Porter, 'Why our calls, and jobs, have been Delhigated', *The Age*, 29 July 2001.
4. Michael Novak, 'Awakening from Nihilism: The Templeton Prize Address', *First Things* 45 (1994).
5. See his remarks reported in Martha Nussbaum, *Sex and Social Justice* (New York: Oxford University Press, 1999), pp. 35–6.
6. Henry Steiner and Philip Alston (ed.), *International Human Rights in Context* (Oxford University Press, 2000) p. 195.
7. In making this threefold distinction, I follow Richard Brandt. See his 'Ethical Relativism' in Paul K. Moser and Thomas L. Carson (eds), *Moral Relativism: A Reader* (New York: Oxford University Press, 2001).
8. Information on Aztec society and the place of human sacrifice within it is drawn from Inga Clendinnen, *Aztecs: An Interpretation* (Cambridge University Press, 1991).
9. F. Barbara Orlans, 'Data on Animal Experimentation in the United States: What They Do and Do Not Show', *Perspectives in Biology and Medicine*, 37, 2. Winter 1994.

10. In contending that it is this thesis that motivates moral relativism, I follow John W. Cook, *Morality and Cultural Differences* (New York: Oxford University Press, 1999).

11. For examples of anthropologically inspired moral relativism, see Melville J. Herskovits, *Cultural Relativism: Perspective in Cultural Pluralism* (New York: Random House, 1972). Herskovits comes to his relativism by way of the enculturation thesis: for him, the notions of right and wrong 'are absorbed as a person learns the ways of the group into which he is born' (15).

12. Friedrich Nietzsche, *The Gay Science* [1882]; trans. Walter Kaufmann (New York: Random House, 1974), p. 181.

13. See Jonathan Glover's *Humanity: A Moral History of the Twentieth Century* (London: Pimlico, 2001) for the influence of Nietzsche upon the Nazis.

14. David Wong argues something like this line in his *Moral Relativity* (Berkeley: University of California Press, 1984), pp. 180–9.

15. Ibid., pp. 189–90.

16. Of course, it does not follow from the fact that we judge a certain behaviour to fall outside this range that we will necessarily want to interfere with it. We might have good reason to believe that such interference will have consequences that are far worse than the acts we wish to prevent. For instance, stopping an abuse of human rights might only be achievable at the cost of a war, which might well be more costly in terms of human lives lost than the original abuse, or might come at the cost of dislocating an entire people and destroying the culture that gave sense and meaning to their lives, which might also be an unacceptable cost.

17. Charles Taylor, 'The Politics of Recognition', in *Multiculturalism: Examining the Politics of Recognition*, Amy Gutmann (ed.) (Princeton University Press, 1994), p. 25.

18. Ibid., p. 70.

19. Ludwig Wittgenstein, *Philosophical Investigations* [1953]; trans. G.E.M. Anscombe (Oxford: Basil Blackwell, 1976), p. 108.

20. The classic analysis of conventions as solutions to co-ordination problems is that developed by David Lewis, in *Convention: A Philosophical Study* (Cambridge: Harvard University Press, 1969).

21. John W. Cook, *Morality and Cultural Differences* (New York: Oxford University Press, 1999), p. 41.

22. John Stuart Mill, *On Liberty* [1859] (London: Penguin Books, 1985), p. 78.

23. Herodotus, *The Histories* [440BCE]; trans. Aubrey de Sélincourt (London: Penguin Books, 1988), pp. 219–20.

24. Michel de Montaigne, 'Of Cannibals', in *The Complete Essays of Montaigne* [1580]; trans. Donald M. Frame (Stanford: Stanford University Press, 1958), p. 152.

25. On this point see, for example, Thomas L. Carson and Paul K. Moser, 'Introduction' to Carson and Moser (eds), *Moral Relativism: A Reader* (New York: Oxford University Press, 2001), p. 1.

26. I take the example, as well as the analysis designed to show that the Dinka do not, in fact, hold different fundamental moral principles to you and me, from John Kekes, 'Pluralism and the Value of Life', in Ellen Frankel Paul, Fred D. Miller Jr and Jeffrey Paul (eds), *Cultural Pluralism and Moral Knowledge* (Cambridge University Press: 1994).

27. Ibid., p. 55.

28. Mary Ann Warren, 'On the Moral and Legal Status of Abortion', in Hugh LaFollette (ed.), *Ethics in Practice: An Anthology* (Cambridge, Mass.: Blackwell Publishers, 1997).

29. I draw this information about the Inuit from James Rachels, *The Elements of Moral Philosophy* (New York: McGraw-Hill, 1993), pp. 23–4. Rachels uses the example to the same end: to show that the fact that exotic people engage in strange practices does not show that these people subscribe to different fundamental moral principles to you and me.

30. See Judith Jarvis Thomson, 'A defence of abortion', *Philosophy and Public Affairs* 1 (1971).

31. All these points are pressed by Michele M. Moody-Adams, *Fieldwork in Familiar Places: Morality, Culture, and Philosophy* (Cambridge, Mass.: Harvard University Press, 1997).

32. My reference here is the *Collins Dictionary of the English Language* (Collins: Sydney, 1979). I might add that *both* forms of the word as listed in this dictionary are wrong relative to German, since in German it would take an initial capital letter.

33. Clifford Geertz has famously defended the notion of cultures as 'webs of significances' in his many writings. See, for example, *The Interpretation of Cultures* (New York: Basic Books, 1973).

34. I am stating Moody-Adams's argument much more fully than she does herself. Thus when I attribute an argument to her, very often I will be stating premises, and even intermediate conclusions, she leaves unstated. Moody-Adams attributes the line of argument to Midgley, but Midgley herself seems to use the example of *tsujigiri* to make a different point. Moody-Adams's discussion of this example is contained in her *Fieldwork in Familiar Places: Morality, Culture, and Philosophy* (Cambridge, Mass.: Harvard University Press, 1997), pp. 81–2. Mary Midgley's original

discussion is 'On Trying Out One's New Sword' in her *Heart and Mind: The Varieties of Moral Experience* (The Harvester Press, 1981).

35. Rousseau considers just this question in *The Social Contract*. Murderers can justly be executed, he holds, because they stand condemned by laws that express their own will. In consenting to the law that condemns murder, I consent to being executed if I violate that law. That I would withdraw my consent, at the point at which the weight of the law is about to fall upon me, does not show that it does not in some sense embody my will. Nor, *a fortiori*, does it show that the law does not express beliefs that are held by my culture. See *The Social Contract* [1762]; trans. Maurice Cranston (London: Penguin Books, 1968), Book II, Chapter V.

36. In this context, it is worth comparing car driving to *tsujigiri*. It is plausible to maintain that Western cultures have consented to having the motor car as a primary form of transportation. When we consent to this, we do so in full knowledge of the risks, to drivers, passengers and pedestrians, of such driving. We might be said implicitly to consent to the risk of dying on our roads. Nevertheless, we would all object strenuously to dying on the roads; consenting to take a risk of dying is not the same as consenting to die, and objecting to dying does not show that we have not consented to the risk.

37. Indeed, the necessity of co-operation might be the basis of the principle of universalizability. If we are to co-operate with one another, we must be confident that our treatment will be responsive to our actions in predictable ways. Thus we will expect to be treated in the same way as anyone else in our situation would be. But this just is the principle of universalizability.

38. Francis Haines, *The Plains Indians* (New York: Thomas Y. Crowell Company, 1976), pp. 200–1.

39. It might be objected that the Sun Dance cannot play the role required of it here for the kinds of reasons advanced by opponents of descriptive relativism: that it is predicated on false empirical beliefs (with regard to supernatural beings and the role they play in human life); which might be seen as somehow overriding the natural responses of the Plains Indians. I suspect that this response misses the point of the example, which is intended to show only that our biological reactions often require cultural elaboration before they play a role in defining the shape of human life. In any case, the same Indians provide us with an example of an activity that involves at least the risk of pain but that does not seem to be predicated on false beliefs. Among them, war – the raiding of enemy camps, in order to steal their horses, to bring back scalps and weapons – was conducted for honour and glory, not for territorial gain or as a result of a conflict over scarce resources. It is, once more, precisely because this activity carried great physical risks that it was

considered so praiseworthy. Upon the basis of the biological fact that we are vulnerable to sudden and violent death, the Indians elaborated a cultural practice of risking their lives. A moment's reflection will reveal that this manner of thinking is not so very foreign to us. We, too, honour those who risk their lives in activities that have little point beyond the risk-taking, whether it be mountain-climbing or performing stunts on a motor bike.

40. David B. Morris, *The Culture of Pain* (Berkeley: University of California Press, 1991), p. 132. For Morris, 'the experience of pain is decisively shaped or modified by individual human minds and by specific human cultures' (p 1)

41. Richard Dawkins, *The Selfish Gene* (Oxford: Oxford University Press, 1989). The example occurs on pp. 183–6.

42. If this melancholy fate befalls our bird population, even worse is in store for it. In a population that consists only of cheats, no bird grooms any other. The ticks that parasite the birds can be expected to flourish; indeed, they may end up completely destroying their hosts.

43. George Will, 'A Radical Proposition', *Washington Post*, 4 February 1999.

44. This example, and the general line of argument, is drawn from Louise M. Antony, 'Nature and Norms', *Ethics* 111 (October 2000).

45. Jon Elster, *Sour Grapes: Studies in the subversion of rationality* (Cambridge: Cambridge University Press; Paris: Editions de la Maison des sciences de l'homme, 1983).

46. Martha C. Nussbaum, *Women and Human Development: The Capabilities Approach* (New York: Cambridge University Press, 2000), p. 139.

47. Martha C. Nussbaum, 'Aristotle, Politics, and Human Capabilities: A Response to Antony, Arneson, Charlesworth, and Mulgan', *Ethics* 111 (2000), 102–140, at 119.

48. Martha C. Nussbaum, *Women and Human Development: The Capabilities Approach* (New York: Cambridge University Press, 2000), p. 137.

49. John Christman, 'Liberalism and Positive Freedom', *Ethics* 101 (January 1991), p. 349.

50. Chief Justice Burger, *Wisconsin V. Yoder*, 406 U.S. 205, 15 May 1972.

51. Martha C. Nussbaum, *Women and Human Development: The Capabilities Approach* (New York: Cambridge University Press, 2000), p.152.

52. Alasdair MacIntyre, 'Epistemological Crises, Dramatic Narrative, And The Philosophy Of Science', *The Monist* 60 (1977).

53. Daniel Bell, *Communitarianism and its Critics* (Oxford: Oxford University Press, 1993), p. 133.

54. Martha C. Nussbaum, 'Aristotle, Politics, and Human Capabilities: A Response to Antony, Arneson, Charlesworth, and Mulgan', *Ethics* 111 (2000), p. 122.

55. Thomas S. Kuhn, *The Structure of Scientific Revolutions* (Second Edition) (University of Chiacgo Press, 1970), p. 111.

56. Benjamin Lee Whorf, *Language, Thought and Reality* (Cambridge Mass.: The MIT Press, 1964), p. 214.

57. See Peter Winch's 'Understanding a Primitive Society', in Bryan R. Wilson (ed.), *Rationality* (Oxford, Basil Blackwell, 1984).

58. See W.V. Quine, *Word and Object* (Cambridge Mass.: The MIT Press, 1960).

59. Donald Davidson, 'On the Very Idea of a Conceptual Scheme' in *Inquiries into Truth and Interpretation* (Oxford University Press, 1984), p. 184.

60. Donald Davidson, 'Radical Interpretation' in ibid, p. 137.

61. David E. Cooper, 'Moral Relativism', in *Midwest Studies in Philosophy*, III (1978), p. 101.

62. Colin Turnbull, *The Mountain People* (London: Jonathan Cape, 1972), p. 135.

63. Pierre Bourdieu, 'The sense of honour', in *Algeria 1960*, trans. Richard Nice (Cambridge: Cambridge University Press, 1979), p. 113.

64. David Pryce-Jones, *The Closed Circle: An Interpretation of the Arabs* (London: Paladin, 1990), p. 35.

65. Sana al-Khayyat, *Honour and Shame: Women in Modern Iraq* (London: Saqi Books, 1990), p. 21.

66. Mansour Khalid, cited in David Pryce-Jones, *The Closed Circle: An Interpretation of the Arabs* (London: Paladin, 1990), p. 36.

67. Tahire Kocturk, *A Matter of Honour: Experiences of Turkish Women Immigrants* (London: Zed Books, 1992), p. 57.

68. Pierre Bourdieu, 'The sense of honour', in *Algeria 1960*, trans. Richard Nice (Cambridge: Cambridge University Press, 1979), p. 127.

69. 'The Price of Honor', *Time*, 18 January 1999.

70. Douglas Jehl, 'Arab Honor's Price: A Woman's Blood', *New York Times*, 20 June 1999.

71. Aristotle, *Nichomachean Ethics* 1095b25; in J.L. Ackrill (ed.), *A New Aristotle Reader* (Princeton: Princeton University Press, 1987), p. 366.

72. Stanley Milgram, *Obedience to Authority: An Experimental View* (New York: Harper and Row, 1974). Milgram told his subjects that he was studying the effects of punishment on learning. Each subject was to ask another subject a series of memory questions, and administer an electric shock of increasing intensity if the subject gave the wrong answer, or no answer at

all. In reality, the other subject was an actor-accomplice of Milgram's, and the shock was faked. A full 65 per cent of the subjects continued to administer shocks to the highest intensity, which was *above* a level marked 'Danger: Severe Shock'.

73. See Gilbert Harmam, 'Moral Philosophy Meets Social Psychology: Virtue Ethics and the Fundamental Attribution Error', *Proceedings of the Aristotelian Society* 99 (1999), pp. 315–31, and John Doris, 'Persons, Situations and Virtue Ethics', *Noûs* 32 (1998), pp. 504–30.

74. Susan Moller Okin argues that we ought to discount the preferences of older women in these cultures, and instead emphasize those of the young. Older women will have reconciled themselves to these values and adopted them as their own, whereas the young might still chafe under them. Moreover, older women receive whatever honour and respect they are granted only by participating in the enculturation of younger females, and by dominating them. They therefore have a vested interest in the continuation of the system (Susan Moller Okin, 'Reply', in Okin and others, *Is Multiculturalism Bad for Women?* (Princeton: Princeton University Press, 1999), pp. 126–7. The problem with Okin's suggestions is twofold. First, as we shall soon see, the contention that younger females as a whole reject the values in question is empirically false. Many identify as strongly with them as do their mothers, or indeed their fathers. Second, even if it is true that rejection of these values is more prevalent among the young than the old, isn't that precisely what we would expect from the young of any culture? A proponent of this system of values will point out that the young frequently lack the wisdom to appreciate the deep point of the values of their elders. We would not advocate that, in general, the views of the young ought to take precedence over those of their elders; on what non-question-begging grounds do we do so now?

75. Douglas Jehl, 'Arab Honour's Price: A Woman's Blood', *New York Times*, 20 June 1999.

76. *Cumhuriyet*, 19 July 1978; cited in Kocturk, *A Matter of Honour: Experiences of Turkish Women Immigrants* (London, Zed Books, 1992), p. 57.

77. Bourdieu points out that among the Algerian Arabs, cousins ideally marry each other. 'Marriage with an outsider is feared as an intrusion; it makes a breach in the protective fence surrounding family intimacy' (Pierre Bourdieu, 'The sense of honour', in *Algeria 1960*, trans. Richard Nice (Cambridge: Cambridge University Press, 1979), p. 128).

78. Afzular Rahman, *Role of Muslim Woman in Society* (London: Seerah Foundation, 1986), p. 9.

79. Ibid., pp. 23–5.

80. Ibid., p. 33.

81. Ibid., p. 38.

82. Ibid., p. 28.

83. Ibid., pp. 28–9.

84. Ibid., p. 367.

85. Loretta M. Kopelman, 'Female Circumcision and Genital Mutilation', in Ruth Chadwick (ed.), *Encyclopedia of Applied Ethics, Vol. 2* (San Diego: Academic Press, 1998), pp. 252–3.

86. Cited in ibid, p. 252.

87. David B. Wong, 'Pluralistic Relativism', in *Midwest Studies in Philosophy* XX (1995).

88. Goh Chok Tong, 'Social Values, Singapore Style', *Current History*, December 1994, p. 417.

89. For examples of the social scientific literature on the manner in which values differ from culture to culture, see the essays collected in Ed Diener and Eunkook M. Suh (eds), *Culture and Subjective Well-Being* (Cambridge, Mass.: MIT Press, 2000).

90. Quoted in James Walsh, 'Asia's Different Drum', *Time Magazine*, 14 June 1993.

91. See, for example, John Kekes, 'Pluralism and the Value of Life', in Ellen Frankel Paul, Fred D. Miller Jr and Jeffrey Paul (eds), *Cultural Pluralism and Moral Knowledge* (Cambridge University Press: 1994). Perhaps the best-known defence of a (supposedly) non-relativistic pluralism is that of Isaiah Berlin, in many essays and books. See, for instance, his *Four Essays on Liberty* (Oxford: Oxford University Press, 1969).

INDEX

219